GLOBAL ISSUES IN
CONTEMPORARY POLICING

International Police Executive Symposium Co-Publications

Dilip K. Das, *Founding President-IPES*

PUBLISHED

Global Issues in Contemporary Policing
John A. Eterno, Arvind Verma, Aiedeo Mintie Das, and Dilip K. Das, ISBN: 978-1-4822-4852-4

Examining Political Violence: Studies of Terrorism, Counterterrorism, and Internal Wars
By David Lowe, Austin Turk, and Dilip K. Das, ISBN: 978-1-4665-8820-2

The Evolution of Policing: Worldwide Innovations and Insights
By Melchor C. de Guzman, Aiedeo Mintie Das, and Dilip K. Das, ISBN: 978-1-4665-6715-3

Policing Global Movement: Tourism, Migration, Human Trafficking, and Terrorism
By S. Caroline Taylor, Daniel Joseph Torpy, and Dilip K. Das, ISBN: 978-1-4665-0726-5

Global Community Policing: Problems and Challenges
By Arvind Verma, Dilip K. Das, Manoj Abraham, ISBN 978-1-4398-8416-4

Global Environment of Policing
By Darren Palmer, Michael M. Berlin, and Dilip K. Das, ISBN: 978-1-4200-6590-9

Strategic Responses to Crime: Thinking Locally, Acting Globally
By Melchor de Guzman, Aiedeo Mintie Das, and Dilip K. Das, ISBN: 978-1-4200-7669-1

Police without Borders: The Fading Distinction between Local and Global
By Cliff Roberson, Dilip K. Das, and Jennie K. Singer, ISBN: 978-1-4398-0501-5

Effective Crime Reduction Strategies: International Perspectives
By James F. Albrecht and Dilip K. Das, ISBN: 978-1-4200-7838-1

Urbanization, Policing, and Security: Global Perspectives
By Gary Cordner, Ann Marie Cordner, and Dilip K. Das, ISBN: 978-1-4200-8557-0

Criminal Abuse of Women and Children: An International Perspective
By Obi N.I. Ebbe and Dilip K. Das, ISBN: 978-1-4200-8803-8

Contemporary Issues in Law Enforcement and Policing
By Andrew Millie and Dilip K. Das, ISBN: 978-1-4200-7215-0

Global Trafficking in Women and Children
By Obi N.I. Ebbe and Dilip K. Das, ISBN: 978-1-4200-5943-4

Policing Major Events: Perspectives from Around the World
by James F. Albrecht, Martha C. Dow, Darryl Plecas, and Dilip K. Das, ISBN: 978-1-4665-8805-9

Economic Development, Crime, and Policing: Global Perspectives
By Garth den Heyer and Dilip K. Das, ISBN: 978-1-4822-0456-8

Civilian Oversight of Police : Advancing Accountability in Law Enforcement
By Tim Prenzler and Garth den Heyer ISBN: 978-1-4822-3418-3

GLOBAL ISSUES IN
CONTEMPORARY
POLICING

Edited by
John A. Eterno
Arvind Verma
Aiedeo Mintie Das
Dilip K. Das

International Police Executive
Symposium Co-Publications

CRC Press
Taylor & Francis Group
Boca Raton London New York

CRC Press is an imprint of the
Taylor & Francis Group, an **informa** business

CRC Press
Taylor & Francis Group
6000 Broken Sound Parkway NW, Suite 300
Boca Raton, FL 33487-2742

Printed on acid-free paper
Version Date: 20161110

International Standard Book Number-13: 978-1-4822-4852-4 (Hardback)

Visit the Taylor & Francis Web site at
http://www.taylorandfrancis.com

and the CRC Press Web site at
http://www.crcpress.com

Printed and bound in the United States of America by
Edwards Brothers Malloy on sustainably sourced paper

Contents

Section I
LEADERSHIP AND ACCOUNTABILITY

Section II
ANALYSIS

Section III
SATISFACTION AND
COMMUNITY CONNECTIONS

11   **Policing by Consent: Exploring the Possibilities
of Functional Linkage between Local Police
Station and Panchayat**   **221**

SONY KUNJAPPAN

Series Preface

The International Police Executive Symposium (IPES) was founded in 1994 to address one major challenge, i.e., the two worlds of research and practice remain disconnected even though cooperation between the two is growing. A major reason is that the two groups speak in different languages. The research is published in hard-to-access journals and presented in a manner that is difficult for some to comprehend. On the other hand, police practitioners tend to not mix with researchers and remain secretive about their work. Consequently, there is little dialogue between the two and almost no attempt to learn from one another. The global dialogue among police researchers and practitioners is limited. It is true that the literature on the police is growing exponentially. But its impact upon day-to-day policing, however, is negligible.

The aims and the objectives of the IPES are to provide a forum to foster closer relationships among police researchers and practitioners on a global scale, to facilitate cross-cultural, international, and interdisciplinary exchanges for the enrichment of the law enforcement profession, to encourage discussion, and to publish research on challenging and contemporary problems facing the policing profession. One of the most important activities of the IPES is the organization of an annual meeting under the auspices of a police agency or an educational institution. The annual meeting, a five-day initiative on specific issues relevant to the policing profession, brings together ministers of interior and justice, police commissioners and chiefs, members of academia representing world-renowned institutions, and many more criminal justice elites from more than 60 countries. It facilitates interaction and exchange of ideas and opinions on all aspects of policing. The agenda is structured to encourage dialogue in both formal and informal settings.

Another important aspect of the meeting is the publication of the best papers presented edited by well-known criminal justice scholars and police professionals who attend the meetings. The best papers are selected, thoroughly revised, fully updated, meticulously edited, and published as books based upon the theme of each meeting. This repository of knowledge under the copublication imprint of IPES and CRC Press–Taylor & Francis Group chronicles the important contributions of the IPES over the last two decades. As a result, in 2011, the United Nations awarded IPES a special consultative status for the Economic and Social Council honoring its importance in the global security community.

In addition to this book series, the IPES also has a research journal, *Police Practices and Research: An International Journal* (PPR). The PPR contains research articles on police issues from practitioners and researchers. It is an international journal in the true sense of the term and is distributed worldwide. For more information on the PPR visit http://www.tandf.co.uk /journals/GPPR.

The IPES holds annual meetings of scholars and practitioners of policing who represent many countries. Additionally, the authors are experts in their fields. A collection of chapters like this is rare and exciting. Readers are treated to up-to-date materials by experts throughout the world.

This collection of chapters on international policing is unique and powerful. The chapters are written by individuals with intimate knowledge of the countries they write about. They include comparative studies of several countries as well as in-depth case analyses. The chapters were initially selected from presentations made at the IPES that were well attended and had excellent reviews. Additionally, the chapters were read by reviewers who suggested changes. The papers were then changed and reread to pass muster. It was a long and arduous process.

IPES advocates, promotes, and propagates that *policing* is one of the most basic and essential avenues for improving the quality of life in all nations, rich and poor, modern and traditional, large and small, as well as peaceful and strife ridden. IPES actively works to drive home to all its office bearers, supporters, and admirers that in order to reach its full potential as an instrument of service to humanity, policing must be fully and enthusiastically open to collaboration between research and practice, global exchange of information between police practitioners and academics, universal disseminations and sharing of best practices, generating thinking police leaders and followers, as well as reflecting and writing on the issues challenging to the profession.

Through its annual meetings, hosts, institutional supporters, and publications, IPES reaffirms that policing is a moral profession with unflinching adherence to the rule of law and human rights as the embodiment of humane values.

Dilip K. Das
Founding President,
International Police Executive Symposium

Book Series Editor, Advances in Police Theory and Practice,
CRC Press, Taylor & Francis Group

Book Series Editor, Interviews with Global Leaders in Criminal Justice,
CRC Press, Taylor & Francis Group

Book Series Editor,
IPES/CRC Press Co-Production Series

Founding Editor-in-Chief,
Police Practice and Research: An International Journal

Acknowledgments

No work of this magnitude can be done without the labor of many. We would like to thank the authors of the chapters and many unnamed assistants for their works. They have done an outstanding job. We also want to thank the International Police Executive Symposium (IPES) for bringing us together. The unique experiences and insights we gain at conferences are especially useful. This book is, in part, a product of those meetings. There was a tremendous amount of behind-the-scenes people in this project. We especially want to thank two graduate students at Molloy College in New York, United States, Gina Passaretti and Kevin Carman. Their edits, diligence, and dedication made this work possible. The editors would also like to thank Scott Phillips for his comments and insights and, of course, CRC Press where many participants were very helpful and accommodating. We especially want to thank Carolyn Spence and Jessica Vega. They worked tirelessly with us. There are many who have reviewed, read, and commented on various drafts of the manuscripts. While they will remain anonymous, we thank them all. These are only a few of the more noteworthy individuals who assisted. If we missed anyone, please forgive us.

Editors

John A. Eterno earned his PhD from the State University of New York at Albany. He is a professor, associate dean, and director of Graduate Studies in Criminal Justice at Molloy College and a retired captain from the New York City Police Department. Molloy College has recognized his accomplishments with specific awards in various areas including research/publication, teaching, and service. He has penned numerous books, book chapters, articles, and editorials on various topics in policing. Some examples of his most recent publications: an op-ed in the *New York Times* entitled "Policing by the Numbers"; several a peer-reviewed articles in *Justice Quarterly*; and three recent books, entitled *The Crime Numbers Game: Management by Manipulation* (with Eli B. Silverman), *The New York City Police Department: The Impact of Its Policies and Practices*, and *The Detective's Handbook* with Cliff Roberson. He lives in a suburb of New York City with his wife JoAnn and two children, Julia and Lauran.

Arvind Verma is a former officer of the Indian Police Service and currently teaches at Indiana University, Bloomington. He has a large number of publications and is the author of several works. His most recent book (coauthored) is *Policing Muslim Communities: Comparative and International Context*. His research interests are in policing of India and computational criminology.

Aiedeo Mintie Das works as a digital media/content marketing specialist. As the director of public relations of the International Police Executive Symposium, she organizes international criminal justice symposia, coordinating with ministries of interior/justice to bring together well-known academics and top police leaders in global venues. Currently, she is pursuing her graduate studies in Helsinki, Finland.

Dilip K. Das is a professor of criminal justice, former police chief, founding editor-in-chief of *Police Practice and Research: An International Journal* (PPR), and a human rights consultant to the United Nations. After serving in the Indian Police Service for 14 years, he moved to the United States, where he later became the founding president of the International Police Executive Symposium (IPES), http://www.ipes.info, which is in special consultative status with the United Nations. He has authored, edited, and coedited more than 30 books and numerous articles, received several faculty excellence awards, and was a distinguished faculty lecturer.

Contributors

Aurel-Mihail Băloi
Intergraph Computer Services SRL
Bucharest, Romania

Sandy Chau
SPEED
Hong Kong Polytechnic University
Hung Hom, Hong Kong

Sorina-Maria Cofan
Institute for Studies on Public Order
Ministry of Internal Affairs
Bucharest, Romania

Maximilian Edelbacher
Austrian Criminal Investigators
    Organization
Vienna, Austria

Creel S. Gallagher
Garland Police Department
Garland, Texas

Jane Goodman-Delahunty
Charles Sturt University
New South Wales, Australia

Robert D. Hanser
University of Louisiana at Monroe
Monroe, Louisiana

Peter C. Kratcoski
Kent State University
Kent, Ohio

Attapol Kuanliang
University of Louisiana at Monroe
Monroe, Louisiana

and

Midwestern State University
Wichita Falls, Texas

Vipul Kumar
Sardar Vallabhbhai Patel National Police
    Academy
Hyderabad, India

Sony Kunjappan
Centre for Studies in Social Management
Central University of Gujarat
Gandhinagar, India

Branko Lobnikar
Faculty of Criminal Justice and Security
University of Maribor
Maribor, Slovenia

Gorazd Meško
Faculty of Criminal Justice and Security
University of Maribor
Maribor, Slovenia

Anthony Minnaar
Department of Criminology and Security
    Science
School of Criminal Justice
College of Law
University of South Africa
Pretoria, South Africa

Maja Modic
Faculty of Criminal Justice and Security
University of Maribor
Maribor, Slovenia

Ida Nguyen
Charles Sturt University
New South Wales, Australia

Bakhit Nurgaliyev
Karaganda University Bolashak
Karagandy, Kazakhstan

Stephen B. Perrott
Department of Psychology
Mount St. Vincent University
Halifax, Nova Scotia, Canada

Branislav Simonovic
Faculty of Law
University of Kragujevac
Kragujevac, Serbia

Chantal Sowemimo-Coker
SUNY College
Old Westbury, New York

Mira Taitz
YouthLaw Aotearoa
Auckland, New Zealand

Krystina Trites
Department of Psychology
Mount St. Vincent University
Halifax, Nova Scotia, Canada

Wing Kwong Yung
SPEED
Hong Kong Polytechnic University
Hung Hom, Hong Kong

Introduction

JOHN A. ETERNO AND ARVIND VERMA

When reading the following chapters, it is important to keep in mind various issues in a democratic society. These issues are the focal points of democratic policing in contemporary times. They are the themes and the subthemes that nearly every scholarly piece in the field will touch upon. They are not only issues of academic interest but of practical importance to all.

Policing in a contemporary democratic society is by its very nature difficult. Officers cannot do as they please with the populace. Fundamental rights must be respected. This necessarily limits the powers of the police to combat crime and terrorism. Are the police essentially controlling their behaviors to work within the law or are they acting as if they are in a police state—acting with impunity on citizens? By studying the police, one can determine the health of a democratic society. One way to gauge this is by thinking about a continuum ranging from the most abusive to the most respectful behavior of police personnel.

It is clear that in times of trouble, the power of the police increases. This is done to address the crisis. Even in such times, however, some semblance of democracy must remain. Once the crisis is addressed and relative calm is restored, the level of police power can be reassessed and reduced to a more healthy level for everyday activity. In the United States, for example, the basic writ of habeas corpus has been curtailed three times—all of which are extreme crises. The first was under President Abraham Lincoln during the American Civil War; the second under, President Franklin Roosevelt during World War II; and the third, after 9/11 under President George W. Bush. In a post-9/11 world that is filled with terrorist activity, striking a proper balance between civil liberties and national security is a challenge. Countries such as Israel, which remain democratic despite constant challenges, need to be examined closely.

Under the rubric of human rights is a host of concerns that must be monitored to ensure democratic policing. Among these, the first priority is minimizing corruption. The police must clean up their own act before they can begin the arduous task of protecting the rights of citizens as well as preventing crime and terrorism. Corruption will prevent a democracy from thriving and, in fact, may kill it outright. Corruption prevents fundamental fairness. The corrupt government and officials working for that government, game the system making due process impossible. There is no equality before the law as corruption prevents any semblance of fairness. Any government attempting democracy must limit corrupt behavior by police and other officials.

Corruption takes many forms. It can be overt. For example, the Russian Federation is well known for its corrupt officials (Gilinskiy, 2009). Officials take bribes, do not enforce various laws, and openly conduct other illegal behaviors. Of concern also is the more covert type of corruption such as the gaming of crime numbers (Eterno and Silverman, 2010, 2012; Eterno, 2015; Eterno, Verma, and Silverman, 2016). This can also have an effect on how victims are treated—less powerful classes' complaints being ignored or downgraded. In either case, the activity threatens the democratic process—directly and/or indirectly. Inevitably, corruption leads to favoritism and, ultimately, if not addressed, the lack of due process will have dire consequences.

Equal protection of the laws is an important aspect of human rights. Importantly, police are public servants, not nobles. They do not lord their individual desires onto an unwary public. They enforce the laws passed by the government of the people, by the people, and for the people, and they are representatives of the same. This must not be lost on law enforcement officers and their leaders in a democratic society. They serve and must have an attitude of humility. Service, not ego or exaggerating one's importance especially from police leaders, must drive the engine of police behavior. There must be a willingness to listen and to serve the interests of the public. In turn, however, the public must obey the laws. This is the essence of the social contract as envisioned by the founding fathers of the United States (see, for example, the study by Eterno [2003]). In a democratic government, power ultimately emanates from the people. There must be some level of consent. This has been lost on many police especially police leaders who vocally proclaim their successes yet fail to hear a wary public. A good example of this is the issue of stop and frisk in New York City. There, the New York City Police Department (NYPD) ran amok stopping millions of mostly minority young men in the span of only a few short years. Between 2003 and 2011, the NYPD forcibly stopped approximately 5 million people. This is about half a million per year. They claimed that the practice was necessary to get guns off the streets and to fight crime. In the years earlier, NYPD generally stopped around 100,000 per year. Additionally, crime was brought down over 60% with the relatively small number of stops being done. A federal court found the actions by the police in violation of basic rights. Not only were the stops unreasonable but the court also found that they were racist. The people spoke in the next mayoral election and a new mayor was elected on a platform to change the police department. The NYPD clearly violated the social contract—failing to heed numerous calls for change for city residents, watchdog groups, and academicians. Indeed, no policy shift was made by the department as they stubbornly held on to their policy even after the courts and the people had spoken. A new police commissioner and a court monitor are in the process of making substantive changes to the policy. The police in India enforcing morality using an outdated law is another example of misuse of authority in the name of law enforcement. Raiding a hotel and dragging out couples who were consenting adults seeking privacy is blatant misuse of policy authority. But the Mumbai police forced the women to prove that they were not prostitutes and even had many of them call their parents as a token of good behavior (Karat, 2015). Despite public outcry, the police in many regions of the country have been questioning and harassing young couples who appear unmarried. The police must work within the law to enforce in the spirit of a democratic society.

One way to understand the difficulties faced by law enforcement is to review Herbert Packer's (1966) seminal article entitled "Two Models of the Criminal Justice Process." Packer divides the criminal justice system into two models that are very instructive. The first he calls the *crime control model*. He likens this to an assembly line. In an efficient and quick process, the crime control model would have the police arrest, the courts convict, and the correctional system jail in a cookie cutter-type system. That is, make the arrest and get that person convicted and in jail with minimal interruption. In my view, such a system has a presumption of guilt. The due process model is the second way to view the criminal justice system. Packer likens this to an obstacle course. Various obstacles are placed before those who work in the system. These obstacles are meant to ensure that the rights of the suspects are protected. One example of this is the Miranda rights being read to arrestees being interrogated. In my view, this model has a presumption of innocence.

Either model can work in a democracy. However, in places like the United States, there is a presumption of innocence, which leans toward the due process model. Police leaders, at times, assume that their job is crime control and will pay less attention to due process concerns.

So which is more important, crime control or due process? There really is no answer to this but we do have some thoughts. Recent events suggest that it changes over time. Further complicating matters is that controlling crime is important but it may not be as important as many police leaders make it out to be. Controlling corruption and respecting rights are, we argue, more important toward democratic law enforcement. A quotation from the Bible is instructive, "You hypocrite, first take the plank out of your own eye, and then you will see clearly to remove the speck from your brother's eye" (Matthew 7:5*). Given the extreme focus on minor quality of life violations such as drinking alcohol, urinating in public, smoking marijuana, and the like by today's law enforcement, one must ponder where corruption prevention now stands. Quota-driven activity, crime report manipulation, civilian

---

* New International Version of the Bible. Retrieved from http://biblehub.com/matthew /7-5.htm, accessed September 9, 2015.

complaints of illegal stop and frisk, and the like seem to be rarely monitored except for an occasional news story. Departments must focus inward before turning to enforcing the laws on the public. The *Floyd* case in New York City is a good example of this. The NYPD at the time made crime control their priority and trampled on the basic rights of its minority citizens.

Another key issue for democratic policing is transparency. Many departments now have sophisticated public information officers. It is their job to disseminate information to the public. However, some of these officers have taken to protecting the department's image rather than getting information out. Police leaders will circle the wagons when faced with criticism. They protect the department at all costs. This may even mean an aggressive public relations campaign. In the case of crime report manipulation, the NYPD waged a public relations blitz against anyone who questioned their accuracy (see the study by Eterno and Silverman [2012]). Similar reactions occurred in the nation's two other largest police departments in Los Angeles and Chicago. In a democracy, to the extent possible, police departments need to get the truth to the public. This means giving out data and information collected at the taxpayers' expense. The NYPD was notorious for holding back figures on lost property, misdemeanor crime, and stop and frisk reports until they were sued in federal court. This is the antithesis of policing in a democratic society.

In summary, we have identified at least three key issues in democratic policing in contemporary society. The first is how limited the police are in their behaviors. Are they properly checked and balanced by other branches of the government? Under this, it should be understood that in times of crisis, the power of the police expands, but it should never become unlimited as in a police state. A second and related issue is ensuring the protection of the basic rights of the citizens. Under this, we discuss three key subthemes: corruption control, equal protection of the laws, and crime control/due process dichotomy. At its most basic level, corruption must be minimized before democratic policing can take place. Officers must be held accountable for their actions. Laws must be enforced equally. Are minorities/immigrants treated differently? If so, that needs to be explained. Also of critical importance to democracy is protecting basic rights—a key function of police that is often left wanting. The last key issue we discussed is transparency. This allows accountability to the people and study of departments. Without it, precious little informed discourse can occur.

With these key issues in mind, we present this book, which is a compilation of papers written by indigenous authors. They are practitioners and scholars who have direct experiences in their respective countries. We divide the papers into three basic sections: leadership and accountability, analysis, and satisfaction and community. Each main section contains three chapters.

The first chapter in the leadership and accountability section is written by Peter Kratcoski. This chapter focuses on the leadership position that the International Police Executive Symposium (IPES) has taken. It traces the history of the organization and also gives a synopsis of a typical meeting. Some of the papers are now in this volume as a chapter. Others have been published in the official journal of IPES entitled *Police Practice and Research*. While the papers highlighted in this chapter are important, the reader should pick up on the leadership position of the organization. IPES brings together researchers and practitioners from all over the world who work together at the symposiums. They do cultural events as well as academic exercises. The events for us have been a source of networking, academic and cultural stimulation, and lifelong friendships. Each of the papers Peter Kratcoski presents contains important information, but the leadership role played by IPES is the key to the chapter.

The second chapter is "Police Executive Leadership and Police Legitimacy" by Vipul Kumar. Leadership, according to Kumar, is the important key to maintaining democratic policing. The article talks about how executives set the tone that officers follow. This is an intuitive argument that is well supported by research and practitioner experiences. With police management today adopting NYPD-style COMPSTAT management principles, in which police managers are browbeaten at meetings, setting a tone of civility and being an example to officers seems to be a prudent approach. This means that police leaders should not bully their own to get results but work as a team (Eterno and Silverman, 2012). The call to better leadership is certainly an important contribution.

The third chapter in this section is by Perrott and Trites entitled "On the Acceptability of Closer Public–Private Policing Partnerships: Views from the Public Side." A sample of 157 officers in Canada was sampled on their feelings toward public–private partnerships among police. This study is exceedingly important, as the role of private policing has expanded immensely. About one-third of those surveyed were outright willing to enter into such partnerships. Two other groups were identified by the authors. This is an exceedingly important article since government officers cannot possibly do the job on their own. They need partnerships with those willing to help. Developing those partnerships may be more difficult than one might think given this research. Leaders need to cultivate a more open agency willing to work with the community including private police.

The last chapter in this section is by Branislav Simonovic, Maximilian Edelbacher, and Bakhit Nurgaliyev. Their study is entitled "Reactive and Proactive Measures of Police Corruption Control: Comparative Study in Three Countries." This study is important for several reasons. First, it is written by authors who are experienced in various countries they study, namely, Austria, Serbia, and Kazakhstan. Second, comparative studies in the field are relatively rare making this one exceptional. Third, the topic of corruption is ripe for study. In essence, they use a survey to ask police officers in each of the countries about the methods used to control corruption and how successful those methods are. The officers surveyed are basically not satisfied with the anticorruption efforts being made. The authors make specific suggestions based on their data. Clearly, the international community needs to focus far more attention on combating corruption. For example, as more information is shared to fight terrorism, other countries need to be confident that the information will not be compromised.

In the second section, "Analysis," the first chapter is "Using Complaints against the Police to Improve Community–Police Relations" by Goodman-Delahunty, Taitz, Sowemimo-Coker, and Nguyen. This chapter is an analysis of the complaints against the police in Australia. The authors give practical feedback from the complaints made by the public. This is a great example of how analysis and feedback to the department can work. Additionally, it shows that the more data are available, the more an informed, intelligent conversation about policing can take place. Transparency is critical to democratic policing.

The second chapter in this section is "Cybercrime, Cyberattacks, and Problems of Implementing Organizational Cybersecurity." While the author Minnaar is in South Africa, this article is certainly written for a world audience. The vulnerabilities of the Internet are explored. Furthermore, how to defend them is even more questionable. How to police the Internet is another question. Minnaar talks about the many types of cybercrimes and outlines the vulnerabilities.

The third chapter in this section is "Intelligence Analysis: A Key Tool for Modern Police Management—The Romanian Perspective." In this chapter, Cofan and Băloi show the importance of new ways to gather and use information. In today's world, gathering and properly analyzing such information is exceedingly important. This is true not only of crime analysis but also of combating terrorism. Sharing information and closely working with police can be more effective.

The last section is "Satisfaction and Community Connections." How satisfied are the citizens with the services of the police. Are the police meeting the needs of the communities they police? In the first chapter "Paradigm Shift in Hong Kong Public Order Policing," Yung and Chau trace the history of the Hong Kong police. The thesis is that the department has moved from a control type of department to a service-oriented one. Given the difficulties of a changing environment in Hong Kong—control has gone from the British to the Chinese—the shift to this model would seem a paradox. Nevertheless, with Hong Kong still operating under a mini constitution and a democratic environment, this shift and what is happening in Hong Kong are not only worthy of study but may also be instructive for democratic police throughout the world. If the police are emblematic of the health of the democracy, Hong Kong, it appears, is doing well. Given the unique situation of Hong Kong, this chapter and the way they police operate are very important to understand.

Hanser, Gallagher, and Kuanliang's chapter on "Citizen Satisfaction with Police: The Effects of Income Level and Prior Victimization Experiences on Citizen Perceptions of Police" helps unravel the key issues about satisfaction with police services. Income and prior victimization were both found to be important to the perceptions of police by the citizens. The authors therefore recommend more focus by the police on those with prior victimizations as well as those in lower socioeconomic groups.

In the next chapter entitled "Transformations in Policing—Two Decades of Experience in Community Policing in Slovenia," Lobnikar, Meško, and Modic discuss and outline the changes of the Slovenian police after gaining their independence. The key to their development is community policing which became the organization philosophy. It is fascinating to see the development of democratic policing and the progress they have made.

The final chapter of the book is "Policing by Consent: Exploring the Possibilities of Functional Linkage between Local Police Station and Panchayat" by Kunjappan. This is a case study that took place in India. It is a unique way to join the communities being served by the police. The author delineates what might be a viable way to have the Indian police be more responsive to local community concerns.

These chapters offer hope in the future for democratic policing. The authors offer their insights and research in the three key areas of leadership and accountability, analysis, and satisfaction and community. Readers should also bear in mind when reading the main themes that we discussed earlier the extent to which police power is limited, ensuring protection of basic rights, corruption control, equal protection of the laws, and crime control/due process dichotomy.

References

Eterno, J. A. 2003. *Policing within the Law: A Case Study of the New York City Police Department*. Westport, CT: Praeger.

Eterno, J. A. ed. 2015. *The New York City Police Department: The Impact of Its Policies and Practices*. Boca Raton, FL: CRC Press–Taylor & Francis Group.

Eterno, J. A., and Silverman, E. B. 2010. NYPD's Compstat: Compare Statistics or Compose Statistics? *International Journal of Police Science and Management*. 12(3): 426–49.

Eterno, J. A., and Silverman, E. B. 2012. *The Crime Numbers Game: Management by Manipulation*. Boca Raton, FL: CRC Press–Taylor & Francis Group.

Eterno, J. A., Verma, A., and Silverman, E. B. 2016. Police performance management: Do managerial pressures influence police manipulation of crime reports? *Justice Quarterly*. 39(5): 811–33.

Gilinskiy, Y. 2009. Chapter Six Police Response in the Russian Federation. In *Police Practices in Global Perspective*. 2010. Eterno, J. A., and Das, D. K., eds. Lanham, MD: Rowman & Littlefield.

Karat, B. 2015, August 10. Mumbai police makes Khap Panchayats look good. *NDTV Opinion*. Accessed October 6, 2015. Retrieved from http://www.ndtv .com/opinion/mumbai-police-makes-khap-panchayats-look-good-1205706.

Packer, H. 1966. The Courts, the Police, and the Rest of Us. *Journal of Criminal Law and Criminology*. 57: 238–40.

Leadership and Accountability

I

Policing
Continuity and Change

1

PETER C. KRATCOSKI

Contents

Abstract

This chapter focuses on global issues in contemporary policing. It is grounded in a summary of the presentations made at the 23rd Annual Meeting of the International Police Executive Symposium. The presentations (papers, addresses, and roundtable discussions) centered on global issues relating to policing, including specialization, corruption, police education and training, leadership, police response to catastrophic events such as natural disasters, mass murders, and terrorist attacks, issues relating to discrimination against minorities and women, and police responses to victims of crime. Additional presentations focused on police organizational models that have been found to be effective in preventing and combating crime.

Introduction: Development of the International Police Executive Symposium

The leadership of any organization from time to time must reflect on where it has been and where it is going, if it is to remain vital. The 23rd annual meeting of the International Police Executive Symposium (IPES), titled "Global Issues in Contemporary Policing," provided such an opportunity. Since its founding by Dilip Das, in 1994, IPES has changed in regard to the number of meeting participants, the formats and the composition of the programs, and the characteristics of the presenters, but the goals and the structure of the IPES have not changed dramatically. The first symposium, held in Geneva, Switzerland, in 1994, had fewer than 20 participants, and they were almost entirely high-level police and government officials. Only a few of those attending were academics or women. Gradually, the topics covered in the symposiums broadened and the characteristics of the participants changed dramatically, with academics, women, and rank-and-file police officers participating in the meetings.

During the next 20 years, the symposia followed the same format in terms of structure, but the content of the presentations and the backgrounds of the participants changed dramatically. The first 10 symposia each focused on a single theme. These themes included community policing, international cooperation, traffic policing, policing crowds and public demonstrations, corruption, trafficking of women and children, terrorism, police education and training, and policing without borders. However, as new and more complex types of crime such as cybercrime, financial crime, and issues pertaining to women and minorities in policing emerged, the themes of the symposia tended to become more diversified. For example, some forms of crime such as theft, murder, robbery, prostitution, and fraud were matters for police concern for centuries, but when other crimes such as those committed on the Internet, child pornography, and various forms of financial crimes became widespread, police administrators realized that some of the old methods used to investigate and prevent crime would no longer suffice. While the nature of police work may have not changed, the types of training and skills needed to be effective changed tremendously. In addition, there has been a growing realization that, in our global society, the leaders of the components of the justice system must reach out for help from the leaders of other private and public agencies and institutions. While those employed in such agencies may not be directly connected to the justice system, those involved in higher education who are training police in specialized topic areas, researchers who provide valuable information on the effectiveness of police practices, and even social service agencies personnel who work with crime victims and abused women and children can make strong contributions to effective police work.

The keynote speeches, papers, and roundtable presentations of the IPES meeting in 2013, in Budapest, Hungary, reflected the issues and the challenges of policing in our contemporary global society. More than 110 persons, representing 40 countries, participated. The changes in the characteristics of the attendees were reflected in the fact that half of those who participated were academics, and approximately one-quarter of the participants were women who were either academics or police and other justice agency practitioners. Although the structure of the symposium was similar to the other symposia, and involved required attendance at all sessions and long working hours, the topics covered included most of the current issues pertaining to police work and even several topics specifically relating to corrections and the judicial component of the justice system.

The theme of the Budapest symposium was "Global Issues in Contemporary Policing." The several subthemes addressed during the meeting, including cybercrime, corruption, terrorism, minorities, women in policing, victims of crime, specialization in policing, and administration of police agencies, all focused to some degree on police and academic collaboration in research, training, and program implementation.

Corruption: A Critical Issue

Hetzer (2012, p. 218) notes that there is no recognized legal definition of corruption and that corruption has been defined from various perspectives, including moral, ethical, political, economic, regulatory, and criminological. He contends that "in principle, corruption is a situation in which a person responsible for performing certain duties pursues improper or unfair advantages for actions or omissions in the performance of those duties." He also believes that corruption is a major reason for the insufficient development of a country and jeopardizes the foundation of any democratic country (p. 217). The keynote address, titled "Corruption," delivered by Martin Kreutner, dean of the International Anti-Corruption Academy, focused on the efforts to combat corruption engaged in by the European Partners against Corruption (EPAC) and the European Contact-Point Network against Corruption (EACN). These groups, along with other authorities throughout Europe, cooperate to develop common standards for anticorruption measures. EPAC/EACN (2012, p. 8) developed the framework for anticorruption agencies in the Council of Europe, the European Union Member States, the European Anti-Fraud office, the European Union Police, and the Eurojust is an organization to stimulate and improve coordination between member states of the European Union "provide a platform for practitioners to exchange expertise and information, assist each other, and cooperate across national borders, both on a practical and professional level." Referring to a survey completed by the International Anti-Corruption Academy, Kreutner (2013) noted that the perception among the majority of the citizens is that corruption has increased during the recent years and the worst offenders are political officials, police, corporate and business leaders, and other public officials. In reference to those organizations investigating corruption, Kreutner (2013) maintained that in order to be successful, these agencies must have independence that is free from any political interference, adequate resources, personnel with the expertise to carry out the investigative activities, transparencies in the structure and the mechanisms used in the corruption investigations, and ability to cooperate with the media and the civil society (Kreutner, 2013). Mills (2012) and Dobovsek and Mastnak (2012) emphasize the importance of the existence of a free mass media communications network that is not politically or economically attached to the national and international efforts to combat corruption. Mills (2012) notes that in countries in which the government is either corrupt or weak, the measures used to silence the investigations of reporters can be threats of physical violence and even death. Mills (2012, p. 207) contends that "on virtually every continent, journalists who report on corruption and organized crime face obstacles. Across Asia, Africa, and Latin America, a favored tool used to silence reporters unveiling corruption is the use of antiquated criminal defamation laws." Dobovsek and Mastnak (2012) note that in some countries, particularly those in a state of economic development, both the economic sector and the political sector may become dependent on organized crime, resulting in widespread corruption in those countries. Needless to say, investigative reporting on corruption, which is very similar in the methods and the procedures followed as those used in criminal investigations, must be free from political and economic influences if it is to be successful. They contend that such investigations by the media are not likely to have much success in countries that are not democratic. Research on citizens' perceived corruption among the police revealed that there seemed to be a direct correlation between the stability of the government and the economic system and the amount of corruption. For example, it was found that in many of the eastern European countries that adopted a democratic form of government after being separated from the Soviet Union, the amount of corruption actually increased until their governments and economic systems had a chance to stabilize (see the study by Das and Marenin [2000]). This finding seems to be confirmed in the comparative study of the perception of corruption among the police by the citizens of Austria, Kazakhstan, and Serbia (Edelbacher, Simonovic, and Nurgaliyev, 2013). In Austria, a country with a stable government and economy, the people tended to trust the police and believed that corrupt police officers would be adequately disciplined by their superiors, while in Serbia and Kazakhstan, two countries that have democratic governments and economies that are still developing, the trust toward police and the belief that police who engaged in corruption and other forms of deviance would be adequately disciplined by their superiors were much lower.

Lobnikar and Mesko (2013) contend that corrupt police officers are made, not born. In order to understand corruption or lack of corruption among the police, it is necessary to understand the culture of the country, the political system, and the organizational structure of the police agency. In the study by Lobnikar and Mesko (2013), police officers were given a questionnaire in which they were asked to evaluate the seriousness of acts that appeared to be deviant engaged in by police. In addition, they were asked to recommend the form of discipline that should be used for officers who had been caught engaging in a specific deviant act. On the basis of their findings, the authors concluded that a just disciplinary policy at all levels must be followed to enhance the integrity of the police organization. Almost half of the officers believed that the discipline given to superior officers was too low, and the officers in the study reported that in some cases no action at all was taken to discipline the higher-ranking officers who engaged in deviant behavior. The researchers suggested that opening the disciplinary policies to the public may be one way to help build trust in the police by the citizenry.

Other presentations (Albrecht, 2013; Antinori, 2013; Haefaele and Hesselink, 2013; Shikwambana, 2013; Storey-White, 2013a) reaffirmed the findings of much of the prior research completed on police corruption and deviance that corruption within the police departments exists because they function within a culture in which corruption is the norm, the code of silence adhered to by police officers prohibits the noncorrupt officers from exposing the deviance of their fellow officers, and the leadership within the police organization is so weak or corrupt that even if the officers who are corrupt are exposed, except in extreme cases, the punishment will likely not be severe enough to deter the corrupt officer. Shikwambana (2013) and Haefaele and Hesselink (2013) note that criminal behavior by the police against women who are under police supervision in South Africa, while widespread, often goes unnoticed, and the offenders are rarely punished. In a survey of such women, the large majority claimed to have either witnessed or personally experienced while in custody such police brutality as women being raped, inappropriately touched or beaten, sworn at by the police, or offered bribes by the police in exchange for sexual favors. Their main reason for not bringing the deviant behavior to the attention of the authorities was the fear of being victimized in the future. While emphasizing that South African police in general are not corrupt, the researchers observed that the traditional values of the South African culture, in which gender-based violence exists, as well as general disrespect for law and order of many police officers, poor training of the police, and negligent police management are all reasons why it will take some time before the situation will change. When South Africa gained its independence, there was a need for a quick turnover in police personnel. Many police officers with serious criminal records were hired, nepotism was prevalent, and the standards for entrance and the pay received by the new recruits were low. There has been a gradual improvement in the methods used to screen new recruits, as well as in the training and the salaries officers receive. However, the transformation of the police is still in a state of transition.

Eterno (2013a), using several research methodologies, including surveys, secondary data analysis, and case studies, concluded that the drastic decrease in index crimes in New York, as reported by the New York Police Department (NYPD), while attributed to the effectiveness of the Computer Statistics (COMPSTAT) organizational model, in actuality can be partially explained by the manipulation of the reports of felony crimes by police administrators. Based on several sources of data gathered from those outside the NYPD, Eterno contended that the pressure to show that COMPSTAT is effective led to a kind of "conditioning among police officers to report many felony crimes as misdemeanor crimes" (slide 4). This widespread practice led to a drastic reduction of felony crimes reported. This prolonged decrease in serious crimes could justify administrative decisions, such as reducing the number of police officers on the force. However, Eterno (2013a) pointed out that research statistics for the period during which COMPSTAT was implemented reveal that, while the number of suspects stopped by the police in New York significantly increased during this period, the number of felony crimes reported significantly declined during this same period, thus adding more evidence of a manipulation of crime statistics. The researcher also surveyed retired police administrators (captains and above), comparing those who retired before COMPSTAT with those who retired after COMPSTAT was implemented. For those who were aware of the manipulation practices, it was found that less than one-third of the officers claimed that they felt pressured to make numbers look better, changed words to downgrade the report, or did not take reports when they should have, while more than half of those who retired after COMPSTAT was implemented claimed that they were pressured to change words to make the numbers look better or downgraded the offense, and almost half claimed that they did not take reports when they should have (Eterno, 2013a). Finally, more than three-quarters of the retired officers reported that these practices were unethical. In conclusion, Eterno (2013a) believed that, with more cooperation between police administration and outside researchers, with researchers having access to police data, the disclosure of information to the public will eventually create an atmosphere in which the public will become less distrustful of the police.

Police Education, Training, and Leadership

While the content and the structure of the training police recruits receive have changed dramatically over the past several decades, there is a need for even more changes, if the police are going to be able to meet the challenges of a global society. Several of the IPES Budapest speakers addressed the need for an international focus in the training of police officers and administrators. Cordner and Shain (2011, p. 281) noted that "police education and training expanded all around the world during the twentieth century and were seen as the cornerstones of police professionalism and modernization." In the twenty-first century, those responsible for police education and training must recognize the need to change the nature of police training, in order to respond to the challenges presented to the police in a global society. Cordner and Shain (2011, pp. 281–82) noted that "police trainers fly around the world to deliver their courses. Organizations like Interpol, Europol, the U.S. International Criminal Investigative Training Assistance Program (ICITAP) and the International Association of Chiefs of Police (IACP) play a growing role in the provision of training, and training content focuses more and more on global issues such as international crime."

Boda (2013a), in his keynote address, stated that policing in the future must bridge the gap between domestic policing and international policing. He observed that "we must learn from each other regarding how to use the most advanced equipment and training and legal standards to fight all forms of international crime and corruption." In Hungary, international specialized crime and corruption prevention units were created.

The International Law Enforcement Academy, located in Budapest, and three other academies located in other countries were started under a US State Department initiative in the late twentieth century. In a program modeled after the Federal Bureau of Investigation (FBI) Training Academy, in Quantico, police officers from various countries complete seven weeks of basic training. There are also 30 to 35 specialized courses offered during the year, each consisting of two-week durations. Various cooperative international training academies have been established in many parts of the world. For example, the Middle European Police Academy was created in the late 1990s. Law enforcement leaders from various middle European countries engage in two to three months of training course, and after returning to their native countries, these law enforcement leaders pass on the information gained to other police officers in their agencies (Kratcoski, 2007, p. 18).

Models for Police Organization

While the current trend in police education and training is to prepare officers to solve policing problems that have international societal implications, the fact remains that the vast majority of police officers throughout the world serve their local communities. Some police officers may work in a jurisdiction that covers a few square miles with a few hundred people being served, while in other jurisdictions, thousands of officers cover hundreds of square miles with millions of people being served. Nevertheless, the focus is still on domestic police matters. With these large differences in the communities served, perhaps there is not one organizational model that can be adapted to best serve the needs of all communities. Often, the organizational model followed by a specific police department is not the result of careful planning and research on what works. Rather, the mission and the goals of a particular police department are often determined by political, social, and economic factors in the community. In certain countries throughout the world, the mission of the police is to protect the state, while in other countries, the mission of the police is to serve and protect the citizens of the community. The mission and the goals of the police change as a result of changes in political thought, changes in the laws, and changes in the sentiments of the public. As missions and goals change, the type of leadership, organizational structure, recruitment and training of personnel, and operating procedures will change to reflect the new goals of the organization. For example, in the United States, the missions and the goals of large city police organizations have changed several times. As large cities began to establish police departments in the mid-nineteenth century, the hiring of police officers was predominately based on political patronage. There were few requirements regarding education and training, and corruption at all levels was widespread. However, there was an emphasis on service to the community, and, since the patrol officers were normally assigned to work in the neighborhoods in which they lived, the communication between officers and residents was generally positive. The negative reaction to the political corruption and the patronage by the press and several reform groups resulted in the police reform movement of the first part of the twentieth century. Those backing police reform attempted to remove the patronage and establish police organizations that had standards for employment based on education and training. The new formally structured professional police departments were more orientated to crime control than service (see the study by Kratcoski and Kempf [1995]). In the 1960s and the 1970s, the civil rights movement, the protests against the Vietnam War, and other factors created a demand for a type of policing that would be more responsive to the needs of the citizenry. This resulted in changes in the missions and the goals as well as changes in the organizational structures of police departments. This so-called new approach to policing, popularized by academics, was labeled community policing and generally called for a decentralization of the structure, less specialization, more decision-making power for the street officers, and more interaction and communications with the citizenry (Kratcoski, 1995; Kratcoski and Dukes, 1995; Mastrofski, 1992; Trojanowicz and Buckueroux, 1990).

At present, political, economic, social, and even technological factors continue to influence the way the leadership of police organizations responds to the demands for strict crime control and the demands for the police to be more responsive to the needs of the community. However, regardless of the differences in beliefs on what should be the mission and the goals of police organizations, they all agree that the police should have high standards for recruitment and that the candidates should be educated and well trained and free from political and criminal influences. The COMPSTAT model was first applied in New York City and rapidly developed in many other cities throughout the United States. It tries to combine the critical elements found in the traditional, centralized, bureaucratic police organizational model with the critical elements of the decentralized community policing model. It is a multifaceted approach to reducing crime and maximizing the effectiveness of personnel and resources while also addressing the quality-of-life matters. In New York City, a decentralized management model has been adopted. High-level police executives from the central headquarters meet with local precinct commanders to discuss problems and develop strategies to try to solve these problems. The precinct commanders have the authority to make decisions on how to address the problems existing in the precincts they command (Wikipedia, 2014).

It should be noted that any police organizational and management model is not inherently superior to another. Too often, in an attempt to implement a model that appears to be effective in another city, a police department may attempt to put in place a model that is either not comparable to the culture and the traditions of the people or for which the resources to properly implement it are not available. In addition, it should be noted that, regardless of the particular environment in which police officers work, the essence of the job is the same all over the world.

In an interview with Mal Hyde, South Australia police commissioner, completed by David Baker (2011, p. 7), it was noted that "policing is a profession where some things change and some things remain the same. The dynamics of policing, the problem of policing, the art of policing, and what policing is all about don't change, because it is a mixture of the behavior of people (innate human behavior that might vary because of different cultures) and then also the way authority interplays with that behavior. The essence of what policing is all about; now that doesn't change. It is the same today as it was 20 years ago or 30 years ago." Commissioner Hyde goes on to note that the details, the crime problems, the technological methods, and the strategies used to investigate crimes may change, but the dynamics of policing do not change. The problems of administering a police agency, in which the tasks related to the job are constantly expanding, while the personnel and the resources available to the agency to complete the tasks are decreasing, were lamented by several speakers at the Budapest symposium. For example, in the case of Brazil (Bruns and Bruns, 2013), the problems of securing the borders are tremendous, since Brazil borders on 10 countries and occupies almost half of the land mass of South America. Although the majority of the crimes in Brazil are committed in the large cities, many crimes such as drug trafficking, trafficking of firearms and humans, pornography, and other forms of crime such as auto theft may originate in smaller population areas of other countries but require the crossing of international borders to reach the targeted distribution areas, that is, the large cities. The Brazilian border police use the latest available crime prevention equipment and techniques, including radar, helicopter patrol, specially trained dogs, and video cameras, to try to curtail the crimes. However, the problems had grown to such proportions that it was necessary to assign interior police to the borders posts. Several possible solutions mentioned by Bruns (2013) were installation of new equipment, better training of the officers, particularly in the area of intelligence-gathering, improvements in cooperation and communications between the interior and the exterior police, as well as more cooperative relations with the governments of other South American countries.

Yung, Chau, and Chi-Wai (2013) noted that, although community policing has been instituted in Hong Kong, there are many challenges that must be overcome, such as police misuse of force, corruption, and tense relations between the community and the police. Research by Salgado (2013) illustrated the universality of police functions and how the most important goals of police organizations were achieved in two cities with large differences in population and inhabited by citizens having different cultures, with the police organizational structures being quite different. In his research comparing the Hague and Tokyo, it was found that while the Tokyo police organization was centralized and the Hague police organization was decentralized, both police agencies had viable strategies and used tactics to prevent crime, solve crime problems, and provide service to the citizenry. The findings of a qualitative study of the effectiveness of the police of Delhi, India, completed by Chhabra and Chhabra (2013), suggests that police effectiveness is determined by many internal factors as well as external factors. For the study, which included both Delhi street officers and police administrators, an effectiveness model was conceptualized and used to measure effectiveness. This model included the dynamic interplay of the external factors that might affect police performance, such as the public's perception of the police or public opinion, confidence in the police, political directives and interference such as continuously changing expectations, and goal priorities of the police. The internal factors affecting police performance that were examined included organization structure of the police agency, inefficient use of personnel and resources, lack of good leadership, and lack of coordination with other policing agencies and criminal justice agencies, such as prosecutors and the judiciary. In regard to the priority of the goals of the Delhi Police, there was a general agreement among the officers included in the research that public order and crime prevention, safety and security, and public service should be the major goals of the police, and the extent to which these goals were achieved should be used to measure police effectiveness. However, as mentioned earlier, there are many factors that interfere with the achievement of the goals. The complexity of police–public relationships relating to such factors as police corruption, incompetence, insensitivity, lack of concern for victims of crime, police being unsympathetic toward the poor and the minorities, as well as public apathy, lack of cooperation from the citizenry, unrealistic expectations, and interference from the public and politicians all increase the difficulty for police to be highly effective on the job. The authors suggest that both organizational changes and individual changes are needed to improve effectiveness. Organizational changes could include capacity building, improvements in the utilization and the management of resources, rigid adherence to a strong ethical code, and improvements in relationships, cooperation, and communications with the public and other justice agencies. The changes in individual factors suggested include better selection of personnel, improvement in training, and development of police officer competencies that are prioritized with the goals of the agency.

De Benedetto (2013) noted that police organizations throughout the world are experiencing reductions in personnel, funding, and other resources, while the tasks of policing are expanding and the political powers, as well as the public, are demanding more from the police in terms of service and safety. Thus, these organizations are forced to develop new management models to improve and assess their performance. He recommends a management model that was initially developed for private corporations but can be adapted by public agencies such as the police.

The key performance metrics of the plan include measuring police performance through quantifiable outcomes and by holding agencies accountable. He notes that performance measurement is an ongoing process that involves systematic efforts to establishing desired outcomes, setting performance standards, and collecting, analyzing, and reporting on data used to improve both individual and collective performances. De Benedetto emphasized that the instruments used to measure police performance in the past, such as number of arrests, response times, and clearance rates, are no longer adequate. Instead, he offered a comprehensive, multidimensional measurement system. The dimensions of this model include the extent to which

- Crime and victimization are reduced
- Offenders are held accountable
- Fear of crime is reduced and security is enhanced
- Safety and order in public places is enhanced
- Police force is used sparingly and fairly
- Citizen satisfaction is enhanced (De Benedetto, 2013, slide 11).

The recommended model can also be useful in determining the health or the dysfunction of an organization and in assessing such matters as police misconduct, abusive behavior, and failure to perform required duties (De Benetetto, 2013, slide 13).

Cofan (2013) suggested that an intelligence analysis model can be utilized to measure the effectiveness of policing in Romania. The fear of crime as well as the belief that the police are not able to do anything about preventing crime is rampant in Romania. The focus of modern police should be on problem solving, and a problem-solving-oriented policing approach can best achieve the goals. The solving approach requires the collection of data, the analysis of data, the establishment of competency performance criteria, the drafting of an action plan, the implementation of the plan, and the evaluation of the results. In addition to the implementation of problem-solving policing, the police leadership must reach out to the community by sharing information with media groups and by instituting measures that will lead to the reduction of the citizens' fear of crime.

The Los Angeles Police Department has developed a special training model to provide officers the type of experience that will lead to improvements in police performance (Putman, 2013). The model can best be described as the use of a combination of community policing techniques and problem-solving policing techniques to achieve the mission and vision values of the policing department. The training is grounded in the notion of the team policing model developed in the 1970s (see the study by Kratcoski and Walker [1978, p. 389]). Officers are trained to function as a team in the social environment to which they are assigned. The Los Angeles Police Department, in collaboration with the University of Los Angeles Graduate School of Psychology, developed the problem-solving model for training officers. Paradigms are used during the training sessions, and both qualitative and quantitative measures are used in the assessment of police performance. Outcome data suggest that the training has a definite impact on improving police performance.

Specialization in Police Education, Training, and Leadership

The type of education and training that will best prepare police officers for the different roles they must perform has been a topic debated by police administrators and by those academics that have completed research on the subject. The matter of preparing officers for a leadership position has also been hotly debated. Several papers and an excellent roundtable discussion by Boda (2013a,b,c), Das (2013a), Edelbacher (2013a,b), and Eterno (2013a,b) focused on police leadership. Presentations by Gottschalk (2013b), Gyebrovszky (2013), and a roundtable by Storey-White (2013a,b), Wuesterwald (2013a,b), Corzine (2013a,b) discussed responding to mass murder situations, cybersecurity and other areas of police work requiring specialized training and expertise. The presentations included identifying potential mass murderers and responding to mass murder situations, preparing for natural disasters, including earthquakes, floods, and tsunamis, and human-made disasters, such as nuclear power plant breakdowns and collapse of the financial system of a country.

Lepard et al. (2013) noted that the investigations of serial murder are the most difficult to conduct and require the officers to have specialized training and skills for various reasons. The absence of bodies, murder sites, physical evidence, and reliable chronology makes it difficult to determine if a missing person report should even require a murder investigation. Generally, if a missing person investigation by the police is started, it will continue as a missing person investigation "even after recognizing the possibility of a serial murderer being responsible in the missing person case" (p. 4).

Mass Murderers

Police decisions for determining if there will be an investigation for a missing person and the strategies for investigations will differ, depending on a number of factors. If there are no bodies and no reports on missing persons, no investigation is completed. There is considerable evidence that a large number of missing persons and possible victims of serial killers are never recorded and investigated (Lepard et al., 2013). A missing person investigation is started when there is a report filed with the police, but if a person or a dead body is not found, the case continues as a missing person investigation. However, if a number of missing person reports are filed and there appear to be some common characteristics associated with the disappearances of the persons, the investigation tends to shift toward a case of a serial murderer. If dead bodies are located, the focus and the strategies of the investigation shift entirely to a murder case (Lepard et al., 2013).

The characteristics of mass murder situations are quite different from serial killing situations and generally call for an entirely different response. Corzine (2013a, slide 1) indicates that while there are several different definitions of mass murder, it usually involves the killing of several people by one or more offenders during a short time span, generally within a few hours or less, within one location or within a short distance from the original murders. She goes on to explain that the terms *spree murder* and *bifurcated mass murder* are often used to designate those mass murder events that happened at more than one location (Corzine, 2013a, slide 6). Corzine (2013b) indicated that, while most sensational mass murder incidents are well covered by the mass media, with the characteristics of the murder/s and the victims recorded by the media as well as the criminal justice investigation agencies, numerous cases of mass murder may receive little attention. The National Incident-Based Reporting System developed by the U.S. FBI, while having limitations (less than one-third of the United States is included, coding errors, and missing information), is nevertheless the most comprehensive and reliable source of information on mass murders. The data collected in this reporting system contain information on the incident, including weapons used, locations, and generally, one is able to determine if a victim–offender relationship existed prior to the mass murder incident (Corzine, 2013b, slide 7). Wilds (2013a, slide 3) summarized the statistics and the research completed on mass murders in the United States. He noted that the most likely locations for mass murder to occur are stores, malls, restaurants, government buildings, and houses of worship, with 50% of the mass murder incidents being at workplaces or schools. Also, from 1982 to the present, there were almost as many wounded as killed in such incidents. Wuesterwald (2013b) referred to typologies developed by Fox and Levin and Holmes to illustrate the types of mass murders and the possible motivations they may have to kill. She noted that the motivation for those who kill in a school could fit into a number of categories, including frustration, social isolation, loss of an intimate friend, revenge, power, loyalty to a leader, profit, terrorism, sexual factors, and execution (slide 25). In addition, many murderers do not seem to fit into any of the profiles mentioned earlier, and their motivations are unexplained (slide 27).

The efforts of psychologists, behavioral scientists, and criminal justice investigators to predict the likelihood of a mass murder incident have not been generally successful. Perhaps the most attention has been given to school shootings resulting in mass murder. Generally, the information on the incidents pertaining to motive, source of the weapon used, and offender/s–victim/s relationship is collected after the fact, and even here, the motive is often difficult to ascertain, since the offender either is killed by the police or dies from a self-inflicted wound. Several typologies of mass murderers include those who have a specific target and those whose killing is random, those who kill for revenge, and those who may be mentally ill. In those cases in which it appears that there is no specific target, perhaps the victims may have just been in the way of the murderer who had one or more specific targets in mind. In the coverage by the mass media as well as in the law enforcement investigations conducted by the police, the characteristics of those victims who were injured during the incident generally do not receive a great deal of attention. For example, in the school shootings that occurred in the United States between 2010 and 2013, in which two or more people were killed, there were also victims injured (shot, stabbed, beaten) in almost 60% of the incidents (Wikipedia, 2014). In summary, considerably more research is needed before criminal justice agencies can say with confidence that they can predict and prevent mass murder.

Prevention of Mass Murder in Schools and Public Places
As previously noted, the vast majority of mass murderers that occurred in the United States happened in workplaces, shopping malls, government

buildings, places of worship, or schools. The prevention strategies followed by each of these types of institutions have varied, depending on the type of institution. The security in specific types of government buildings, such as courthouses and places that house city, state, or federal workers, has been considerably enhanced. Generally, the establishment of new security measures in private establishments such as office buildings, places of worship, and shopping centers has been piecemeal, depending on such factors as the size of the establishment, the potential for a mass murder situation to develop, and the ability to pay for the new security programs. On the other hand, the administrations of schools throughout the United States have instituted many new school security measures to protect the students against school violence and particularly school shootings.

In a study of school security programs (Kratcoski, Edelbacher, and Graff, 2010), in which the school security in the United States was compared with that of Austria, it was found that the school security measures adopted in the United States varied considerably. However, the strategies and the programs adopted tended to include the following:

- Zero-tolerance policies
- Cooperative planning developed by administrators, teaching staff, local police, and community residents
- Enhancement of existing communications systems
- Improvements in physical security measures, including having lighting, installing video cameras, locking entrance doors during school hours, requiring staff and students to wear identification tags, and in some cases using metal detector screens
- Enhancement of security at special events such as sporting events and musical concerts
- Coordination of intelligence gathering and attempt to identify those youths who may be a high risk for becoming violent
- Provision of special training for the staff and the students on how to respond to bomb threats, school shootings, and natural disasters that might occur on school grounds
- Presence police officers (student resource officers) in schools on a regular schedule

In Austria, the threat of violence and mass murder in the schools is minimal compared to the threat in many of the schools in the United States. However, the growing citizen concern about this problem resulted in the members of the national government acknowledging that a problem existed and taking action in the form of new legislation that provided for a nationwide strategy focused on the prevention of school violence. This legislation consisted of the following:

- Providing information to the public on the causes of school violence
- Networking and cooperating with teachers, parents, school officials, medical staff, police, and academic researchers
- Instituting prevention and intervention programs in the schools that include the public, the parents, and the teachers
- Completing systematic documentation and evaluation of the general strategy plan and providing feedback

Police Response to Catastrophes, including Terrorism and Natural Disasters

The research completed by Yokoyama (2013) revealed that Japan had put in place a comprehensive plan for responding to crises. The following steps were taken soon after the earthquake and the tsunami occurred in Japan in March 2011, when a command system prescribed under the Basic Law on Disaster Countermeasures was immediately put into operation. The actions taken included the following:

1. The umbrella plan of the national government authorized the response from a number of police agencies to the disaster area. In addition, the prime minister and other high-level government officials became directly involved in rescue efforts.
2. The prime minister used the mass media to appeal to the public to remain calm and not to panic.
3. The private sector engaged in a number of relief activities. For example, the Interpreffectual Emergency Rescue Unit was employed. In addition, volunteers served as firefighters, emergency vehicle drivers, assisted the police by patrolling evacuated areas, and provided medical and food supplies to those affected by the earthquake and the tsunami.
4. The riot squad was dispatched to the damaged areas to maintain public order.
5. The police and other rescue units established good communications with the mass media agencies to the extent that these communication networks were very helpful in rescue and relief activities.
6. The police, the medical teams, and the firefighters units coordinated their efforts to assure that food, clothing, water, electric power, and medical supplies were brought to those in need as quickly as possible.
7. Power units from other parts of Japan not hit by the earthquake were brought in to assist the police stationed in the hardest hit areas.
8. Data were immediately collected and analyzed, and the information was fed back to those agencies that could find the information helpful in the rescue efforts.

Terrorism

How to prevent terrorist attacks and destroy terrorist organizations has been a hotly debated subject throughout the world, particularly in the United States, after terrorists destroyed the World Trade Center buildings on September 11, 2001. Hundreds of books and articles have been written on the subject, and those countries that feel that they might be targets for terrorism have created new national security agencies and spent huge amounts of money to increase the personnel and the resources devoted to the prevention of terrorism. A keynote address by Janos Hajdu at the annual meeting of the IPES held in Budapest, in 2013, titled "Issues on Crime and Terrorism," was devoted to the ways to combat terrorist organizations. Other speakers at the symposium, Weyers, Sim, Paul, and Antinori, demonstrated models for identifying those individuals and groups who were vulnerable to accepting violent extremism as a method to address real or perceived transgressions against them. The mass communications, in particular, the Internet, has been used by various extremist groups to spread their messages and to recruit new followers. It was noted that all countries have some internal (domestic) terrorist organizations and external internationally based left- and right-wing extremist groups whose sole purpose is to cause confusion or fear and to convince the public that the government cannot protect its citizens and guarantee their security. Some internal and external terrorist organizations do not adhere to any political ideology, and these are the most difficult to understand, to determine their motivations, and to predict their behavior. In Hungary, Hajdu (2013) reported that specialized units were created to combat both internal and external terrorism. Several speakers at the IPES Budapest meeting emphasized that maintaining communications and information exchanges among law enforcement agencies throughout the world is critical in combating terrorist organizations. The development of international laws and binding legal agreements must be a high priority for all countries that have concerns about international terrorist organizations. This is true, even if the terrorist organizations do not base their operations in the country but merely use it as a pass-through country (Hajdu, 2013).

The topics of cybercrime and how cybercrime can threaten the national security of a country were discussed by Tamas Gyebrovszky (2013), who gave a detailed description of the methods used in Hungary to provide internet security. The difficulty in controlling the effects of cybercrime was also discussed at the symposium. While the techniques used by the police and the security agencies are constantly improving, the Internet methods used by criminals to commit financial crimes, direct terrorist operations, and promote organized criminal activities are becoming so sophisticated that it is very difficult for police and other government agencies to develop the techniques to establish appropriate prevention and control mechanisms.

Peak (2013) reported on the security measures used by the gaming casinos. He stated that the role of these private security officers is very similar to that of a public police officer, with the exceptions of the limitations on the jurisdiction of the private security officers. In the United States, the gaming industry is legal in a number of states, and it is expected to become legal in the majority of states in the future. Security personnel are responsible for protecting billions of dollars of assets and personal property of those who visit the gaming facilities. Security protective measures include closed-circuit television cameras and highly trained personnel. The security measures have now expanded to include preventive and response patterns for responding to crises. For example, security officers can intercept and question suspects and are trained to respond to bomb threats, robbery attempts, accidents, and all types of disturbances within the facility. The use of various electronic devices and the specialized training of the security personal provide protection against cheaters, potential robbers, and those bent on creating a crisis.

The rational choice model demonstrates how this model can be a useful tool to identify potential terrorist individuals and groups. However, when using such models, there is always the danger of violating privacy rights and the potential for profiling innocent individuals.

The Role of Mass Media

The mass media often plays a critical role when law enforcement, security, and rescue agencies of a nation, a city, or a community respond to crisis situations such as natural disasters, terrorism, taking of hostages, and mass murders. The mass media can be very helpful and assist the efforts of specialized safety units, as demonstrated in the assistance given during rescue efforts following the earthquake and the tsunami in Japan (Yokoyama, 2013). In addition, the media can make positive contributions to an understanding of the causes of human-made disasters as in the cases where investigative reporters uncover extensive corruption among government officials who overlook violations of safety during their inspections of factories, dams, mines, buildings, bridges, energy plants, and entertainment centers. On the other hand, the media can inhibit and actually interfere with the work of the specialized safety units. Wilds (2013b) reported that the safety forces had a real problem with the mass media during and after the school crisis at Fort Gibson, Oklahoma, in which several children were killed and others held hostage. During the hours immediately after the crisis, the parents, the critical response teams, the community, and the political officials were in constant communication. All the national, international, and local news media converged at the scene of the disaster, with helicopters, equipment trucks, cameras, and other vehicles.

These were intermixed with police vehicles, ambulances, and hospital rescue helicopters, resulting in breakdowns in communications, lack of coordination, and much wasted effort. Wilds (2013b) noted that although mass murder incidents are generally spontaneous and dynamic, it is still possible to be prepared for such an event by developing a plan that includes the mass media in the response efforts. The media can be given short answers to key questions as to what happened, who are the victims, if known, and who is in charge of the situation.

Minorities, Women in Policing, and Victims of Crime

A major theme that developed during the IPES conference in Budapest, focused on minorities, women in policing, and assistance for victims of crime. The keynote address on "Policing Multicultural Problems" (Holdaway, 2013a) and the presentations that focused on police–minority group relations emphasized the importance of officers' culture, attitudes, values, and personal experiences and how they can affect their perceptions of the victims of crime from other cultures and races and how the cultures and the values of minority groups can affect how the police are perceived by them. This is a topic area that clearly demonstrated the contributions of the academics. The findings from research and the assistance of academics in the training of the police on human relations topics have had a significant effect in changing the way the police respond to victims of crime, particularly violent crimes against women and children, and in some cases have led to police developing specialized units to work with these victims. The importance of collaboration and cooperation of the police with service agencies such as victim services, battered women shelters, and children's service agencies is readily acknowledged by most police administrators.

Taylor et al. (2013) and Leukhina (2013) revealed that those police administrators responsible for the planning and the implementation of specialized police training pertaining to sexual violence often commit one or more errors by not taking into account how the response to sexual violence may be driven by the resources available, the organizational structure of the police organization, and, in particular, the culture, the values, and the attitudes of the officers. The authors noted that the research on police training, sex crime investigations, and management of procedures for responding to sex crimes is often ad hoc, not based on policy, and inconsistent (slide 9). In addition, regardless of the specialized training they have received on sex crimes and victims of sex crimes, the particular police response to the crime is more often based on the officers' attitudes than on the policies and the official procedures (slide 10). The authors recommended that some form of systematic assessment be used in the recruitment and the selection of police officers. While many departments use some form of assessment of police officer attitudes, it is generally not an integral part of the selection decision or an ongoing process followed in the supervision and the management of police officers. The authors acknowledged that police administrators and prosecutors are generally becoming more aware of the research completed on the importance of attitudes in the decision making of the police and that many police organizations, including the Victoria Police in Australia, are using these research findings to improve the selections and the training of officers.

In a report on crime trends in Japan, Oyaizu (2013) contended that official crime statistics showing a drastic decrease in crime in Japan are misleading, since a large number of victims of crime never report the victimizations to the police. This is particularly true for crimes committed against children, such as physical and sexual abuse, child pornography, physical abuse of women and elderly, and fraud (slide 13). A great amount of personal abuse and violence against these groups is hidden, because they occur in the home and the perpetuators are either members of the family or close acquaintances of the family. In nationwide surveys, more than 80% of the respondents indicated that the crime situation in Japan is not any better than it was 10 years ago (slide 6). The author attributed much of the increase in crimes against the vulnerable to the changes in the international and global societies, which have had an effect on the people of Japan. These include economic recession, natural disasters, involvement of the mass media, particularly the Internet, and changes in the family, the culture, and the values (slide 19).

Barkhuizen (2013) pointed out that males who are victims of domestic violence are often subjected to ridicule by the South African police who investigate domestic violence cases, since the culture of the South African people emphasizes that males are stronger and more dominant than females, and thus, the victimization of a man by a woman is an abnormal incident.

Hanser (2013a) suggested that section 287 (9) of the 1996 U.S. Immigration and Nationality Act that broadened immigration and enforcement powers for local police actually created discrimination against Native American citizens, particularly those of Mexican descent (slide 1). The passage of this act by the U.S. Congress in 1996 created more responsibilities and additional demands for services relating to immigration but did not provide for additional budgetary assistance (slide 4). In addition, on matters relating to immigration, the local police are under the direct supervision of the federal government. Although the local police are not obligated to participate in the federal cooperative policing programs, they experience a great deal of pressure to do so from the public, the federal agencies, and the local politicians. Several states, including Arizona (Hanser, 2013a), have passed legislation more aggressive than the federal legislation in regard to police investigation of possible illegal entry and residence of aliens. The negative results coming from this aggressive approach to law enforcement are claims of violations of minority citizens' rights pertaining to arrests without probable cause, stop and frisk, profiling, and harassment (slide 8). In those states having a large minority population, such practices as those described earlier tend to lead to considerable resentment by the minority groups toward the police and reduce the opportunities for the police to engage in community policing, since the minority population is less likely to cooperate with the police by reporting crimes and providing information. The ways to reduce the negative effects include having states discard discriminatory laws and, in regard to the relationship between the federal and local law enforcement agencies, developing a more equal partnership between these agencies by giving local policing agencies more say in decision making.

Several of the presenters at the IPES conference, in Budapest, in 2013 reflected on the low proportion of women and minorities in police forces throughout the world. The reasons for the imbalance in the ratio of men and women in the police forces are still not completely understood. In several states, there are tremendous pressures from political figures and citizenry for the police to curb the flow of illegal immigrants into their communities, and thus, the local police often feel that they must accept these additional responsibilities, such as increased surveillance and investigation of suspected illegal immigrants. These enhanced tactics have often resulted in charges against the local police of racial profiling, harassment, discrimination, illegal arrests, and other violations of the rights of minority citizens (slide 8).

In a study focusing on women who commit white-collar crimes, Gottschalk (2013a) found that the extent and the role of women in the commission of white-collar and financial crimes have been generally overlooked in the research. In his study of 255 convicted white-collar criminals, more than 90% were men. He found that the male and female criminals were very similar for some characteristics. For example, he could not find any evidence of discrimination in the type and the length of sentences received for men and women who were convicted of similar types of white-collar crimes. The differences in the two groups by gender were that the male white-collar criminals had significantly higher personal income, paid more taxes, and had greater personal wealth than the female white-collar criminals. He concluded that the major reason why women were so underrepresented in white-collar crime relates to the fact that women have far less opportunity to commit these types of crimes, since they are less likely to be heads of corporations or leaders in banking and stock exchange or to hold high level positions in the government.

Perrott (2013) suggested that the question is still open regarding the extent to which minorities and women are treated fairly and equally in the recruitment of police into the Canadian police forces. The goals of recruiting minorities and women resulting from the civil rights movement of the

1960s and the desire to improve police services and enhance relationships (slide 2) appear not to have been met, since women and visible minorities are still underrepresented in most police departments in Canada (slides 5 and 6). In addition, more research is needed to determine if minorities and women are being given equal treatment in regard to assignments, promotions, and relationships within the police organizations. He concluded that many questions related to workplace harassment, tension with the organizations, and discriminatory practices with the public need to receive more attention and are areas in which the police and the academics can collaborate in research.

Some police departments that have recognized this matter as being a problem have adopted management strategies developed for business corporations for recruiting women and minorities into police work. Linn (2013) illustrated how new initiatives at the national, state, and local levels resulted in some very positive programs to assist victims of sex trafficking in Brooklyn, New York. She noted that although the federal and state laws on sexual trafficking are somewhat different in terminology and scope, they are nevertheless compatible, since the laws address offenders' involvement in recruitment, harboring, transportation, provision, or obtaining of a person for the purpose of a commercial sex act. The commercial sex legislation relates to persons being induced by force, fraud, or coercion or, in the case of minors, the person now having attained 18 years of age (Linn, 2013, p. 22). In the past, the major initiatives by federal, state, and local governments have focused on the prevention or the curtailing of sex crimes through legislation, interagency task forces, and specialized training for the police. However, the focus has gradually changed as a result of federal initiatives such as the Trafficking Victims Protection Reauthorization Act of 2013 and various state and local initiatives designed to protect and assist victims of sex crimes. The Trafficking Victims Protection Act renewed critical federal antitrafficking programs and provided resources for human trafficking victims, It granted new tools for the prosecution of human traffickers and enhanced the opportunities to form partnerships to curtail human trafficking with those countries in which human trafficking is most prevalent. Locally, the city of New York (Linn, 2013) has instituted new initiatives to combat sex crimes and to assist victims of human trafficking for the purpose of engaging in sex crimes. The 2013 Safe Harbor Law provided resources for the office of the district attorney of Kings Colony, Brooklyn, to

- Initiate a public information campaign on preventing human trafficking
- Provide for special training for laws enforcement officers
- Provide for relief services to victims of human trafficking

- Provide the resources to enable the police to rigidly enforce the laws for those who engage in human trafficking, especially if the victim is under the age of 18 (slide 8).

The research completed by Barrow (2013) focused on the extent to which urban minority youths perceived themselves as being victims of police practices in such areas as being harassed, discourteously treated, verbally abused, not provided with assistance when needed, and being victims of excessive force. Using a qualitative research design that involved face-to-face interviews, the researcher found that the youths interviewed had both positive and negative attitudes toward the police. For example, several youths indicated that the police were responsive in time of need and helped the community but that they also witnessed negative attitudes and disrespect from the police. It was also mentioned that the response time to a call for service was often very slow, and some youth complained of being constantly stopped and searched by the police. These youths indicated that they were constantly afraid of doing anything wrong and that they dressed in clothing that would not attract police attention, even though they would have preferred other styles of clothing. She concluded that the youths welcomed more police presence in the neighborhood because they were needed to maintain social control but recommended that the police become more proactive and fair in their administration of law enforcement.

Berlin (2013a) reported that prior research confirmed that when the attitudes of minority group members toward the police are compared with those of nonminority group members, the attitudes of the minority population toward the police are significantly less positive. He completed a survey of attitudes toward the police. The respondents were students attending a university located in a large eastern city in the United States. The large majority of the respondents were African-American. More than half of the respondents had experienced contact with the police during the past four years, as victims of crime, as witnesses to a crime, being questioned as a suspect of a crime, or being arrested (slide 10). He found that the respondents' attitudes toward the police were predominately shaped by their first personal experiences and, in descending order, experiences of family and friends, the media, and from conversations with friends and peers and classroom conversations on the subject (slide 11). He found that a slight majority of the respondents who answered the questions believed that the police were fair, courteous, friendly, and respectful and showed concern. Less positive were the responses to questions pertaining to police misuse of their power, particularly the use of force, responsiveness to the needs of lower-class citizens, and conclusions that the police never believe that you are telling the truth. Berlin (2013a) concluded that the attitudes of minority citizens toward the police could become more positive if changes in the organizational structure and the management of the police were made through the creation of a decentralized structure, some form of participatory management, more input from the community, and better training of officers in interpersonal communications, problem-solving, and communications skills.

Police Collaboration with Other Justice Agencies

A special feature of the Budapest 2013 symposium was the roundtable presentations on interviews of police, judges, and corrections leaders. A positive point regarding these roundtable sessions is that they tended to show how the components of the justice system are interrelated and that, regardless of the positions the persons hold in the justice system, police chief, judge, or corrections administrator, they must cooperate with each other. By using an ethnographic or case study approach, the participants (Boda, 2013a,b,c; Das, 2013b; Edelbacher, 2013a; Eterno, 2013a,b; Holdaway, 2013b; Kratcoski, 2013a,b; Storey-White, 2013b; Wuesterwald, 2013a) of the police leaders roundtable and the presenters (Berlin, 2013b; Boda, 2013b,c; Bruns, 2013; Das, 2013b; Edelbacher, 2013b; Ikram, 2013) of the judges roundtable after completing extensive in-depth interviews of judges and police administrators concluded that there is value in knowing how leaders in justice occupations progressed throughout their careers. The in-depth information obtained in the interviews pertaining to their motivations for entering the field, their major challenges and setbacks, as well as the current problems they face cannot be obtained by reading a book on careers in criminal justice.

The discussants for the workshop on corrections (Barooah, 2013; Chokprajakchat, 2013; Das, 2013b,c; Hanser, 2013b; Horne, 2013; Juhasz, 2013; Kratcoski, 2013a; Kuanliang, 2013; Sim, 2013a,b), in 2013, represented leaders in corrections administration and academics who have completed research on correctional administration. Several continents were represented on the panel. The speakers first presented an overview of the administrative structure of the correctional systems of the countries they represented. The leadership and administrative structure in those countries having a national corrections system is very centralized and much closer to a military model than what will be found in a country such as the United States that has several corrections systems, including the National Bureau of Prisons, a corrections system for each of the states, county jails and community correctional facilities, and a number of privately administered correctional facilities. However, regardless of the jurisdiction of the corrections administrator and the manner in which the corrections system is administered, there was a consensus among the speakers from the countries represented that all or at least some of the following factors create security and administrative problems. The factors mentioned include the following: The prisons are filled beyond capacity; the lack of employment and the idleness of the inmates create major security problems; inmate violence is a major problem in some prisons; poorly trained and low-paid corrections officers create problems relating to low motivation and frequent turnover of officers, drugs, terrorist gangs, insufficient resources, corruption; and political interference in the administration of the correctional facilities. The fact that the governments often passes knee-jerk legislation, laws that are poorly defined and motivated by a desire to please the public, such as many of the laws pertaining to illegal drugs, often causes considerable problems.

In summary, during the course of their careers, the leaders of police organizations, judicial systems, and corrections systems met many challenges and often had experiences that interfered with the pursuits of their career goals. Typically, the major problems they encountered relate to the factors already discussed in this chapter, such as insufficient resources, political interference, lack of cooperation from other justice agencies, lack of coordination with other agencies, and failure of the agency to adapt to the changes in the laws and the changes in the needs of the community.

Summary

In the realm of policing, as well as in other components of the justice system, there is a need for continuity but also a need for change. This need was demonstrated in the presentations of the contributors at the IPES held in Budapest, in August 2013, as well as in the prior research cited.

It was noted in the introduction of this chapter that the IPES, under the direction of its founder, Dilip Das, has kept abreast of the changes in the demands placed on policing agencies worldwide, as well as the need to be innovative and make adjustments in the recruitment policies, training programs, and administration of policing agencies. The IPES held in many different countries throughout the world, while maintaining a core of old-time regular participants, have also attracted many new participants since the IPES' founding more than 20 years ago. Regardless of the specific theme of each symposium, the program organizers have always recognized the importance of policing agencies being able to adapt to the changing needs of a global society, as well as being sure to maintain the basic components of police work that define the police as being unique. As mentioned by one author, police work does not change, but the type of tasks and knowledge needed to complete these tasks do change. The presenters at the IPES held in Budapest, in 2013, reflected on the ever-changing goals of policing, including crime prevention, provision of security for the community, and provision of service to the citizenry, and it also discussed some of the problems that police agencies have always had to deal with such as corruption, misuse of police powers, citizen complaints, and lack of public satisfaction with police performance. In addition, many of the presenters focused on fairly recent developments in police work, including how to cope with and respond to Internet crimes, financial crimes, natural and human-made disasters, terrorism, and international crimes.

Several of the major themes of the symposium were highlighted in the presentations. First, the fact that the policing component of the criminal justice system is intricately connected to the other components, that is, the judiciary and the corrections, was emphasized through several roundtable discussions focusing on police, judicial, and correctional leaderships. In addition, a number of other presentations addressed special issues related to victims of crime. Another major theme was the fact crime and crime control have has become global concerns. No longer can nations protect their borders without the cooperation and the assistance from other nations. Finally, another major theme permeating the symposium was the degree to which academics and police leaders have collaborated in research, program development, education and training of police officers, and many other areas.

References

Albrecht, J. 2013, August. Effective leadership principles and pre-employment screening mechanisms to deter police deviance and corruption: Lessons learned from the NYPD. Paper presented at the 23rd Annual Meeting of the International Police Executive Symposium, Budapest.

Antinori, A. 2013. Mafia new strategies of dominance during crisis. Paper presented at the Annual Meeting of the International Police Executive Symposium, Budapest.

Baker, D. 2011. Interview with Commissioner Mal Hyde. In *Trends in Policing*, Vol. 3. Marenin, O. and Das, D., eds. Boca Raton, FL: CRC Press: 1–22.

Barkhuizen, M. 2013, August. Police reaction to the male victim of domestic violence in South Africa. Paper presented at the Annual Meeting of the International Police Executive Symposium, Budapest.

Barooah, P. 2013, August. Corrections administration roundtable. Presented at the 23rd Annual Meeting of the International Police Executive Symposium, Budapest.

Barrow, C. 2013, August. Growing up with New York's finest: Youth perceptions of policing in urban communities. Unpublished paper presented at the Annual Meeting of the International Police Executive Symposium, Budapest.

Berlin, M. 2013a, August. Minority youth attitudes toward the police: Implications for police practices. Paper presented at the Annual Meeting of the International Police Executive Symposium, Budapest.

Berlin, M. 2013b, August. Leaders of the judiciary round table. Presented at the 23rd Annual Meeting of the International Police Executive Symposium, Budapest.

Boda, J. 2013a, August. Cyber security. Keynote address presented at the 23rd Annual Meeting of the International Police Executive Symposium, Budapest.

Boda, J. 2013b, August. Police leaders roundtable. Presented at the 23rd Annual Meeting of the International Police Executive Symposium, Budapest.

Boda, J. 2013c, August. Leaders of the judiciary roundtable. Presented at the 23rd Annual Meeting of the International Police Executive Symposium, Budapest.

Bruns, D. 2013, August. Leaders of the judiciary roundtable. Presented at the 23rd Annual Meeting of the International Police Executive Symposium, Budapest.

Bruns, D., and Bruns, J. 2013, August. Police misconduct: Does a college education make a difference? Paper presented at the Annual Meeting of the International Police Executive Symposium, Budapest.

Chhabra, M., and Chhabra, B. 2013, August. Police effectiveness: An inside story, a study of Delhi Police. Unpublished paper presented at the Annual meeting of the International Police Executive Symposium, Budapest.

Chokprajakchat, S. 2013, August. Corrections administration roundtable. Presented at the 23rd Annual Meeting of the International Police Executive Symposium, Budapest.

Cofan, S. M. 2013, August. Intelligence analysis: A key tool for modern police management—The Romanian perspective. Paper presented at the Annual Meeting of the International Police Executive Symposium, Budapest.

Cordner, G., and Shain, C. 2011, August. The changing landscape of police education and training. *Police Practice and Research.* 12, 4: 281–85.

Corzine, L. 2013a, August. Defining mass murder: What it is and what it is not. Paper presented at the 23rd Annual Meeting of the International Police Executive Symposium, Budapest.

Corzine, J. 2013b, August. Data sets on mass murders, 2013. Paper presented at the Annual Meeting of the International Police Executive Symposium, Budapest.

Das, D. 2013a, August. Leaders of the judiciary roundtable. Presented at the 23rd Annual Meeting of the International Police Executive Symposium, Budapest.

Das, D. 2013b, August. Police leaders roundtable. Presented at the 23rd Annual Meeting of the International Police Executive Symposium, Budapest.

Das, D. 2013c, August. Corrections administration roundtable. Presented at the 23rd Annual Meeting of the International Police Executive Symposium, Budapest.

Das, D., and Marenin, O. eds. 2000. *Challenges of Policing Democracies.* Amsterdam: Gordon and Breach Publishers.

De Benedetto, R. 2013, August. Best practices in police performance measurement and management. Paper presented at the Annual Meeting of the International Police Executive Symposium, Budapest.

Dobovsek, B., and Mastnak, M. 2012. Police detectives and investigative reporters working hand in hand against organized crime. In *Financial Crimes: A Threat to Global Security.* Edelbacher, M., Kratcoski, P., and Theil, M., eds. Boca Raton, FL: CRC Press/Taylor & Francis Group: 289–300.

Edelbacher, M. 2013a, August. Police leaders roundtable. Presented at the 23rd Annual Meeting of the International Police Executive Symposium, Budapest.

Edelbacher, M. 2013b, August. Leaders of the judiciary. Presented at the 23rd Annual Meeting of the International Police Executive Symposium, Budapest.

Edelbacher, M., Simonovic, B., and Nurgaliyev, B. 2013, August. Perceptions of corruption among the police by the citizens of Austria, Kazakhstan, and Serbia. Paper presented at the Annual Meeting of the International Police Executive Symposium, Budapest.

Eterno, J. 2013a, August. The new corruption: Manipulation of crime numbers. 2013. Paper presented at the Annual Meeting of the International Police Executive Symposium, Budapest.

Eterno, J. 2013b, August. Police leaders roundtable. Presented at the 23rd Annual Meeting of the International Police Executive Symposium, Budapest.

European Partners against Corruption/European Contact-Point Network against Corruption. 2012. Anti-corruption authority standards and police oversight principles, Laxenburg: International Anti-Corruption Academy, Austrian Ministry of the Interior.

Gottschalk, P. 2013a, August. A conceptual model for pink-collar criminals. Paper presented at the 23rd Annual Meeting of the International Police Executive Symposium, Budapest.

Gottschalk, P. 2013b, August. What happened in Norway? The Anders Brevik case. Paper presented at the 23rd Annual Meeting of the International Police Executive Symposium, Budapest.

Gyebrovszky, T. 2013, August. Cyber security. Presentation at the 23rd Annual Meeting of the International Police Executive Symposium, Budapest.

Haefaele, B., and Hesselink, A. M. 2013, August. The extent of police brutality in South Africa. Paper presented at the 23rd Annual Meeting of the International Police Executive Symposium, Budapest.

Hajdu, J. 2013, August. Issues on crime and terrorism. Presentation at the 23rd Annual Meeting of the International Police Executive Symposium, Budapest.

Hanser, R. 2013a, August. Using local law enforcement to enhance immigration law in the United States: A legal and social analysis. Paper presented at the 23rd Annual Meeting of the International Police Executive Symposium, Budapest.

Hanser, R. 2013b, August. Corrections administration roundtable. Presented at the 23rd Annual Meeting of the International Police Executive Symposium, Budapest.

Hetzer, W. 2012. Financial crisis or financial crime: Competence and corruption. In *Financial Crimes: A Threat to Global Security*. Edelbacher, M., Kratcoski, P., and Theil, M., eds. Boca Raton, FL: CRC Press/Taylor & Francis Group: 217–64.

Holdaway, S. 2013a, August. Policing multicultural problems. Presentation at the Annual Meeting of the International Police Executive Symposium, Budapest.

Holdaway, S. 2013b, August. Leaders of the judiciary roundtable. Presentation at the 23rd Annual Meeting of the International Police Executive Symposium, Budapest.

Horne, A. 2013, August. Corrections administration roundtable. Presented at the 23rd Annual Meeting of the International Police Executive Symposium, Budapest.

Ikram, T. 2013, August. Leaders of the judiciary roundtable. Presented at the 23rd Annual Meeting of the International Police Executive Symposium, Budapest.

Juhasz, A. 2013, August. Corrections administration. Presented at the 23rd Annual Meeting of the International Police Executive Symposium, Budapest.

Kratcoski, P. 1995. Perspectives on community policing. In *Issues in Community Policing*. Kratcoski, P. and Dukes, D. Eds. Cincinnati, OH: Anderson, pp. 21–33.

Kratcoski, P. 2007. The challenges of police education and training in a global society. In *Police Education and Training in a Global Society*. Kratcoski, P. C. and Das, D. K., eds. Lanham MD: Lexington Books: 3–21.

Kratcoski, P. 2013a, August. Police leaders roundtable. Presented at the 23rd Annual Meeting of the International Police executive Symposium, Budapest.

Kratcoski, P. 2013b, August. Corrections administration roundtable. Presented at the 23rd Annual Meeting of the International Police Executive Symposium, Budapest.

Kratcoski, P., and Kempf, K. 1995. Police reform. In *Encyclopedia of Police Science*. 2nd edition, W. Bailey ed. New York: Garland Publishing, pp. 609–613.

Kratcoski, P., and Dukes, D. 1995. Perspectives on community policing. In *Issues in Community Policing*. Cincinnati, OH: Anderson: 21–33.

Kratcoski, P., and Walker, D. 1978. *Criminal Justice in America: Process and Issues*. Glenview, IL: Scott Foresman and Company.

Kratcoski, P., Edelbacher, M., and Graff, D. 2012. School security: A comparison between Austria and the United States. In *The Administration of Juvenile Justice*. Kratcoski, P., ed. Boca Raton, FL: CRC Press: 197–216.

Kreutner, M. 2013, August. Corruption. Key note address given at the Annual Meeting of the International Police Executive Symposium, Budapest.

Kuanliang, A. 2013, August. Corrections administration roundtable. Presented at the 23rd Annual Meeting of the International Police Executive Symposium, Budapest.

Lepard, D., Demers, S., Langan, C., and Rosno, K. 2013, August. Challenges on serial murder investigations involving missing persons. Paper presented at the 23rd Annual Meeting of the International Police Executive Symposium, Budapest.

Leukhina, A. 2013, August. Public distrust of the police in the Ukraine. Paper presented at the 23rd Annual Meeting of the International Police Executive Symposium, Budapest.

Linn, E. 2013, August. New initiatives to combat sex trafficking. Paper presented at the 23rd Annual Meeting of the International Police Executive Symposium, Budapest.

Lobnikar, B., and Mesko, G. 2013, August. The level of police integrity among Slovenian police officers. Paper presented at the 23rd Annual Meeting of the International Police Executive Symposium, Budapest.

Mastrofski, S. 1992. What does community policing mean for daily policy work? *National Institute of Juvenile Justice*. 225: 23–27.

Mills, A. 2012. Fighting corruption: The role of the media in the broader global context. In *Financial Crimes: A Threat to Global Security*. Edelbacher, M., Kratcoski, P., and Theil, M., eds. Boca Raton, FL: CRC Press/Taylor & Francis Group: 205–16.

Oyaizu, N. 2013, August. Unseen crimes on vulnerable people in closed settings: Changes needed for the public's safety and reassurance. Paper presented at the Annual International Police Executive Symposium, Budapest.

Peak, K. 2013, August. Private policing in the casino gaming environment: Legal and practical perspectives and problems. Unpublished paper presented at the Annual meeting of the International Police Executive Symposium, Budapest.

Perrott, S. 2013, August. The recruitment of women and visible minorities into Canadian police forces: Mission accomplished? Paper presented at the Annual Meeting of the International Police Executive Symposium, Budapest.

Putman, K. 2013, August. The good cop factor. Paper presented at the 23rd Annual Meeting of the International Police Executive Symposium, Budapest.

Salgado, J. 2013, August. A tale of two cities' police departments: Community oriented policing in The Hague and Tokyo. Paper presented at the 23rd Annual Meeting of the International Police Executive Symposium, Budapest.

Shikwambana, D. 2013, August. Sub-cultural norms: The case of whistle blowing vs. occupational survival within the law enforcement departments in South Africa. Paper presented at the 23rd Annual Meeting of the International Police Executive Symposium, Budapest.

Sim, S. 2013a, August. Leveraging terrorists dropouts for countering violent extremism in Southeast Asia. Presentation at the 23rd Annual Meeting of the International Police Executive Symposium, Budapest.

Sim, S. 2013b, August. Corrections administration roundtable. Presented at the 23rd Annual Meeting of the International Police Executive Symposium, Budapest.

Storey-White, K. 2013a, August. Corruption, conspiracies, weasel-words, bad language. Paper presented at the 23rd Annual Meeting of the International Police Executive Symposium, Budapest.

Storey-White, K. 2013b, August. Police leadership roundtable. Presented at the 23rd Annual Meeting of the International Police Executive Symposium, Budapest.

Taylor, S., Cowan, E., Doyle, K., and Lea, S. 2013, August. Attitudes: What attitude? Paper presented at the Annual Meeting of the International Police Executive Symposium, Budapest.

Trojanowicz, R., and Buckueroux, B. 1990. *Community Policing: A Contemporary Perspective*. Cincinnati, OH: Anderson.

Wikipedia. 2014. ComStat. Accessed February 11, 2014. Retrieved from https://en.wikipediaorg/wki/CompStat.

Wilds, M. 2013a, August. Mass murder: An international dialogue on mayhem and madness. Paper presented at the Annual Meeting of the International Police Executive Symposium, Budapest.

Wilds, M. 2013b, August. Eye of the storm: Dealing with the media after a school crisis, 2013. Paper presented at the Annual Meeting of the International Police Executive Symposium, Budapest.

Wuesterwald, T. 2013a, August. Police leadership roundtable. Presented at the 23rd Annual Meeting of the International Police Executive Symposium, Budapest.

Wuesterwald, M. 2013b, August. Mass murder typologies. Paper Presented at the Annual Meeting of the International Police Executive Symposium, Budapest.

Yokoyama, M. 2013, August. Policing at catastrophe: Special policing after earthquake and tsunami in Japan on March 11, 2011. Paper presented at the Annual Meeting of the International Police Executive Symposium, Budapest.

Yung, W., Chau, S., and Chi-Wai, A. 2013, August. Higher education for policing in the city of protest-Hong Kong. Paper presented at the 23rd Annual Meeting of the International Police Executive Symposium, Budapest.

Police Executive Leadership and Police Legitimacy

2

VIPUL KUMAR

Contents

Abstract

Executive leadership plays a vital role in promoting legitimacy for policing in the democracies around the world. The process of building legitimacy within policing organizations is put into effect not only through
policy and procedures, but also through leadership behavior and styles.
In this chapter, the author explores how a value-based relationship
between leaders and followers (or between leadership and followership)
reflecting the norms of empowerment, motivation, trust, transparency,
emotional involvement, and shared vision is the key catalyst to the
legitimization of police authority in the eyes of the public.

Introduction

The key is that change begins with leadership. This applies to all levels and areas
of management. The more it is practiced, the more it will become productive.
Having worked in the West, I realize that this principle is no different any-
where in the world. This is a human need and needed most. (Bedi, 2008, p. 106)*

---

* Kiran Bedi (born June 9, 1949) holds the distinction of being the first lady Indian Police
Service (IPS) officer. She joined the IPS in 1972 and retired in 2007. She not only made her
mark as a distinguished police officer, but also became a role model and an inspirational
leader for the younger generation of police officers.

Leadership in a police organization as in any organization, public or private, is a complex behavioral process. A good and effective leadership at the executive level is essential not only for the achievement of organizational objectives, but also for establishing the means of that achievement. It is equally, if not more, true for the police as a public sector organization whose processes and outcomes are subjected to constant scrutiny by the media and the civil society, as well as to formal oversight by governmental and judicial authorities. Policing in today's democratic world has become a complex and difficult task with leadership burdened with the onerous responsibility of leading police performance to the satisfaction of the community it serves.

As this chapter submits, it is the processes rather than the outcomes of policing that crucially impact the citizens' understanding of good policing. This understanding is the main ingredient of legitimate authority of policing in the democratic world. Therefore, building legitimate authority for policing has become the core function of police executive leadership. Police leaders can achieve this organizationally through framing suitable policing policies, laying clear-cut procedures, providing sufficient resources to field/frontline officers, and upholding the key traditions of the department. However, more than this, it is cultivation of the right leadership behavior at the top level in a police organization, which promotes police legitimacy and, hence, a healthy and positive police–public relationship in its jurisdiction. An exploration of this argument requires an unraveling of the processes of police executive leadership and police legitimacy in order to develop a theoretical structure robust enough for further scholarly examination.

Police Executive Leadership and Transformational Behavior

"As in all matters involving how law enforcement is conducted, the role of top police executives is key" (Community Relations Service, 2003). Police executive leadership sets the climate for the "much needed police organizational reform" (Wakefield and Fleming, 2009). It influences the relations between the police supervisors and the frontline police officers (internal relationship) and also between the frontline police officers and the public they serve (external relationship). Unfortunately, despite its highly significant role in the modern social setup, police leadership suffers from a lack of scholarly studies (Haberfeld, 2006; Wakefield and Fleming, 2009). In contrast, the literature in corporate/business leadership continues to grow (Storey, 2011). Whatever little research is available on police leadership, there is a common finding that the traditional transactional behavior of leadership—dependent on the hierarchical rank-and-file structure of the organization, along with rewards and punishments as the motivational factors—is just good enough to maintain the status quo and play-safe environment within the organization at the cost of the inability to initiate and manage the changes desired in the modern rapidly changing globalized world (Densten, 1999; Long, 2003). Such leadership does not help the growth of an organization.

The demands of policing a modern democratic society require police organizations that are open to new ideas, new directions, and new opportunities. The new leadership behavior, defined as a transformational style of leadership, is suited to such demands—challenging the status quo and embracing change (Long, 2003). Such behavior is underpinned by the four I's, viz., *idealized influence* (developing trust and followership), *inspirational motivation* (putting up a shared vision), *intellectual stimulation* (encouraging new ideas), and *individualized consideration* (having concern for the growth and the welfare of every follower) (Bass and Avolio, 1994). The transformational leadership provides a strong value-based platform for mutual trust and respect, emotional involvement of both the leader and the followers, and shared vision for personal and organizational growth. Interestingly, as in business management and other public sectors, the transformational leadership in the police organizations as well has been found to be strongly correlated with positive work behavior of the staff (Dobby, Anscombe, and Tuffin, 2004). So how does transformational leadership relate to police legitimacy?

Police Legitimacy

In a modern democracy, people need to have trust and confidence not only in the ability of the police to maintain public order and control crime but also in the fairness of police actions in the treatment of people and decision making during police–public interactions and processes involved therein. Once this is reposed, research shows that the likelihood of the public's intention to cooperate with the police willingly, comply with the law voluntarily, and defer to police directions unquestioningly is higher (Tyler, 2006a). Further to it, the likelihood of people engaging in crime prevention activities with other community members and reporting suspicious activities in a neighborhood increases. This is the essence of police legitimacy. As a renowned police scholar spearheading the relentless research in this field, Tom Tyler (2006b, p. 375) defines police legitimacy as "a psychological property of an authority, institution, or social arrangement that leads those connected to it to believe that it is appropriate, proper and just."

This perception can be measured by the level of trust, satisfaction, and confidence of people in the police. For example, in the United States, the *Sourcebook of Criminal Justice Statistics* annually reports the public confidence in the police as a measure of police legitimacy (Tyler, 2011a). Similarly, in Australia, the measurement of police legitimacy is related to the annual National Survey of Community Satisfaction with Policing conducted by the Australian and New Zealand Policing Advisory Agency

(Goodman-Delahunty, 2010). However, this idea of police legitimacy is not completely new, and its root can be traced back to the following nineteenth century Peelian principles of policing* advocating policing by consent.

> The ability of the police to perform their duties is dependent upon public approval of police actions.
>
> Police must secure the willing cooperation of the public in voluntary observance of the law to be able to secure and maintain the respect of the public.
>
> The degree of cooperation of the public that can be secured diminishes proportionately to the necessity of the use of physical force.
>
> Police, at all times, should maintain a relationship with the public that gives reality to the historic tradition that the police are the public and the public are the police; the police being only members of the public who are paid to give full-time attention to duties which are incumbent on every citizen in the interests of community welfare and existence.

In a systematic review of police legitimacy by the Campbell Collaboration last year, it was concluded that "legitimacy policing is an important precursor for improving the capacity of policing to prevent and control crime" (Mazerolle et al., 2013, p. 78) thus providing an evidence base to policy makers and practitioners to enhance the public perceptions of legitimacy in policing—a strong case for the police executive leadership to promote police legitimacy. The big question is how. Is procedural justice an answer?

Procedural Justice Model of Police Legitimacy

The police executive leadership influences various factors that contribute to the building of police legitimacy. These include, as mentioned earlier, sound legal structure, supportive political executive, quality policing policies, clear-cut and well-laid out police procedures, sufficient resources, strong traditions, etc. However, research has identified procedural justice as the most effective intervention to improve police legitimacy (Tyler, 2001). Procedural justice is simply put the fair treatment and the fair decision making by police officers whenever they come in contact with the people. The literature identifies four essential components of procedural justice, also referred to as the

---

* Sir Robert Peel, then home secretary of the United Kingdom and founder of the Metropolitan Police (Met), London, is credited to have propounded nine principles of policing in 1829 to guide the functioning of the newly created police force. Despite some scholars raising doubts about their precise origins (Lentz and Chaires, 2007), these principles "remain nevertheless a foundational document for modern policing in Britain and other commonwealth countries" (Bronitt and Stenning, 2011, p. 323).

four key ingredients of the group values relational model developed by Lind and Tyler (1988), namely, trustworthiness (to what extent the public perceives the police as working for the best interests of the community), respectful treatment (to what extent the police behaves with respect and dignity with people during police–public interactions), neutrality (to what extent police is neutral, transparent, and nondiscriminatory in its decision making), and voice (to what extent police considers the public's views and opinions in decision making). The presence of these ingredients in the police–public interface improves the perception of police legitimacy by increasing public satisfaction and confidence in police (Goodman-Delahunty, 2010). Thus, the purpose of procedural justice is to engage the police and the public in a healthy and positive relationship in order to control crime and creating a win-win situation even during potentially more conflictual engagements like search and arrest (Tyler and Huo, 2002). Today, many policing interventions in the form of community-oriented policing (COP) and problem-oriented policing incorporate the elements of procedural justice as a means of enhancing police legitimacy.

Research has further established that the impact of procedural justice, especially the quality of treatment by the police, outweighs the impact of police performance or effectiveness as far as the people's belief in police legitimacy is concerned (Sunshine and Tyler, 2003; Tyler, 2004). In other words, the public perceives the police to be legitimate more by the police use of procedural justice than the delivery of police outcomes despite the latter remaining an important predictor of police legitimacy. This supremacy of procedural justice has firmly propped the wide acceptance of the procedural justice model of police legitimacy.

The responsibility to implement procedural justice falls on the shoulder of frontline or field officers as they have contact with the public on a day-to-day basis. It is a big task expected of them by senior police managers and police executives. The key ingredients of procedural justice discussed earlier are value based and normative in nature, and these cannot be instilled in frontline officers merely by preaching them through catechism classes, training courses, or workshops. It leads to the argument that the elements of procedural justice must be first implemented internally within the organization before expecting them to be applied in frontline police work. This application of procedural justice within the organization engenders organizational justice.

Organizational Justice and Internal Legitimacy

The key driver of organizational justice within a police organization is an effective police leadership, right from putting in place procedurally fair policing practices to conducting proper training of police officers to rewarding them for enhancing police image (Tyler, 2011a). But it is the attitude and the behavior of the police executive leaders that primarily instill the desired norms and values in the subordinate officers leading to organizational justice, that is, how good and committed they feel about their organization (Tyler, 2014). The procedurally fair treatment of the officers during their interaction with police leadership propagates the organizational satisfaction. Organizational justice enhances the legitimacy of police executive leadership within the organization. It empowers the frontline officers and encourages a belief of internal legitimacy—a belief in their own authority vis-à-vis enforcement of law.

The elements of organizational justice, like trust, openness, respect, involvement, empowerment, shared vision, are by default the characteristics of the transformational style of leadership. It signifies that a transformational police executive leadership will naturally foster organizational justice and internal legitimacy and therefore procedural justice and external legitimacy of policing. Police scholars like Tyler (2011a,b) and Myhill and Bradford (2013) are in agreement with this argument. This argument can be represented as a theoretical model connecting the transformational behavior of police executive leadership with the legitimated policing as illustrated in Figure 2.1.

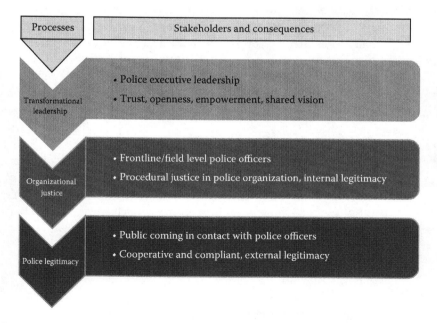

Figure 2.1 A theoretical model connecting the transformational style of leadership to the police legitimacy.

To support this argument, field cases from two diverse policing cultures are discussed as follows.

Durham Constabulary

This case was presented by the Durham Constabulary of England and Wales during the Excellence in Policing Conference of the Association of Chief Police Officers in 2012. A staff survey conducted in the Durham Constabulary in association with the National Policing Improvement Agency (NPIA),* titled "Behavioral Consequences of Organizational Justice," mapped the outcome of organizational justice in terms of internal and external legitimacies of the constabulary (Porter and Quinton, 2012). The indicators of organizational justice were fair, consistent, and impartial decisions; explaining decisions and their rationale; giving people a voice in the process; giving people a sense of influence; good quality communication; fair and respectful interpersonal contact; and openness and honesty. The outcome performance measured 90% staff satisfaction with the whole experience of organizational justice—a direct indicator of the improved internal legitimacy, apart from other various indicators like reduced victim-based crime, reduced antisocial behavior, and significant reduction in repeat locations and victims. Although the study did not include any public survey to find the impact on public trust and external police legitimacy, it was concluded that engaging the staff in positive work behaviors based on organizational justice was a necessary condition for building public trust and internal and external legitimacies. As is obvious from the indicators of the organizational justice in this case, the default style of leadership was transformational.

The Indian Police

India is yet to come to terms with the process-based policing, and it is very much reflected in the distrust and the suspicion of members of public toward the police. Unfortunately, there is little empirical research on the Indian police to gauge its legitimacy that, based on media reports and general perception, seems to be very low. The Indian police is yet to completely come out of its colonial garb and is still struggling with a slow and painful transition from the ruler's police to the people's police.

This is despite a Supreme Court directive to enforce certain reform measures directed toward reducing the political interference in the police organizational affairs and operations and putting in place civil authorities for oversight.[†]

---

* Home Office closed NPIA in October 2013, distributing its functions to various other agencies. The function of research, analysis and information was handed over to the newly created College of Policing.

† In 2006, on a public interest litigation to enforce police reforms in India, the Supreme Court of India issued seven major directives binding the central and state governments to implement them henceforth in order to insulate the police from political interference and improve police accountability. The compliance has been tardy and far from satisfactory (Commonwealth Human Rights Initiative, 2010).

These external reforms are taking their own time to get implemented and, even if implemented, cannot guarantee the legitimacy in the absence of internal reforms of the organization. The key to internal reforms lies with the police executives, belonging to the elite IPS,* separately recruited and trained to occupy the leadership positions. These leaders need to walk extra miles to bridge the big divide between the management cops and street cops in India, and that would be the first step in improving organizational justice and hence police legitimacy. Two examples from south Indian states, Kerala and Karnataka, have shown the way forward in this direction.

The Kerala State Police initiated its community policing program called Janamaithri Suraksha Project in 2008 breaking the barriers of old traditional policing. Facing the same constraints as any other state police agency in India, the executive leadership of the day in Kerala State Police stretched itself beyond the traditional role and empowered its subordinates by providing them a platform to get closer to the members of public and build police legitimacy. It had its desired impact, and the project was hailed as a bold initiative not only by the public but also even by the political establishment. However, a few years later, the project started encountering difficulties. In a review of this program undertaken by an independent agency, the Tata Institute of Social Sciences (TISS) (2013), it was found that the project had lost its initial steam due to various reasons such as lack of human and material resources and transfer of trained officers. But the most important aspect, sticking out as an obstruction, was the lack of transformational leadership, which is evident from the following passage:

> ...The discontent that civil police officers face within the police hierarchy is an issue that affects the manner in which they discharge their official responsibilities, particularly so when they are required to undertake new responsibilities such as making beat visits. Before we talk of Janamaitri, let us have some Maitri† within the department is what they say.
>
> There is a latent discontent amongst civil police officers who are located at the lowest rung of the department hierarchy. They are unhappy with the way in which they are treated by senior officials. The more educated amongst them are unhappy about the fact that even today they are only expected to "obey orders"; that they are not treated as an intelligent force. ... A democratisation process within the police force is as necessary as the democratisation process envisaged under Janamaitri. (TISS, 2013, pp. 135–136)

---

* IPS is an elite cadre in the Indian police setup. The IPS officers are selected through a highly competitive national civil services examination attracting bright young university graduates. Immediately after an initial training period of two years, they are posted as assistant superintendent of police. The other levels of entry into the Indian police are constable, subinspector, and deputy superintendent.
† *Maitri* is a Sanskrit word, which means friendship. *Janamaitri* means friendship with the people. This sentence accentuates the feeling that a congenial atmosphere inside the police organization is a precursor for the COP programs.

Another example is from the neighboring Karnataka State Police. During the period of 2009–2011, the executive leadership of Karnataka State Police wanted to create an evidence base before taking up any intervention for the improvement of police performance and hence requested an independent nongovernment organization, the Public Affairs Centre to conduct an assessment of the services provided by the police stations in the state of Karnataka. The findings (Nair, Prabhakar, and Rao, 2010) were on expected lines: people remaining afraid of approaching police and getting their complaint registered, a weak system of follow-up of enquiry or investigation, the existence of corruption ostensibly to compensate less material resources available to police, and hardly any awareness among the public about police procedures accompanied by an absence of any proactive step by the police to address these issues. It also explored the issues faced by the police staff and found a rigid hierarchy, lack of openness, unfair treatment of subordinates by superiors, lack of material resources for investigation, and lack of human resources leading to work–life imbalance as the main organizational impediments.

Based on these findings, the police leadership—cutting across the hierarchy—discussed and analyzed them at various levels in order to chalk out the collective goals (shared vision) of organizational reforms and better policing. In this process, communication channels were devised to ensure that every voice, irrespective of rank and position, was heard. It was followed by several people-friendly policing measures: easy accessibility of public to police officers, ensured registration of complaints, systematic follow-up of all cases under investigation by holding meetings with the complainants/informants, creation of a separate investigation fund, speedy return of stolen property to the victims of crime, modified police beat system, and increased formal and informal interactions with the citizens. At the same time, the Supreme Court's guidelines on police reforms were leveraged to safeguard the police machinery from rampant political interference for strengthening police authority and improving police accountability.

This process affirmed the necessity of internal reforms (see Organizational Justice and Internal Legitimacy section) in order to reap the benefits of external reforms. There was a palpable sense of association with this policing mission among police staff and common public as well. Police officers felt empowered and so did the public at large. However, this experiment, like in the previous case of Kerala Police, subsequently lost its momentum with the changing of the guard.

Conclusion

This chapter has attempted to develop a theoretical model, a hypothesis relating the transformational behavior of the police executive leadership with police legitimacy, based on the academic research findings and field experiences. If the police officers are respected, empowered, trusted, made to feel involved and important in decision making by their leaders, such police officers bring the same values, norms, and practices in their work environment, on to the streets. The route of organizational justice to procedural justice and hence police legitimacy is natural, logical, and simple. Yet the dearth of empirical research in this area is a matter of scholarly concern. It is hoped that both academics and practitioners will join their hands together to expand the research for corroboration and confirmation of the hypothesis presented in this chapter.

References

Bass, B. M., and Avolio, B. J. 1994. *Improving Organizational Effectiveness through Transformational Leadership.* Thousand Oaks, CA: Sage.

Bedi, K. 2008. *Indian Police... As I See...* New Delhi, India: Sterling Publishers.

Bronitt, S., and Stenning, P. 2011. Understanding discretion in modern policing. *Criminal Law Journal.* 35(6): 319–32.

Commonwealth Human Rights Initiative. 2010. Seven steps to police reform. Accessed March 5, 2014. Retrieved from http://www.humanrightsinitiative.org/programs/aj/police/india/initiatives/seven_steps_to_police_reform.pdf.

Community Relations Service. 2003. Principles of good policing: Avoiding violence between police and citizens. Retrieved from http://www.justice.gov/archive/crs/pubs/principlesofgoodpolicingfinal092003.pdf.

Densten, I. L. 1999. Senior Australian law enforcement leadership under examination. *Policing: An International Journal of Police Strategies & Management.* 22(1): 45–57.

Dobby, J., Anscombe, J., and Tuffin, R. 2004. *Police Leadership: Expectations and Impact.* London: Home Office.

Goodman-Delahunty, J. 2010. Four ingredients: New recipes for procedural justice in Australian policing. *Policing.* 4(4): 403–10.

Haberfeld, M. R. 2006. *Police Leadership.* Upper Saddle River, NJ: Prentice Hall.

Lentz, S. A., and Chaires, R. H. 2007. The invention of Peel's principles: A study of policing 'textbook' history. *Journal of Criminal Justice.* 35(1): 69–79.

Lind, E. A., and Tyler, T. R. 1988. *The Social Psychology of Procedural Justice.* New York: Plenum.

Long, M. 2003. Leadership and performance management. In *Handbook of Policing.* Newburn, T., ed. Cullompton, UK: Willan Publishing: 628–54.

Mazerolle, L., Bennett, S., Davis, J., Sargeant, E., and Manning, M. 2013. *Legitimacy in Policing: A Systematic Review.* Oslo, Norway: The Campbell Collaboration.

Myhill, A., and Bradford, B. 2013. Overcoming cop culture? Organizational justice and police officers' attitudes toward the public. *Policing.* 36(2): 338–56.

Nair, M., Prabhakar, K., and Rao, P. 2010. *A Mirror to the Police: A Bottom-Up Assessment of the Karnataka Police.* Bangalore, India: Public Affairs Centre.

Porter, G., and Quinton, P. 2012. Behavioral consequences of organizational justice. Accessed March 14, 2014. Retrieved from http://www.excellenceinpolicing.org .uk/wp-content/uploads/2012/09/1-5_Organisational_Justice.pdf.

Storey, J. 2011. Signs of change: "Damned rascals" and beyond. In *Leadership in Organizations: Current Issues and Key Trends*, second edition. Storey, J., ed. New York: Routledge: 3–13.

Sunshine, J., and Tyler, T. R. 2003. The role of procedural justice and legitimacy in shaping public support for policing. *Law & Society Review*. 37(3): 513–48.

Tata Institute of Social Sciences (TISS). 2013. *An Evaluation of the Community Policing Programme in Kerala*. Trivandrum, India: TISS Mumbai.

Tyler, T. R. 2001. Public trust and confidence in legal authorities: What do majority and minority group members want from the law and legal institutions? *Behavioral Sciences & the Law*. 19(2): 215–35.

Tyler, T. R. 2004. Enhancing police legitimacy. *The ANNALS of the American Academy of Political and Social Science*. 593(1): 84–99.

Tyler, T. R. 2006a. *Why People Obey the Law*. Princeton, NJ: Princeton University Press.

Tyler, T. R. 2006b. Psychological perspectives on legitimacy and legitimation. *Annual Review of Psychology*. 57(1): 375–400.

Tyler, T. R. 2011a. Trust and legitimacy: Policing in the USA and Europe. *European Journal of Criminology*. 8(4): 254–66.

Tyler, T. R. 2011b. *Why People Cooperate: The Role of Social Motivations*. Princeton, NJ: Princeton University Press.

Tyler, T. R. 2014. Legitimacy and procedural justice: A new element of police leadership. In *The Police Executive Research Forum*. Fischer, C., ed. Washington, DC: Bureau of Justice Assistance, U.S. Department of Justice.

Tyler, T. R., and Huo, Y. J. 2002. *Trust in the Law: Encouraging Public Cooperation with the Police and Courts*. New York: Russell Sage Foundation.

Wakefield, A., and Fleming, J. 2009. *The Sage Dictionary of Policing*. London: Sage.

On the Acceptability of Closer Public–Private Policing Partnerships
Views from the Public Side

3

STEPHEN B. PERROTT
KRYSTINA TRITES

Contents

Abstract

As the private-policing sector continues to grow, the willingness of public officers to form closer relationships with their private counterparts remains in doubt. In this study, a sample of 156 municipal police officers situated themselves on a continuum of public–private partnership acceptance, based on a model proposed by Stenning in 1989. Officers also provided judgments of their respect for the private police, the competence they attributed to them, and how adequate they believed their education and training to be. A measure of right-wing authoritarianism (RWA) was used as a proxy for in-group–out-group sentiment to determine whether this was related to the appraisals. Results showed that respondents split into three relatively equal groups: (1) those who were simply unwilling to develop closer relations, (2) those who cited deficits in training and education as obstacles to closer relationships, and (3) those who were willing to work in partnerships. The ratings on the three appraisal measures reinforced just how poorly trained and regulated the private police were perceived to be. Authoritarianism was not correlated with the placement on the partnership continuum or with any of the appraisal measures. The discussion focuses on the implications of these findings for the prospect of partnership building with a conclusion addressing the need for the government to assume greater responsibility for the professionalization of private policing.

Introduction

When the first author was hired as a constable with a municipal Canadian police force in 1976, *private policing*, had such a term been in use, might have evoked images of bouncers, security guards, and private investigators. Security guards, in particular, were viewed as underpaid and poorly trained; many were seen as wannabes aspiring to become public police officers (see the study by Nalla and Hummer [1999]). They were perhaps viewed with a modicum of sympathy, or even derision, and certainly never as potential partners.

Much has changed since then both in the numbers and in the scope of private policing practices. For example, in the United States, a 1.4:1 ratio of public over private officers in the 1970s reversed direction such that there were three private agents for every public officer just 30 years later (Joh, 2004). A similar phenomenon has been observed in the United Kingdom and continental Europe (Van Steden and Sarre, 2007), Australia (Prenzler, Earle, and Sarre, 2009; Sarre, 2005, 2013), New Zealand (Bradley and Sedgwick, 2009), and Canada where this study was conducted (Shearing and Stenning, 1983; Swol, 1998).

The burgeoning private policing industry came with pressures for the private and public sectors to form partnerships. Although the prospect of such partnerships was initially met with fierce resistance by the public side, more recent research suggests a softening of views at least insofar as this is seen as an inevitable development (Joh, 2004; Johnston and Stenning, 2013). Nonetheless, the public police retain considerable ambivalence about sharing functions, and Nalla and Hummer (1999; Hummer and Nalla, 2003) summarize the situation as one where private agents hold a positive view of the public police but perceive themselves as being viewed negatively in return. The public police are actually fairly neutral about their private sector counterparts, although this view seems premised on private agents remaining cognizant of their status as junior, even subordinate, partners. Stenning (2009) characterizes the growing pluralistic policing family as "not always a very harmonious one … frequently riven with jealousies, enmity, competition, conflict, and lack of mutual respect and common goals" (p. 23).

The Public–Private Dichotomy and Blurred Lines

The official roles of the public and private police remain distinct in theory, if not practice. Simply put, the public police are "backed by the authority of the state, paid for by public funds, and accountable to democratic institutions" (Joh, 2004, p. 61). They are, therefore, public servants with the responsibility for the public good.* The private police, in contrast, serve a client (Shearing and Stenning, 1983; Wakefield, 2012); although their efforts may also further the public good, at least situationally, such an outcome is incidental to achieving the goals of whatever private entity or person pays their wages. There is also the seemingly clear separation in how the public and private police exercise their authority, with the public police having more discretional latitude and greater powers of arrest (Stenning, 2000). When framed differently, the public police role can be seen as one of governance, whereas the private police focus on management and are motivated by the pursuit of profit (Joh, 2004).

In practice, however, the lines become blurry (Johnston and Stenning, 2013; Rigakos and Greener, 2000). Is the public interest best served, for example, when public officers are hired and paid for by private entities (Stenning, 2009) or with the increasing trend for public police forces to competitively bid for public contracts? (Rigakos, 2002). What is the status of private agents when carrying out duties traditionally the domain of the public police? In Rigakos' study (2002) of the parapolice, we learn

---

* Obviously, many minority group members, a sizable proportion of criminologists, and virtually all critical theorists would challenge this premise.

how Intelligarde International's agents patrol high-risk housing projects in Toronto wearing uniforms remarkably similar to those of public officers. In such situations, where private agents combine landowner powers with the rights of all citizens, even the distinction in powers of arrest is considerably narrowed (Joh, 2004).

The ever-increasing salary costs of public officers against the pressure to cut government deficits and rationalize services in Canada (Burbidge, 2005; Murphy, 2004) and elsewhere (Ruddell, Thomas, and Patten, 2011), an elevated societal concern about risk impervious to evidence (Ericson and Haggerty, 1997; Williamson, Ashby, and Webber, 2006), and the current prevailing neoliberal Zeitgeist in Western nations (Bradley and Sedgwick, 2009; Johnston and Stenning, 2013; Murphy, 2007) all point toward the further growth in private policing (Grover, 2009; Ransley and Mazerolle, 2009). It seems inevitable that this growth will be accompanied by even greater pressures for private–public partnerships. Given that the public police are both the more resistant and more powerful partner, it is important to update where they are in their contemplation of closer relationships, what roadblocks they perceive to be impeding progress, and the degree to which these articulated obstacles should be viewed as legitimate.

Public Police Objections to Private–Public Partnerships

We propose a three-category typology of public police objections to private policing: (1) philosophical/conceptual, (2) practical/legitimate, and (3) nonrational/illegitimate. The first category focuses on the degree to which the private police can focus upon the public good when serving a specific client. This concern, especially viewed from more radical perspectives that already emphasize police oppression and actions that serve only the powered interests in society (Cohen, 1985), is amplified when considered in the context of private policing. Public officers need, in theory at least, to balance the goals of landowners against the needs and the intrinsic rights of all citizens, even those who are marginalized and lacking in power. By comparison, the private agent needs only to represent the needs of the landowner. Although a clear articulation of the objections to the comodification or the marketization of the functions hitherto the responsibility of the state remains primarily the domain of academics, policy makers, and social critics (see the studies by Johnston and Stenning [2013] and Rigakos [2002]), frontline public officers also likely perceive this as a conflict of interest even if conceived of in more concrete and visceral ways.

The practical/legitimate objections that the public police have in partnering with private agencies involves the concern about the attributes of the agents at intake, the quality of their training, and the need for greater regulations governing their practice. All Western English-speaking countries have scrambled to deal with perceived shortcomings and developed regulatory frameworks and mandatory/minimum standards for training. However, such legislation is highly variable and we are nowhere near achieving uniformity even within countries (Joh, 2004; Manzo, 2011).* Moreover, Button (2009) contends that the level of training, although better, has failed to keep abreast of the expansion of the private sector, and Burbidge (2005) has referred to an ongoing lack of accountability in the private sector as a governance deficit. Thus, when public police officers object to the encroachment of private agents in areas that were hitherto theirs, the resistance is based, arguably at least, in realistic, legitimate concerns.†

That articulated objections are restricted to ideological and, especially, these practical grounds, does not mean that public police resistance is not also motivated by less rational, illegitimate reasons. This final category of resistance involves turf protection (see the study by Shearing [1992]), whereby the objections of the public police are based in their resentment that private agencies are encroaching into territory that they consider to be rightfully in the public domain. Police unions are clearly motivated to object as they stand to lose revenue, and therefore, their power to extend their membership is diminished due to work being assumed by the private sector.

Beyond these objections, however, is the mythical police personality and subculture with its pronounced *us versus them* sentiments (Skolnick, 1966). Even if traditional conceptions of police ethnocentrism have developed into overblown stereotypes (Perrott and Taylor, 1994), there is little doubt that public policing is characterized by a working culture emphasizing the need for solidarity and the threat faced from external forces. From this perspective, the growth of private policing represents a challenge to social identity and collective efficacy that is likely greater than that experienced by other public sector groups facing the prospect of privatization.

Study Purpose

This study was designed to assess the degree to which a sample of municipal Canadian public police officers have evolved in willingness to engage in public–private partnerships on a continuum ranging from complete rejection to complete acceptance where private police agents are viewed

---

* The lack of uniformity in regulation is particularly problematic when private agencies provide transnational services (see Johnston and Stenning [2013]).
† Stenning (2009) challenges the conventional wisdom that there is a huge deficit in the accountability of the private police; furthermore, while recognizing the differential emphases placed in policing activities by the two sectors, he argues that the public–private dichotomy has been exaggerated in the self-serving interests of both (Stenning, 1989).

as equal partners. We further sought respondent views of how much they respected the private police, the degree of competence with which they perceive them to act, and the adequacy of the education and training they believe them to have. Finally, a measure of RWA was used as a proxy for in-group–out-group sentiment to determine if there was any relationship between the construct, the appraisal ratings, and the continuum placement scores.

A Developmental Model toward Public–Private Police Partnerships

A quarter of a century ago, then Canadian-based private policing expert Philip Stenning (1989) proposed a seven-stage model to encompass the evolving nature of public–private policing partnerships. Stenning argued that Canadian police forces had already moved beyond the first stage characterized by denial about the existence of private policing but have yet to enter a hypothetical future seventh stage where, following a redefinition of the policing role, the public and private would work together as equal partners. His model is summarized as follows:

Denial

Denial involves holding the position that there is no such thing as private policing and, therefore, nothing to be discussed or debated. This is the stage that Stenning held is now behind us.*

Grudging Recognition and Denigration

Grudging recognition and denigration is the resentful acknowledgement of the growth and the reality of private policing qualified by the contention that it is not real policing. Although this stage was mostly eclipsed by the mid-1970s, according to Stenning, some public police leaders maintain such sentiments.

Competition and Open Hostility

Competition and open hostility is the increasing recognition of the threat posed by private policing as it became clear that the public police no longer held a monopoly on the provision of policing services. This perception of threat and competition is coupled with the recognition that the private sector

---

* Fifteen or so years ago, the first author attempted to elicit the views of the deputy chief of a Canadian municipal police force on private policing and evoked a response indicating that such a conversation was not possible given that the term *private policing* was an oxymoron.

provides postretirement opportunities for public officers, resulting in considerable ambivalence overall.

Calls for More Controls

Calls for more controls is the stage where the public police lead the call to demand more controls on private policing and, simultaneously, situate themselves as the developers and administrators of these controls.

Regulation

Stage 5 involves further attempts to impose a regulatory framework on private policing, insofar as possible, to be under the control of the public police, with the premise that it is "a necessary evil, which should be the subject of strict governmental control and public police supervision, and kept within as narrow bounds as possible" (Stenning, 1989, p. 176).

Active Partnership

By the early 1980s, the reality of private policing as a significant force had become sufficiently clear that it was no longer plausible to deny that police forces and private agencies would increasingly need to come together in various forms of partnership. These relationships were, however, characterized with the public police as the senior and the private police as the junior partner. When Stenning proposed this model 25 years ago, this stage was the end point to which any partnership had evolved.

Equal Partnership

Stenning's final level was a hypothetical, and in his view desirable, stage to which public–private partnerships might evolve. At this stage, the public and private sectors ultimately come together to work as equal partners, and the unique qualities offered by both sides are complementary to optimize the provision of policing services.

Although Stenning's model was meant to explain change over time, we use it cross-sectionally here to gauge where a Canadian sample of police officers situated themselves on the continuum in 2014. Although Stenning's conceptualization involved considerable overlap between stages 3, 4, and 5, we see a clear demarcation between stage 3 (competition and open hostility) and stages 4 (call for more controls) and 5 (regulation). Specifically, whereas an officer endorsing any of the first three stages seems to be rejecting partnerships, those situated at the calls for more controls and regulation stages may simply be raising concerns in what we noted earlier as in the legitimate/practical realm (in developing the instrument for this study, we used a single item to capture the concerns at these two stages). Of course, as also noted, this expression of concerns may also serve as subterfuge, in whole or in part, to justify resistance actually motivated by the public police protecting their turf.

Right-Wing Authoritarianism

According to Altemeyer (1981), RWA is a unidimensional construct that simultaneously captures three qualities: a conservative worldview, a readiness to acquiesce to established authority figures, and a predisposition to denigrate and to be punitive toward persons deviating from the established social order. RWAs tend to be rigid in thought and are equal opportunity bigots in their across-the-board disparagement of minority group members. The RWA construct, and Altemeyer's gold standard scale to measure it, evolved out of the work of Adorno et al. (1950) and their historically important F (fascism) scale.

It is often assumed that the police are an especially authoritarian occupational group with debate focused on whether this is predispositional or the result of socialization (Gratto et al., 2010). However, Perrott and Taylor (1994) challenged the basic premise of the inordinate levels of authoritarianism in the police overall with the findings that a sample of Canadian officers reported normative of RWA, varying only on the basis of whether or not they were university educated. Based on their review of the literature, Perrott and Taylor (1994) further conceptualized RWA as analogous to ethnocentrism, albeit at the personality rather than at the group level. Ethnocentrism is a construct of interest in this study insofar as it captures the inclination toward rigid in-group–out-group distinctions, or tribalism, another characteristic often attributed to the police. In this study, we use RWA as an individual difference variable and as a proxy for ethnocentrism to investigate the potential role of turf protection as a predictor of where respondents score on the partnership continuum.

To sum up, in this study, we investigated where a sample of police officers situated themselves on a six-point continuum of relative acceptance of the prospect of developing partnerships with private policing agencies. We anticipated that concerns about training and regulation would be widely cited as reasons for resisting partnerships. In order to gain insight into whether these objections should be viewed as legitimate (as opposed to cover for what is really turf protection), we added two strategies. First, we examined how choices on the continuum related to the officers' overall appraisal of the private police with the assumption that these measures would be intercorrelated. Second, we used a measure of RWA as a proxy for ethnocentrism to gauge whether the articulated objections should be seen as legitimate. As the approach was exploratory and descriptive, we posed no specific hypotheses.

Method

Participants

One hundred and fifty six municipal police officers (124 men, 32 women) from a medium-sized city in eastern Canada completed an online questionnaire.

A 31% response rate was achieved. One hundred and twenty-two participants were constables, and 33 were supervisors (i.e., sergeants or staff sergeants), and the years of service ranged from 2–36 years (M = 15.7, SD =
8.7). Twenty respondents completed high school; 30, a community college
program; 38, at least one year of university; 65, a bachelor's degree; and
3 had achieved graduate degrees. The participants were invited to self-
identify either as being a member of a visible minority group or as having
First Nations status with the caveat that this item was optional. Only three
respondents chose to self-identify, precluding any analyses on the basis of
majority–minority status.

Measures

Demographic Queries
Participants first provided responses indicating sex, length of service, rank,
and level of education; as noted earlier, there was an optional query about
minority status.

Partnership Acceptance
A six-stage partnership acceptance continuum was written with narrative descriptors intended to capture Stenning's (1989) seven-stage model
described earlier, but with stages 4 (calls for more controls) and 5 (regulation)
collapsed into a single stage. The item stem was worded as follows:

Let's assume that the private security/policing sector spends money to
better select and train its people and let's assume that the governments pass
the regulations that you see as necessary. Under these circumstances, how
would you, as a public police officer, see your optimal partnership to be with
para-police agencies? (Check only one box.)

Response options were as follows (intended stage from Stenning model
in parentheses):

i. This is kind of a stupid question. The private security sector has
nothing to do with real policing so it is pointless to ask questions
about partnerships. (Denial)

ii. It seems unavoidable that the private security sector is going to be a
reality in my life as a public police officer. Still, I don't accept that the
word "police" should be connected to anything they do and, accordingly, they can never be any kind of a partner. (Grudging Recognition
and Denigration)

iii. The private security sector is really over-stepping boundaries; governments need to push this movement back and leave policing to
the real police. Still, given government cut-backs I can see why there
has been an increase in this sector and this growth may have the

side benefit of providing employment for retired police officers. (Competition and Open Hostility)

iv. It seems governments are determined to save money by letting the private sector take over more and more policing functions. So be it. If this is the way of the future, governments better get busy getting appropriate regulations and training in place. Otherwise, there's real trouble ahead and, when it's all said and done, no money will be saved. (Calls for More Controls and Regulation, Stenning's Stages 4 and 5)

v. The private security sector is here to stay. When sufficient training and regulation is put in place, I will have no problem partnering with private security agencies providing the public police remain the "senior partner" and the private agency the "junior partner." (Active Partnership)

vi. Providing that sufficient training and regulation is put into place, I am OK working with private security agencies as full partners. (Equal Partnership)

Appraisal of Private Policing

Three questions eliciting perceptions of the private police were posed: (1) How much respect do you have for the private policing sector now? (2) How competent do you believe the private policing sector is to be handling the functions its personnel are performing now? And (3) how well trained and educated do you believe the private policing sector is to be handling the functions its personnel are performing now? These items were rated on seven-point Likert scales ranging from 1 (disrespect greatly/extremely incompetent/extremely poor) to 7 (respect greatly/extremely competent/extremely well).

Right-Wing Authoritarianism

Manganelli Rattazzi, Bobbio, and Canovas' (2007) abbreviated 10-item RWA scale, based on Altemeyer's (1981) original 30-item measure, was used to measure RWA. The internal consistency on this shortened scale was found to be adequate ($\alpha = 0.72$).

Procedure

All officers below the commissioned rank of inspector (i.e., constables, sergeants, and staff sergeants) were sent a Fluid surveys link via the force's internal e-mail system and invited to participate on a voluntary and anonymous basis. The link was left up for three weeks, and two reminder letters were sent. The survey was approved by the University Research Ethics Board at Mount St. Vincent University in accordance with the Canadian Tri-Council policy.

Results

The frequency of the responses for each of the six levels of the Stenning partnership continuum is provided in Table 3.1. Only 9 of the 156 respondents reported not recognizing private policing at all, while 21 officers acknowledged a willingness to act as equal partners.

The largest single category endorsed and the distribution median, as was expected, was at the calls for greater controls stage where fully one-third of the respondents situated themselves.

Repeated measures of one-way analysis of variance (ANOVA) on the three appraisal measures revealed that the officers respected the private police (M = 4.27, SD = 1.3) significantly more than they thought them to be competent (M = 3.9, SD = 1.4) but nonetheless rated them significantly higher in competence than in the belief that they were adequately trained or educated (M = 3.6, SD = 1.3, $F [2, 304] = 20.81$, $p < .001$, $\eta^2 = 0.12$).

Given the ordinal nature of the continuum, Spearman's rho correlations were calculated between the partnership variable, the three appraisal measures, the years of service, and the RWA scores. As can be seen in Table 3.2, the partnership variable was positively and significantly correlated with the

Table 3.1 Private–Public Partnership Continuum (Frequency of Responses)

Stage	n	Percentage (%)
Denial	9	5.8
Grudging recognition	19	12.2
Competition and open hostility	20	12.8
Calls for greater controls	52	33.3
Active partnership	35	22.4
Equal partnership	21	13.5

Table 3.2 Correlation Matrix of Partnership, Appraisal, Years of Service, and RWA Scores

	Partnership	Respect	Competence	Training	Years of Service	RWA
Partnership	1.0	0.40[a]	0.26[b]	0.31[b]	0.05	−0.11 ns
Respect		1.0	0.38[b]	0.45[b]	0.05	−0.05 ns
Competence			1.0	0.39[b]	0.03	−0.08 ns
Training				1.0	0.06	−0.05 ns
Years of service					1.0	−0.24[a]

Note: $n = 156$.

[a] Spearman's ρ $p < .01$.

[b] Spearman's ρ $p < .001$.

56   Global Issues in Contemporary Policing

three appraisal variables (as they were to each other). There was a significant, but modest, negative relationship between the years of service and the RWA, but these variables were related neither to the partnership scores nor to any of the appraisal measures.

Both the six-item partnership continuum and the five-level education variables were not only written to reflect ordinal scaling but could also be viewed as nominal in nature. In order to improve their usability as categorical variables, and be consistent with our conceptualization of the partnership continuum, the stages/categories for both variables were collapsed into three-level nominal variables. In the case of education, those respondents indicating either high school or community college completion were placed into a no-university group (n = 50, 32.1%); those indicating at least one year of university were the some university group (n = 38, 24.4%); and those having finished a degree or a graduate degree were collapsed into the university group (n = 68, 43.6%). Our modified partnership variable divided our group into three levels each comprising about one-third of the sample: (1) The reject partnership group were those respondents endorsing stages 1, 2, or 3 (n = 48; 30.8%); (2) the call for controls group were those endorsing stage 4 (n = 52, 33.3%); and (3) the partnership group comprised those endorsing willingness to engage in an active or equal partnership, stages 5 and 6 (n = 56, 35.9%).

Cross tabulations were conducted between this three-level partnership variable against the modified education variable, officer sex, and officer rank. chi-square tests with sex and education proved to be nonsignificant, but the test with rank showed that sergeants and staff sergeants were significantly less likely to shut out the possibility of forming partnerships with the private police than were constables (χ^2 (2) = 6.48, $p < .05$; see Table 3.3).

In order to test whether authoritarianism was related to any of the grouping variables, one-way ANOVAs were conducted on RWA scores with sex, level of education, and rank as independent variables. Male and female officers did not differ in RWA nor were there significant differences across the three-level education variable. However, a significant effect of rank showed that constables were significantly higher (M = 37.18, SD = 12.52) in RWA than were their supervisors (M = 31.34, SD = 13.37; F [146], $p < .05$). Given the

Table 3.3   Cross Tabulations of Rank and Partnership Acceptance

| Rank | Level of Partnership Acceptance | | Active or Equal Partnership n (%) |
	Reject Partnership n (%)	Calls for Control and Training n (%)	
Constables	43 (35.2)	35 (28.7)	44 (36.1)
Sergeants and staff sergeants	5 (15.2)	16 (48.5)	12 (36.4)

Note: χ^2 (2) = 6.48, $p < .05$.

potential importance of authoritarianism in this study, one final check of a possible relationship between RWA scores and placement on the continuum was conducted with the three-level modified partnership variable treated as an independent variable and RWA scores as the dependent measure. A one-way ANOVA proved to be nonsignificant.

Discussion

We investigated where a sample of public police officers would place themselves on a continuum of acceptance toward public–private policing partnerships based on a model proposed by Stenning in 1989. Approximately 3 out of every 10 respondents were clear that they did not, for a variety of reasons, support any type of partnership, whereas exactly one-third, although more receptive at least in theory, reported significant ambivalence on the basis that they found the training levels of, and regulatory framework for, private agents to be wanting. The final third of the respondents were willing to work in partnerships, although the majority of these officers viewed the appropriate model to be one where they, the public police, would remain in control.

Stenning's model was a hypothetical one, unaccompanied by data, and meant to describe a developmental process. He did not postulate what proportions of officers would spread across the stages of the continuum. Nonetheless, the distribution of responses here suggests that he may have been overly optimistic in his judgment or, at the very least, that there has been little evolution in attitudes across the 25 years since his proposal was made. In describing the model, he either discussed the police generically or, in some instances, referenced police leaders. To the extent that he had leaders in mind, it is interesting that the sergeants and the staff sergeants in this sample were significantly less likely to preclude the possibility of partnerships than were constables. (Constables and supervisors reported being willing to work in partnerships in equal proportions. It was the greater likelihood of constables to endorse the bottom three stages of the continuum, i.e., reject the possibility of partnerships, that was responsible for the significant rank difference.)

It is difficult to move beyond speculation about what this distinction with supervisors, in isolation, means. It may be that by virtue of their roles, they are more able to step back from the vicissitudes of the street for a more macrolevel look at where policing has been and where it is going. Or it may be that they were simply reflecting, consciously or not, what they perceived to be the position of senior management. This caveat aside, findings here suggest that much further evolution is necessary before public officers are willing, en masse, to move into any sort of closer relationship with the private sector, let alone one where the partnership is of equal status.

It is noteworthy that the sample overall reported holding private agents in reasonably high esteem, found them to be competent at a lesser, although still moderate level, but were quite critical about the levels of education, training, and regulation. These appraisal variables qualified but were consistent with the scores on the partnership continuum. An optimistic view of these ratings is that the participants thought fairly highly of the private police and believed them to be doing a reasonable job given that with which they were given to work. It was that with which they were given to work that was seen as the real problem. It may be that there was a certain social desirability bias at the core of these ratings (i.e., the respondents did not wish to be perceived as hostile or unwilling to contemplate change) but, given the very real problems with training and regulation in private policing that remain outstanding, it may simply be a reasonable assessment.

The means by which we sought to assess the reasonableness of these appraisals was via RWA scores. These scores did not vary on the basis of years of service, officer sex, or even on level of education where, based on past research, we could have reasonably predicted differences (Lee and Punch, 2007). The only difference to emerge was again on officer rank with the supervisors scoring significantly lower than the constables. Perrott and Taylor (1995) observed a similar finding in a work conducted more than 20 years ago.

Given our interest in the possibility that line officers seek to protect their turf covertly by offering plausible reasons for not wanting closer relationships makes these rank-based findings a potentially interesting starting point from which to pursue this hypothesis. However, the trail went cold beyond this point, and we are left with findings that fail to provide direct evidence of anything. The stronger evidence, although still circumstantial, would be the findings showing RWA levels to be linked to appraisal ratings or to placements on the partnership continuum. However, there was a striking absence of a relationship between RWA scores and any sentiments expressed toward the private police.

Thus, there is no evidence to suggest that the respondents resisted closer relationships to private policing agencies on the basis of in-group–out-group processes, rigid thinking, or any sort of intolerant views. Of course, the failure to find evidence of such does not disqualify the presence of these factors. It may be, for example, that even though there was a sound theoretical basis for linking authoritarianism with ethnocentrism, RWA was simply not a salient proxy for this purpose. Conversely, were we to take the objections the respondents offered at face value policy makers might heed their advice in pressing for more professional training and establishment of uniform regulatory frameworks for the private policing industry.

It seems clear that the private policing sector has little motivation to do more than it must in this regard given the tight profit margins in the industry, a factor that also impacts the level of pay most agents receive. Although the wages improved somewhat in recent years, the wages generally paid to private policing agents in Canada are not only paltry compared to their public counterparts but very low compared to the workforce as a whole (Sanders, 2005). It is odd to think that the public and private sectors can come together on an equal basis and meet societal performance expectations in the face of such disparity.

Conclusion

It may be time to shift immediate attention away from the concerns about the extent to which the public police are willing to work with the private sector to a focus on the state itself as a partner to private policing. Any development in this regard would be premised on the governmental responsibility extending beyond simply developing regulatory frameworks to circumstances where tax revenues are used to support, and perhaps even subsidize, the professionalization of private policing. Given that the main driver of private policing is cost savings and deficit reduction, such an investment would obviously be limited. One possibility would be for governments to assume the costs, and perhaps the actual responsibility, for basic training and some level of continuing education for private policing. This would free up the private agencies to focus on operations and, provided that bidding wars were not allowed to eat up all the savings, might allow the latitude to provide private agents with salaries that are a little more commensurate with the responsibilities they are increasingly taking on.

The largest roadblock in implementing an initiative of this sort may not be in the ability of governments to make the monies available so much as the challenge entailed in tackling the neoliberal mindset currently driving privatization without regard to social cost. However, as Stenning (2009) points out, "the current dichotomous arrangements ... are no longer adequate to ensure effective and accountable policing in the public interest" (p. 31). The continuing growth in the privatization of policing functions, without government responsibility ensuring that the services are delivered in an equitable and integrated manner, may ultimately prove to challenge the very basis of what it means to live in a democratic society.

References

Adorno, T. W., Frenkel-Bruswick, E., Levinson, D., and Sanford, N. 1950. *The Authoritarian Personality*. Oxford, UK: Harper and Brothers.
Altemeyer, R. A. 1981. *Right-Wing Authoritarianism*. Winnipeg, Canada: University of Manitoba Press.

Bradley, T., and Sedgwick, C. 2009. Policing beyond the police: A "first cut" study of private security in New Zealand. *Journal of Policing and Society*. 19: 468–92.

Burbidge, S. 2005. The governance of deficit: Reflections on the future of public and private policing in Canada. *Canadian Journal of Criminology and Criminal Justice*. 47: 63–86.

Button, M. 2009. The private security industry act 2001 and the security management gap in the United Kingdom. *Security Journal*. 24: 118–32.

Cohen, S. 1985. *Visions of Social Control*. Cambridge, UK: Polity Press.

Ericson, R. V., and Haggerty, K. D. 1997. *Policing the Risk Society*. Oxford, UK: Oxford University Press.

Gratto, J., Dambrun, M., Kerbrat, C., and De Oliveira, P. 2010. Prejudice in the police: On the process underlying the effects of selection and group socialisation. *European Journal of Social Psychology*. 40: 252–69.

Grover, C. 2009. Privatizing employment services in Britain. *Critical Social Policy*. 29: 487–509.

Hummer, D., and Nalla, M. K. 2003. Modeling future relations between the private and public sectors of law enforcement. *Criminal Justice Studies*. 16: 87–96.

Joh, E. E. 2004. The paradox of private policing. *The Journal of Criminal Law and Criminology*. 95: 49–132.

Johnston, L., and Stenning, P. C. 2013. Challenges of governance and accountability for transnational private policing. In *International Police Cooperation: Emerging Issues, Theory, and Practice*. Lemieux, F. ed. Hoboken, NJ: Taylor & Francis.

Lee, M., and Punch, M. 2007. Policing by degrees: Police officers' experience of university education. *Policing and Society: An International Journal of Research and Policy*. 14: 233–49.

Manganelli Rattazzi, A. M., Bobbio, A., and Canova, L. 2007. A short version of the right-wing authoritarianism (RWA) scale. *Personality and Individual Differences*. 43: 1223–34.

Manzo, J. 2011. On the practices of private security officers: Canadian security officers' reflections on training and legitimacy. *Social Justice*. 38: 107–27.

Murphy, C. 2004. The rationalization of Canadian public policing: A study of the impact and implications of resource limits and market strategies. *The Canadian Review of Policing Research, 1*. Accessed April 2, 2014. Retrieved from http://crpr.icaap.org/index.php/crpr/article/viewArticle/11/11.

Murphy, C. 2007. "Securitizing" Canadian policing: A new policing paradigm for the post 9/11 security state? *Canadian Journal of Sociology*. 32: 449–75.

Nalla, M. K., and Hummer, D. 1999. Relations between police officers and security professionals: A study of perceptions. *Security Journal*. 12: 31–40.

Perrott, S. B., and Taylor, D. M. 1994. Ethnocentrism and authoritarianism in the police: Challenging stereotypes and reconceptualising ingroup identification. *Journal of Applied Social Psychology*. 24: 1640–64.

Perrott, S. B., and Taylor, D. M. 1995. Attitudinal differences between police constables and their supervisors: Potential influences of personality, work environment, and occupational role. *Criminal Justice and Behaviour*. 22: 326–9.

Prenzler, T., Earle, K., and Sarre, R. 2009. Private security in Australia: Trends and key characteristics. *Trends and Issues in Crime and Criminal Justice*. 374: 1–6.

Ransley, J., and Mazerolle, L. 2009. Policing in an era of uncertainty. *Police Practice and Research*. 10: 365–81.

Rigakos, G. S. 2002. *The New Parapolice: Risk Markets and Commodified Social Control*. Toronto, Canada: University of Toronto Press.

Rigakos, G. S., and Greener, D. R. 2000. Bubbles of governance: Private policing and the law in Canada. *Canadian Journal of Law and Society*. 15: 145–85.

Ruddell, R., Thomas, M. O., and Patten, R. 2011. Examining the roles of the police and private security officers in urban social control. *International Journal of Police Science & Management*. 13: 54–69.

Sanders, T. 2005. Rise of the rent-a-cop: Private security in Canada, 1991–2001. *Canadian Journal of Criminology and Criminal Justice*. 47: 175–90.

Sarre, R. 2005. Researching private policing: Challenges and agendas for research. *Security Journal*. 18(3): 57–70.

Sarre, R. 2013. Public-private cooperation in policing crime and terrorism in Australia. In *Policing Global Movement: Tourism, Migration, Human Trafficking, and Terrorism*. Taylor, C., Torpy, D., and Das, D., eds. Boca Raton, FL: CRC Press.

Shearing, C. D. 1992. The relationship between public and private policing. *Crime and Justice*. 15: 399–434.

Shearing, C. D., and Stenning, P. C. 1983. Private security: Implications for social control. *Social Problems*. 30: 493–506.

Skolnick, J. H. 1966. *Justice without Trial*. New York: Wiley.

Stenning, P. C. 1989. Private police and public police: Toward a redefinition of the police role. In *Future Issues in Policing: Symposium Proceedings*. Loree, D. J., ed. Ottawa, Canada: Ministry of Supply and Services Canada: 169–92.

Stenning, P. C. 2000. Powers and accountability of private police. *European Journal on Criminal Policy and Research*. 8: 325–52.

Stenning, P. C. 2009. Governance and accountability in a plural policing environment— The story so far. *Policing* 3: 22–32.

Swol, K. 1998. Private security and public policing in Canada. *Juristat*. 18(13): 1–12.

Van Steden, R., and Sarre, R. 2007. The growth of private security: Trends in the European Union. *Security Journal*. 20: 222–35.

Wakefield, A. 2012. *Selling Security: The Private Policing of Public Space*. Portland, OR: Willan Publishing.

Williamson, T., Ashby, D. I., and Webber, R. 2006. Classifying neighbourhoods for reassurance policing. *Policing and Society*. 16: 189–218.

Reactive and Proactive Measures of Police Corruption Control

Comparative Study in Three Countries

4

BRANISLAV SIMONOVIC
MAXIMILIAN EDELBACHER
BAKHIT NURGALIYEV

Contents

Abstract

In this chapter are shown the results of the research with police officers from Austria, Serbia, and Kazakhstan about their attitudes concerning the implementation of reactive and proactive measures that are applied in the control of police corruption. Firstly, the respondents were asked to comment about whether certain anticorruption measures are applied in the police system of their country and the frequency of their application. After that, they were asked to rate each measure by its effectiveness. The results show that respondents are not satisfied with the effectiveness of anticorruption measures applied and that they consider that the application of some other measures used around the world, but not in their system, would have a bigger anticorruption effect.

Introduction

The consequences of police corruption are different and very huge. Police corruption undermines the legitimacy of police organization and police effectiveness (Bayley and Perito, 2011, p. 5; Punch, 2000, p. 301) and causes a decline in public support for police, loss of trust in the rule of law, and general mistrust of the police organization at large (Jenks, Johnson, and Matthews, 2012, p. 4; Kutnjak Ivković, 2009, p. 777; Sellbom, Fischler, and Ben-Porath, 2007, p. 985; Tankebe, 2010, p. 297; Weitzer, 2002). Corruption destroys the fundamental values of human dignity and political equality, making it impossible to exercise most other human rights. When corruption is widespread, people do not have access to justice, are not secure, and cannot protect their livelihoods (Kolthoff, 2010, p. 7). The problem is that small police corruption and abuses of office may later lead to greater corruption and abuses of office (Moran, 2005, p. 74). Corruption is a "virus capable of crippling government, discrediting public institutions and having a devastating impact on the human rights of populations, and thus undermining society and its development" (Fijnaut and Huberts, 2002, p. 15).

The level of corruption in the society affects the level of corruption in the police as well (Kutnjak Ivković, 2009; Kutnjak Ivković and Kang, 2012, p. 84). Any anticorruption strategy depends on the willingness of the political leadership to take corruption problems seriously, to make anticorruption policy a priority, and to assign sufficient resources to the relevant institutions (Bayley and Perito, 2011, p. 9; Fijnaut and Huberts, 2002, p. 16).

The control of police corruption can be internally and externally extended to civilian oversight agencies (Criminal Justice Commission, 2001, p. 3). This chapter researches the strategies and the methods of the internal control of police corruption.

Punch (2000, p. 301) noted that police corruption is not an individual aberration of an incidental nature that can be readily combated with temporary, repressive measures. The new realism on this maintains that corruption and police misconduct are persistent and constantly recurring hazards generated by the organization itself. Rather what should be studied is the context, the wider environment, and the system within which corruption takes place. Of course, bad apples exist, as does the individual element, but because the individual operates in a social context, it is the interaction between individual and social contexts that matters (Kolthoff, 2010, p. 4).

It is very important that the measures have a balance between negative and positive social controls and rest on two pillars: aggressive investigations and promoting integrity (Punch, 2000, pp. 317, 322; Ward and McCormack, 1987, p. 163). Anticorruption measures should provide support for corruption opponents and intimidate those prone to it. On one hand, the strategies directed toward the control of police corruption should be based on increased risk from revealing corruptive behavior, while, on the other hand, long-term strategies should be directed toward adopting new ethical standards and strengthening the integrity (McCormack, 2001, p. 107). An anticorruption strategy should strive to accomplish three goals: (1) to eliminate possibilities for corruption by introducing measures that hinder corruption; (2) to combat corruption through efficient revelation, investigation, and prosecution; and (3) to educate the public about the dangers corruption bears and to strive to achieve the public's support in combating this phenomenon (Mutonyi, 2005, p. 77).

Various documents and literature written by committees that have researched major corruption scandals recommend a great number of measures for the control of police corruption. These measures and the recommendations involve reforms to police culture, management, recruitment and training, disciplinary processes, promotion and assignment, and external environment (Bayley and Perito, 2011, p. 1).

The most cited recommendations and measures that can be found in the literature are strong leadership (Punch, 2000, p. 314); police supervision, (Marché, 2009, p. 471); strengthening of internal investigative capacity, (Punch, 2000, p. 301); intelligence gathering (Mollen Commission Report, 1994, p. 70); vigorous pursuit of suspects of police deviance through criminal prosecutions, disciplinary procedures, and enforced early retirements (Punch, 2000, p. 314); adoption of proactive strategies/methods against corrupt officers as you would against organized criminals, integrity testing officer; use of informants, checking of rumors and indications of a serious corruption problem, various electronic or surveillance devices, telephone intercepts, and sting operation, strategic analysis of intelligence (Fijnaut and Huberts, 2002, p. 18; Kolthoff, 2010, p. 18; Moran, 2005, p. 64; Prenzler and Ronken, 2003, p. 158; Punch, 2000, pp. 314, 318); improvement of organizational structure (Marché, 2009, p. 471); risk and danger zones detecting (Kolthoff, 2010, p. 18; Punch, 2000, p. 319); registration, an extensive record of corruption in public life in general and in the police in particular (Huberts, Lamboo, and Punch, 2003, p. 229; Kolthoff, 2010, p. 3); command accountability and supervision (Mollen Commission Report, 1994, p. 70); holding leaders responsible for deviance on their own territory (Bayley and Perito, 2011, p. 1; Kolthoff, 2010, p. 18; Punch, 2000, p. 314); training programs in integrity and improvement of police culture (Marché, 2009, p. 471; Kolthoff, 2010, p. 18; Osse, 1997).

The mentioned measures of control of police corruption are written by theoreticians and recommended by various committees that have done research on current corruption affairs in the police, while legislators regulate the enforcement of these measures in practice. However, no research has been done on how police officers rate (evaluate) the measures of corruption control. These questions deserve attention, considering the fact that police officers apply anticorruption measures directed toward the control of corruption within a police organization. They have a direct experience in the implementation of these measures, and they are aware of the limitations and the difficulties that arise in the process. The research of the attitudes and the evaluations of police officers concerning the control of corruption in the police is a multidimensional and complex issue, bearing in mind the indisputable facts that result from the complexity of this phenomenon, the problems with integrity (Jenks, Johnson, and Matthews, 2012; Kutnjak Ivković, 2005, 2009; Kutnjak Ivković and Kang, 2012; Kutnjak Ivković and Shelley, 2005), and the existing code of silence among the police officers (Moran, 2005; Skolnick, 2002, 2005; Rothwell and Baldwin, 2007).

This chapter is a part of a wider research, and it is focused only on the attitudes of police officers concerning the application of reactive and proactive measures that are applied in the control of corruption in the police.

Methods and Data

Comparative studies in the field of corruption are gaining more significance in criminology and police research, considering the fact that the globalization process brings the increased knowledge transfer between countries. The value of comparison is much greater than its utility for describing observed variations between states and societies. It is an essential device for understanding what is distinctive (and problematic) about domestic arrangements (Zimring and Johnson, 2005, p. 794). However, comparative research faces challenges because different systems (Kääriäinen, 2007), as well as the structure of the police (Kutnjak Ivković and Kang, 2012, p. 78) can affect the results, as can possible linguistic and cultural differences (Huberts, Lamboo, and Punch, 2003, p. 219).

Comparative research regarding corruption in the police and integrity of police profession represent a special challenge in the states with a long history of political interference in the police, in which the police served the interests of the communist state rather than the interests of the individual (Kutnjak Ivković and Shelley, 2005, p. 438).

This research was conducted with the help of police officers in three states: Austria, Serbia, and Kazakhstan. The countries in question are significantly different, in terms of political and economic developments, democratic tradition, police structure, and anticorruption policy. Austria is a developed country with strong democratic tradition of a civil society, a member of the European Union, ranked 25th (score: 69) according to the Corruption Perceptions Index (CPI) in 2012 (whereas in 2011, it was ranked 16th). Serbia is not a member of the European Union; it is currently going through a transition process, ranked 80th according to CPI (score: 39). Kazakhstan is an Asian country, in transition, ranked 133rd according to CPI (score: 28). The Serbian and Kazakhstan police are going through a difficult period of democratization, depolitization, and professionalization, which makes the development of anticorruption tendencies a special challenge in these countries.

We used a questionnaire that encompasses the reactive and proactive measures whose application is most frequently recommended in literature and reports of the committees, which have been researching corruption in police, and other documents (e.g., Anti-Corruption Investigation and Trial Guide [USAID, 2005], Benchmarking Police Integrity Programmes [ACPO, 2013], Mollen Commission Report [1994]). Apart from the standard measures, the questionnaire contains questions formulated relating to the measures that are known to be unusual in the police of the countries being studied. The intention was to determine the opinion of the respondents about the effectiveness of these measures and the prospective need for introducing them in an anticorruption model.

The same questionnaire was used for police officers in Austria, Serbia, and Kazakhstan. The original version was made in English. For the purposes of the interviews in Serbia and Kazakhstan, the questionnaire was translated into Serbian and Russian, respectively. Austrian police officers filled in the questionnaire in English.

There were the general parts to the questionnaire including questions about age, years of service, education, rank, police service, and position in police management. The special part of the questionnaire contained questions related to the dependent variables concerning reactive and proactive measures applied in the control of police corruption. The questionnaire was created in two levels. The first level asked the respondents to express their opinion, within each variable, about whether a particular anticorruption measure (or several similar measures) is applied and to what extent, within the police system of their country. The goal was to determine the awareness of the respondents about the application of particular reactive and proactive measures in the field of suppressing and controlling corruption. The second part of the questionnaire had the goal to determine how respondents evaluate the effectiveness of each measure in particular, in combating police corruption.

The quantification of the responses resulted in the possibility to compare the pairs of the variables on level 1 (evaluation of the frequency of measure implementation) with level 2 (evaluation of measure effectiveness). We started from the supposition that the comparison of these two levels will show possible directions in which the array of measures should be lead. Apart from that, the aim was to determine opinions about the anticorruption measures in the police of those who apply the measures, as well as the correlations in the responses between the interviewed police officers from these three very different countries.

The structured interview was conducted in Austria with 27 police officers, whereas in Serbia and Kazakhstan, the number of interviewed police officers was 50. The interviews with police officers were conducted in the period of February–April 2013 in such a way that each respondent was familiarized with the aim of the research and the meaning of particular variables. The research was conducted in the home cities and states of the coauthors. Each coauthor had organized and conducted the research in his respective city and state. The research was conducted in one day in the premises of the city police. The selections of the interviewed police officers were performed on the basis of random sampling. It was done on the occasion of police management meetings about fighting crime, which gathered mostly criminal police officers and fewer uniformed police. After the official meeting of the police management, the police officers were asked to stay in the room with the researcher if they wished to participate in the interview about police corruption. In Austria, the police management meeting included active police officers as well as retired police officers who have great experience in police work and wish to share it with younger colleagues. The average number of years of work experience of the police for the respondents form Serbia is 17.3; from Kazakhstan, 12.4; and from Austria, 30.6. The sample was appropriate, having in mind that the respondents have more years of experience in the police and with higher educational degree. Overall, the sample included 127 police officers. The data were processed in computer program SPSS 18. This study is exploratory, and the results should be considered valid in terms of preliminary research.

The research started with a general hypothesis: Attitudes of the police officers about the frequency of the application and the effectiveness of particular measures that are applied in the control of police corruption are significant for forming (defining, directing, correcting) anticorruption strategies.

Results of the Research

The results of the research are presented in three parts, i.e., three tables that are discussed in this chapter.

Overview of the Results on the Entire Sample

In the processing of gathered data, all 12 pairs of the variables on level 1 (measure implementation) were, firstly, compared with the variables on level 2 (evaluation of measure effectiveness) within a collective response of all 127 respondents from the three states (descriptive statistics for each variable as well as correlations for each variable pair). The results are shown on Table 4.1.

The first level of research (measure implementation), encompassed the respondents' evaluation for each of the 12 listed anticorruption measures

Table 4.1 Descriptives and Correlations (Entire Sample)

Level 1: Measures Implementation	Descriptives of Variables: a1_1–a12_1	Pearson's Correlation (For N ≈ 127)	Descriptives of Variables: a1_2–a12_2	Level 2: Estimated Efficiency
a1_1: Mandatory suspension	M = 4.57; SD = 0.88 1 = 3.9%, 2 = 0%, 4 = 23.6%, 5 = 63.8% (3) Not informed = 8.7%	r = −0.192[a]	M = 2.81; SD = 1.42 1 = 27.6%, 2 = 12.6%, 3 = 25.2%, 4 = 18.9%, 5 = 15.0%	a1_2: Estimated efficiency
a2_1: Disciplinary action, criminal charges, providing evidence	M = 4.47; SD = 0.94 1 = 3.9%, 2 = 1.6%, 4 = 26.8%, 5 = 57.5% (3) Not informed = 9.4%	r = 0.119	M = 2.97; SD = 1.43 1 = 22.8%, 2 = 11.0%, 3 = 26.8%, 4 = 15.7%, 5 = 18.9%	a2_2: Estimated efficiency
a3_1: Special investigative techniques (simulated offering bribes, undercover agents, etc.)	M = 3.79; SD = 1.24 1 = 7.1%, 2 = 7.1%, 4 = 37.8%, 5 = 20.5% (3) Not informed = 25.2%	r = −0.285[b]	M = 3.11; SD = 1.29 1 = 11.0%, 2 = 21.3%, 3 = 30.7%, 4 = 13.4%, 5 = 20.5%	a3_2: Estimated efficiency
a4_1: Recording direct communication/phone tapping	M = 4.29; SD = 0.91 1 = 3.1%, 2 = 1.6%, 4 = 37.8%, 5 = 34.6% (3) Not informed = 00.0%	r = −0.120	M = 3.03; SD = 1.31 1 = 14.2%, 2 = 20.5%, 3 = 23.6%, 4 = 19.7%, 5 = 15.7%	a4_2: Estimated efficiency
a5_1: Covert surveillance of space and cars	M = 3.74; SD = 1.24 1 = 5.5%, 2 = 8.7%, 4 = 33.1%, 5 = 17.3% (3) Not informed = 32.3%	r = −0.245[a]	M = 3.15; SD = 1.33 1 = 11.8%, 2 = 17.3%, 3 = 26.8%, 4 = 13.4%, 5 = 20.5%	a5_2: Estimated efficiency

(Continued)

Table 4.1 (Continued)　Descriptives and Correlations (Entire Sample)

Level 1: Measures Implementation	Descriptives of Variables: a1_1–a12_1	Pearson's Correlation (For $N \approx 127$)	Descriptives of Variables: a1_2–a12_2	Level 2: Estimated Efficiency
a6_1: Targeted polygraph testings	M = 2.74; SD = 1.53 1 = 23.6%, 2 = 15.0%, 4 = 24.4%, 5 = 9.4% (3) Not informed = 24.4%	r = −0.220[a]	M = 3.36; SD = 1.39 1 = 13.4%, 2 = 11.8%, 3 = 24.4%, 4 = 17.3%, 5 = 27.6%	a6_2: Estimated efficiency
a7_1: Using internal informants	M = 4.1; SD = 1.03 1 = 3.9%, 2 = 2.4%, 4 = 33.9%, 5 = 25.2% (3) Not informed = 33.1%	r = −0.073	M = 2.75; SD = 1.22 1 = 16.5%, 2 = 24.4%, 3 = 29.1%, 4 = 13.4%, 5 = 10.2%	a7_2: Estimated efficiency
a8_1: Targeted integrity testing	M = 2.24; SD = 1.55 1 = 27.6%, 2 = 11.0%, 4 = 8.7%, 5 = 7.9% (3) Not informed = 43.3%	r = −0.502[b]	M = 3.11; SD = 1.46 1 = 18.9%, 2 = 15.0%, 3 = 24.4%, 4 = 11.8%, 5 = 25.2%	a8_2: Estimated efficiency
a9_1: Random integrity testing	M = 2.42; SD = 1.59 1 = 26.8%, 2 = 10.2%, 4 = 12.6%, 5 = 8.7% (3) Not informed = 8.7%	r = −0.344[b]	M = 3.08; SD = 1.41 1 = 18.9%, 2 = 10.2%, 3 = 30.7%, 4 = 11.8%, 5 = 22.0%	a9_2: Estimated efficiency
a10_1: Control polygraph testing	M = 1.6190; SD = 1.01678 1 = 41.7%, 2 = 16.5%, 4 = 7.1%, 5 = 0.8% (3) Not informed = 33.9%	r = −0.174	M = 3.41; SD = 1.40 1 = 13.4%, 2 = 11.8%, 3 = 22.8%, 4 = 18.9%, 5 = 29.9%	a10_2: Estimated efficiency
a11_1: Psychological and ethical testing	M = 2.88; SD = 1.72 1 = 25.2%, 2 = 9.4%, 4 = 14.2%, 5 = 18.9% (3) Not informed = 30.7%	r = −0.574[b]	M = 2.98; SD = 1.38 1 = 19.7%, 2 = 16.5%, 3 = 23.6%, 4 = 20.5%, 5 = 16.5%	a11_2: Estimated efficiency

(Continued)

Table 4.1 (Continued) Descriptives and Correlations (Entire Sample)

Level 1: Measures Implementation	Descriptives of Variables: a1_1–a12_1	Pearson's Correlation (For $N \approx 127$)	Descriptives of Variables: a1_2–a12_2	Level 2: Estimated Efficiency
a12_1: Unhidden video–acoustic recording of official activities	M = 3.48; SD = 1.46 1 = 12.6%, 2 = 13.4%, 4 = 307%, 5 = 22.8% (3) Not informed = 18.1%	r = −0.401[b]	M = 3.29; SD = 1.37 1 = 12.6%, 2 = 16.5%, 3 = 24.4%, 4 = 18.1% , 5 = 26.0%	a12_2: Estimated efficiency

Pearson's correlation (for $N = 12$): r = −0.663.[a]
Sig. (two-tailed): $p = .019$

Spearman's rho correlation (for $N = 12$): $\rho = -0.671$.[b]
Sig. (two-tailed): $p = .017$

Note: Values of answer modalities, for variables a1_1–a12_1, are as follows: not applied or are planning to introduce it = 1; it does not apply, but I think its introduction is planned = 2; it is used occasionally = 4; it is used regularly = 5.

[a] Correlation is significant at the 0.05 level (two-tailed).
[b] Correlation is significant at the 0.01 level (two-tailed).

concerning the degree of the application of the given measure in the respective countries. The scale of possible answers ranged from not applied or are planning to introduce it; it does not apply, but I think its introduction is planned; I am not informed in this regard; it is used occasionally; and it is used regularly. The second level of research encompassed the estimated efficiency of each of the 12 listed measures. The scale of possible answers ranged from 1 to 5 (the most efficient measure in police corruption control being 5 and the least efficient measure being 1). The modalities of the responses are shown in percentages. Based on such quantification, the mean values (M) were calculated and shown in Table 4.1 with corresponding standard deviations (SD), for all variables of implementation (from a1_1 to a12_1) and for all variables of effectiveness (from a1_2 to a12_2). Table 4.1 represents the overview of the results in all three countries (descriptive and correlation analyses for the entire sample of 127 respondents).

The results of the correlation analysis are shown in Table 4.1, as 12 Pearson's r coefficient of bivariate correlation and one Spearman's rho coefficient. Pearson's r coefficient is adequate for large samples (with $N > 30$); therefore, our research applied it to a unified sample of respondents, $N = 127$. The calculation of this coefficient determined the correlation between implementation (estimated degree of implementation of the measure) and effectiveness (opinion of the efficiency of the measure in controlling police corruption) for each of the 12 observed anticorruptive measures.

As seen in Table 4.1, almost all of correlations are negative, while more than half of them are statistically significant. Therefore, a general conclusion can be drawn that the higher the degree of application of a particular anticorruptive measure, the lower the evaluation of its effectiveness.

The same conclusion is indicated by statistically significant and comparatively high negative value of Spearman's rho coefficient of correlation between the means of the variables on level 1 and the means of the variables on level 2, ($\rho = -0.671^b$) shown in the bottom row of the table. Spearman's coefficient is used here because the number of cases was only 12, which represents a small sample.

Respondents' Evaluation of the Frequency of Application of Reactive and Proactive Measures in the Control of Corruption in the Police of Their Countries

A descriptive statistical analysis was conducted in this research, and it showed the respondents' evaluation of the implementation of reactive and proactive measures in the control of the corruption in the police of their countries. Reactive measures are undertaken after committing the crime (for example, mandatory suspension). Proactive measures are undertaken before committing the crime with the aim of providing evidence (for example, phone tapping) or preventing/detracting the crime (for example, control polygraph testing).

The responses of the interviewed police officers from each state are shown in separate columns and expressed in percentages of the received responses. The mean value (M) and the standard deviation (SD) were determined for each response in each state with regard to each variable. The frequencies of the responses (expressed in percentages) are shown as follows: (1) = Not applied or are planning to introduce it. (2) = It does not apply, but I think its introduction is planned. (3) = "I am not informed in this regard" (variable 3 was omitted from the scale and was not used in future statistical calculations). (4) = It is used occasionally. (5) = It is used regularly. Additionally, Table 4.2 shows the statistical significance of the differences in the distribution of the responses to questions about the measures implementation of particular anticorruptive measures, among the respondents from different countries using the t-test for the equality of means for independent samples.

Mandatory suspension (a1_1) is applied in the case of police officers where it was determined that they have received a bribe, but its implementation is not equal and unconditional in all three countries, although there is a legal obligation to pronounce suspension. Only 46% of the respondents from Serbia believe that this measure is regularly applied (36% chose the response *used occasionally*). Police officers from Kazakhstan cited the same percentage (66% of the respondents chose the response *used regularly*; 20% chose *occasional use*). There is a significant difference in the responses from the interviewed police officers from Austria, where practically all of them stated that mandatory suspension is regularly applied in cases of police officers suspected of bribery (92.6%) (M = 4.93, SD = 0.27). The application of t-test showed the existing significance of the differences in the application of mandatory suspension between Serbia and Austria at a level $p < .01$, as well as the significance of the differences between Kazakhstan and Austria at a slightly lower level of $p < .05$.

Similar responses were received for the question about repressive measures, *initiation disciplinary action, file criminal charges, provide evidence,* relating to the offense of any officer, regardless of the rank or the position, if there is a reasonable suspicion of committing a criminal act (a2_1). Only 46% of police officers in Serbia responded with *used regularly* (38% responded with *used occasionally*). Half of the respondents from Kazakhstan stated that this measure is applied regularly (26% occasionally). Unlike them, almost all interviewed police officers from Austria stated that this measure is also applied in the case of every suspect, without exception (92.6%, M = 4.93). Undoubtedly, the attitudes of the police officers that these two repressive measures are applied irregularly in the police of Serbia (M = 4.26) and

Table 4.2 Significance of Differences between Implementation of the Measures

Level 1: Measures Implementation	Serbia	Kazakhstan	Austria	Significance of Difference		
				S–A	S–K	K–A
a1_1: Mandatory suspension	M = 4.48; SD = 0.74; (3) 16.0%[a] %: (1) 2.0; (2) 0.0; (4) 36.0; (5) 46.0	M = 4.45; SD = 1.14; (3) 8.0% %: (1) 8.0; (2) 0.0; (4) 20.0; (5) 66.0	M = 4.93; SD = 0.27; (3) 0.0% %: (1) 0.0; (2) 0.0; (4) 7.4; (5) 92.6	c	–	b
a2_1: Disciplinary act., crim. charges, prov. evidence	M = 4.26; SD = 1.06; (3) 8.0% %: (1) 8.0; (2) 2.0; (4) 38.0; (5) 46.0	M = 4.41; SD = 1.00; (3) 16.0% %: (1) 4.0; (2) 2.0; (4) 26.0; (5) 50.0	M = 4.93; SD = 0.27; (3) 0.0% %: (1) 0.0; (2) 0.0; (4) 7.4; (5) 92.6	c		c
a3_1: Spec. investigative techniq. (simul. offer brib.)	M = 3.44; SD = 1.05; (3) 30.0% %: (1) 4.0; (2) 14.0; (4) 48.0; (5) 2.0	M = 3.90; SD = 1.39; (3) 16.0% %: (1) 12.0; (2) 4.0; (4) 32.0; (5) 36.0	M = 4.25; SD = 1.00; (3) 33.3% %: (1) 3.7; (2) 0.0; (4) 29.6; (5) 25.9	c	–	–
a4_1: Recording direct communication/phone tapp.	M = 4.15; SD = 0.57; (3) 32.0% %: (1) 0.0; (2) 2.0; (4) 50.0; (5) 14.0	M = 4.25; SD = 1.20; (3) 12.0% %: (1) 8.0; (2) 2.0; (4) 28.0; (5) 50.0	M = 4.57; SD = 0.51; (3) 14.8% %: (1) 0.0; (2) 0.0; (4) 33.3; (5) 44.4	c	–	–
a5_1: Covert surveillance of space and cars	M = 3.04; SD = 1.20; (3) 50% %: (1) 4.0; (2) 18.0; (4) 24.0; (5) 2.0	M = 3.98; SD = 1.23; (3) 20.0% %: (1) 8.0; (2) 4.0; (4) 38.0; (5) 30.0	M = 4.17; SD = 0.92; (3) 22.2% %: (1) 3.7; (2) 0.0; (4) 40.7; (5) 22.2	c	c	–

(Continued)

Table 4.2 (Continued) Significance of Differences between Implementation of the Measures

Level 1: Measures Implementation	Serbia	Kazakhstan	Austria	Significance of Difference		
				S–A	S–K	K–A
a6_1: Targeted polygraph testings	M = 4.11; SD = 0.76; (3) 24.0% %: (1) 2.0; (2) 2.0; (4) 54.0; (5) 18.0	M = 2.23; SD = 1.15; (3) 38.0% %: (1) 14.0; (2) 36.0; (4) 8.0; (5) 4.0	M = 1.17; SD = 0.83; (3) 0.0% %: (1) 81.5; (2) 0.0; (4) 0.0; (5) 3.7	c	c	c
a7_1: Using internal informants	M = 3.82; SD = 0.96; (3) 56.0% %: (1) 2.0; (2) 4.0; (4) 32.0; (5) 6.0	M = 4.25; SD = 1.19; (3) 20.0% %: (1) 8.0; (2) 0.0; (4) 28.0; (5) 44.0	M = 4.24; SD = 0.70; (3) 14.8% %: (1) 0.0; (2) 3.7; (4) 48.1; (5) 25.9	—	—	—
a8_1: Targeted integrity testing	M = 1.52; SD = 0.75; (3) 58.0% %: (1) 24.0; (2) 16.0; (4) 2.0; (5) 0.0	M = 3.45; SD = 1.53; (3) 42.0% %: (1) 10.0; (2) 10.0; (4) 20.0; (5) 18.0	M = 1.25; SD = 0.91; (3) 18.5% %: (1) 66.7; (2) 3.7; (4) 0.0; (5) 3.7	—	c	c
a9_1: Random integrity testing	M = 1.74; SD = 1.16; (3) 46.0% %: (1) 34.0; (2) 10.0; (4) 10.0; (5) 0.0	M = 3.29; SD = 1.44; (3) 44.0% %: (1) 8.0; (2) 14.0; (4) 22.0; (5) 12.0	M = 2.11; SD = 1.79; (3) 22.2 %: (1) 48.1; (2) 3.7; (4) 0.0; (5) 18.5	—	c	c
a10_1: Control polygraph testing	M = 1.90; SD = 1.26; (3) 42.0% %: (1) 32.0; (2) 14.0; (4) 10.0; (5) 2.0	M = 1.93; SD = 0.98; (3) 44.0% %: (1) 20.0; (2) 28.0; (4) 8.0; (5) 0.0	M = 1.00; SD = 0.00; (3) 0.0% %: (1) 100.0; (2) 0.0; (4) 0.0; (5) 0.0	c	—	c

(Continued)

Table 4.2 (Continued) Significance of Differences between Implementation of the Measures

Level 1: Measures Implementation	Serbia	Kazakhstan	Austria	Significance of Difference		
				S–A	S–K	K–A
a11_1: Psychological and ethical testing	M = 1.65; SD = 1.20; (3) 48.0% %: (1) 34.0; (2) 12.0; (4) 2.0; (5) 4.0	M = 3.56; SD = 1.38; (3) 28.0% %: (1) 10.0; (2) 10.0; (4) 34.0; (5) 18.0	M = 3.21; SD = 2.00; (3) 3.7% %: (1) 37.0; (2) 3.7; (4) 0.0; (5) 48.1	c	c	—
a12_1: Unhidden video–acoustic recording of official activities	M = 3.11; SD = 1.23; (3) 22.0% %: (1) 6.0; (2) 28.0; (4) 36.0; (5) 6.0	M = 3.88; SD = 1.43; (3) 16.0% %: (1) 12.0; (2) 6.0; (4) 28.0; (5) 38.0	M = 3.33; SD = 1.74; (3) 14.8% %: (1) 25.9; (2) 0.0; (4) 25.9; (5) 25.9	—	c	—

Note: Values of answer modality are as follows: Not applied or are planning to introduce it = 1; it does not apply, but I think its introduction is planned = 2; it is used occasionally = 4; it is used regularly = 5.

[a] Answer modality 3: I am not informed in this regard.

[b] Sig. (two-tailed): $p < .05$ (t-test for equality of means for independent samples).

[c] Sig. (two-tailed): $p < .01$ (t-test for equality of means for independent samples).

Kazakhstan (M = 4.41) represent a great weakness in the anticorruption policy of these states. The application of *t*-test showed existing differences in the implementation of this measure between Austria and Serbia on one hand and Kazakhstan and Austria on other, at level $p < .01$.

The targeted proactive police techniques, simulated offering bribes, undercover agents, etc. (a3_1), record direct/telephone conversation (a4_1), covert surveillance of space and cars (a5_1), are applied in each of the three states. Based on the responses of the interviewed police officers, the most frequently applied measure is recording of direct/telephone conversation and phone tapping. The application of *t*-test showed that there are statistically significant differences in the implementation of these three special techniques between Serbia and Austria. Apart from that, a statistically significant difference was noticed between Serbia and Kazakhstan concerning the application of covert surveillance of space and cars.

The polygraph testing of police officers suspected of corruption (a6_1) is most frequently applied in Serbia (M = 4.11. *Used regularly* was the chosen response of 18%, while 54% chose *used occasionally*). The responses lead to a conclusion that this measure is rarely applied in Kazakhstan (M = 2.23), while it is not applied at all in Austria (M = 1.17). The application of *t*-test showed existing statistically significant differences in the implementation of this measure between all three states.

The classic police measure of using internal informants (a7_1) with the aim of gathering information about corrupted police officers is applied in all three states, with regard to the fact that the frequency of using this measure is almost equal in Kazakhstan (M = 4.25) and Austria (M = 4.24), while it is slightly lower in Serbia (M = 3.82). The application of *t*-test did not show a significant deviation between the states.

Targeted integrity testing (a8_1) is not applied in Serbia (M = 1.52) or Austria (M = 1.25), whereas the application in Kazakhstan exists to a certain extent (M = 3.45; 18% responded with *used regularly*; 20% responded with *used occasionally*). The statistical analysis of the responses by using *t*-test showed significant statistical difference between Serbia and Kazakhstan and between Kazakhstan and Austria in implementation of this measure.

Random integrity testing (a9_1) is applied in Kazakhstan to a certain degree (M = 3.29; used regularly: 12%, used occasionally: 22%; not informed: 44%; and not applied: 22%). The mean value of the responses from Austria is M = 2.11, while in Serbia, M = 1.74, i.e., it is practically not applied. The statistical analysis of the responses by using *t*-test showed significant statistical difference between Serbia and Kazakhstan and between Kazakhstan and Austria.

Polygraph testing as a control, screening measure, (a10_1), is not applied in Austria (M = 1.00), whereas it is rarely applied in Serbia (M = 1.90) and Kazakhstan (M = 1.93). The statistical analysis of the responses by using *t*-test showed a significant statistical difference in the application of this measure between Serbia and Austria and Kazakhstan and Austria.

Psychological and ethic testings (a11_1) in the police applied with the aim to discover individuals who are prone to corruption and also prone to other misuse of the orders. The responses show that these measures are practically not applied in Serbia (M = 1.65), whereas in Kazakhstan (M = 3.56) and Austria (M = 3.21), they are applied to a certain extent. The statistical analysis of the responses by using t-test showed a significant statistical difference in the implementation of this measure between Serbia and Austria and Kazakhstan and Austria.

Unhidden video–acoustic recording official activities (a12_1) are applied almost the same in all three states (Serbia, M = 3.11; Kazakhstan, M = 3.88; and Austria, M = 3.33). The statistical analysis of the responses by using t-test showed a significant statistical difference in the implementation of this measure between Serbia and Kazakhstan.

A certain percentage of the respondents from each of the three states (which is not insignificant) did not respond to the question about the application and the frequency of particular anticorruption measures. They chose the response that is marked in the table as (3) "I am not informed in this regard." The most frequent reason given why they were unable to answer the question whether a particular measure is applied in the control of police corruption was that they cannot give a reliable answer with regard to its implementation.

Respondents' Evaluation of the Effectiveness of Reactive and Proactive Measures in the Control of the Corruption in the Police

The second level of the research shows the quantitatively expressed results of the respondents' evaluation of the effectiveness (anticorruption potential) of the measures given in 12 variables (1 being the lowest and 5 being the highest effectiveness). The statistical overview of the evaluated effectiveness of each of the measures and for each state in particular is given in Table 4.3. Additionally, Table 4.3 shows the statistical significance of the differences in the distribution of the responses to the questions about the estimated efficiency of the particular anticorruptive measures, among the respondents from different countries by using t-test for equality of means for independent samples.

Mandatory suspension (a1_2) was rated with a higher number by the interviewed police officers from Serbia than in the two other countries. Police officers rated this measure with the average score of 3.74; that is to say, this measure got the highest score (4 and 5 on the scale) in 60% of the responses. The police officers from Kazakhstan rated this measure with a slightly lower average score of 2.78; that is to say, in 40% of the responses, the lowest scores of 1 and 2 were dominant. The police officers from Austria rated mandatory

Table 4.3 Significance of Differences between Estimated Efficiency (Country Samples)

Level 2: Estimated Efficiency of	Serbia (1)%	(2)%	(3)%	(4)%	(5)%	Kazakhstan (1)%	(2)%	(3)%	(4)%	(5)%	Austria (1)%	(2)%	(3)%	(4)%	(5)%	S–A	S–K	K–A
a1_2: Mandatory suspension	M = 3.74; SD = 1.01					M = 2.78; SD = 1.27					M = 1.08; SD = 0.27					b	b	b
	2.0	8.0	30.0	34.0	26.0	20.0	20.0	34.0	14.0	12.0	88.9	7.4	0.0	0.0	0.0			
a2_2: Disciplinary act, crim. charges, prov. evidence	M = 3.66; SD = 1.26					M = 3.00; SD = 1.21					M = 1.24; SD = 0.70					b	b	
	8.0	10.0	22.0	28.0	32.0	14.0	14.0	46.0	10.0	16.0	66.7	7.4	0.0	3.7	0.0			
a3_2: Spec. investigative techn. (simul. offer brib.)	M = 3.78; SD = 1.16					M = 2.92; SD = 1.26					M = 2.17; SD = 0.82					b	b	b
	2.0	14.0	24.0	22.0	36.0	14.0	24.0	34.0	12.0	16.0	22.2	29.6	37.0	0.0	0.0			
a4_2: Recording direct communication/phone tapp.	M = 3.68; SD = 1.02					M = 3.04; SD = 1.29					M = 1.59; SD = 0.59					b		b
	2.0	10.0	26.0	34.0	22.0	14.0	20.0	32.0	16.0	18.0	37.0	40.7	3.7	0.0	0.0			
a5_2: Covert surveillance of space and cars	M = 3.87; SD = 1.06					M = 2.90; SD = 1.31					M = 1.88; SD = 0.78					b	b	b
	2.0	6.0	28.0	24.0	34.0	16.0	24.0	32.0	10.0	18.0	22.2	25.9	14.8	0.0	0.0			
a6_2: Targeted polygraph testings	M = 3.44; SD = 1.05					M = 2.63; SD = 1.36					M = 4.74; SD = 0.92					b	b	b
	4.0	14.0	28.0	36.0	14.0	28.0	16.0	32.0	8.0	14.0	3.7	0.0	3.7	0.0	77.8			
a7_2: Using internal informants	M = 3.26; SD = 1.02					M = 2.66; D = 1.32					M = 1.91; SD = 0.85					b	b	b
	4.0	14.0	40.0	22.0	12.0	24.0	22.0	32.0	8.0	14.0	25.9	48.1	3.7	7.4	0.0			
a8_2: Targeted integrity testing	M = 3.37; SD = 1.29					M = 2.26; SD = 1.24					M = 4.28; SD = 1.17					b	b	b
	10.0	12.0	26.0	22.0	22.0	36.0	24.0	26.0	6.0	8.0	3.7	3.7	18.5	3.7	63.0			

(Continued)

Table 4.3 (Continued) Significance of Differences between Estimated Efficiency (Country Samples)

Level 2: Estimated Efficiency of	Serbia					Kazakhstan					Austria					Significances of Difference		
	(1) (%)	(2) (%)	(3) (%)	(4) (%)	(5) (%)	(1) (%)	(2) (%)	(3) (%)	(4) (%)	(5) (%)	(1) (%)	(2) (%)	(3) (%)	(4) (%)	(5) (%)	S–A	S–K	K–A
a9_2: Random integrity testing		M = 3.53; SD = 1.31					M = 2.62; SD = 1.34					M = 3.21; SD = 1.50							
	10.0	6.0	28.0	18.0	28.0	28.0	18.0	30.0	12.0	12.0	18.5	3.7	37.0	0.0	29.6	–	b	–
a10_2: Control polygraph testing		M = 3.40; D = 1.14					M = 2.66; SD = 1.35					M = 4.88; SD = 0.43							
	8.0	10.0	26.0	36.0	14.0	26.0	20.0	30.0	10.0	14.0	0.0	0.0	3.7	3.7	88.9	b	b	b
a11_2: Psychological and ethical testing		M = 3.42; SD = 1.09					M = 2.62; SD = 1.19					M = 2.84; SD = 1.93							
	6.0	12.0	28.0	36.0	14.0	20.0	28.0	30.0	14.0	8.0	44.4	3.7	3.7	3.7	37.0	–	b	–
a12_2: Unhidden video–acoust. recording of official activ.		M = 4.08; D = 0.96					M = 2.86; SD = 1.23					M = 2.65; SD = 1.57							
	2.0	2.0	22.0	30.0	40.0	16.0	22.0	34.0	16.0	12.0	25.9	33.3	11.1	0.0	25.9	b	b	–

Note: Question: Estimate the efficiency of a measure connected to the fight against corruption using points 1–5.

[a] Sig. (two-tailed): $p < .05$ (*t*-test for equality of means for independent samples).
[b] Sig. (two-tailed): $p < .01$ (*t*-test for equality of means for independent samples).

suspension unanimously with lowest score. Scores 1 and 2 are dominant in 96% of the responses (M = 1.08, SD = 0.27). It is an interesting observation that mandatory suspension is not regularly applied in Serbia (see Table 4.2), and the police officers in Serbia rated it highly. Such results could be interpreted as the fact that Serbian police officers are not satisfied, having in mind that mandatory suspension is not applied in all cases that require suspension, and it can be understood as the attitude of the respondents that it should be regularly applied, since it would contribute to combating corruption in the police. The results from Austria are very interesting, when the responses about the frequency level of the implementation of this measure (92.6% of the respondents chose *used regularly*; M = 4.93; see Table 4.2) is compared with the responses about the evaluation of the effectiveness of this measure in combating corruption (M = 1.08). Evidently, the measure of mandatory suspension of police officers suspected of corruption is regularly applied in Austria; while on the other hand, interviewed police officers rated it as inefficient. Perhaps the reason can be found in the dissatisfaction of the police officers with the inefficiency of the anticorruption policy that is enforced in their country, which shows the rigidness of the problem of corruption control.

Similar responses were given concerning several repressive measures predicted in the variables, *initiation disciplinary action, file criminal charges, provide evidence* (a2_2), relating to the offense of any officer, regardless of the rank or the position, if there is a reasonable suspicion of committing a criminal act corruptly. Again, Serbian respondents rated these measures with higher scores than others (M = 3.66; i.e., 60% of the respondents gave scores of 4 and 5). The police officers from Kazakhstan's medium score was 3. The police officers from Austria unanimously (SD = 0.7) rated the effectiveness of these measures, same as the previous variable, with a very low score (M = 1.24; 74.1% of the responses rated it with lowest score points of 1 and 2). Also, in the case of this variable, a clear difference between level 1 (evaluation of the frequency of measure implementation) and level 2 (evaluation of the effectiveness of the measure) can be observed, especially in the responses of Serbian and Austrian police officers. Serbian police officers have, on the one hand, rated this measure higher than the respondents from the two other countries did, while on the other hand, a high percentage of them stated that this measure is not regularly applied. There is no doubt that based on the opinion of the interviewed police officers from Serbia, it can be concluded that this measure should be applied in practice more regularly than it is currently the case, since the respondents rated its anticorruption potential highly. On the other hand, the police officers from Austria have a completely contrary opinion. According to the opinion of Austrian police officers, this repressive measure is regularly applied in practice (92.6% of the responses—Table 4.2), but at the same time, it is rated low on the scale of effectiveness (M = 1.24—Table 4.3), viewed from the aspect of evaluated anticorruption potential. Probably the reason can again be found in the dissatisfaction of the Austrian police officers with the inefficiency of the anticorruption policy enforced in their country, which shows the rigidness of the problem of control of police corruption.

The variables based on special investigative techniques (*simulated offering bribes, undercover agents* [a3_2]; *record direct and telephone conversation* [a4_2]; and *covert surveillance of space and cars* [a5_2]) show the evaluation of the effectiveness of particular investigating techniques (targeted proactive methods) that are applied in the case of police officers suspected of corruption. As stated, these measures are applied in each of the three states. Interviewed Serbian police officers believe more in the implementation of covert investigation techniques than their colleagues from the two other states. The mean values of the Serbian police officers' evaluation of the effectiveness of these measures are high, and they range from 3.68 to 3.87, with a significant dispersion of the responses that ranges from SD = 1.02 up to 1.16. The police officers from Kazakhstan rated the effectiveness of covert investigation techniques with an average score of 3. The highest evaluated measure was *recording of direct and telephone conversation* (M = 3.4). Interviewed Austrian police officers gave a low score to the effectiveness of these investigating techniques (dominant score points are 1 and 2). The highest rated measure was simulated offering bribes and undercover agents (a3_2) (M = modest 2.17), and the lowest rated was record direct communication/record telephone conversations (M = 1.59). Based on the results, it can be concluded that Austrian police officers evaluated covert investigating techniques in these three variables as highly inefficient in combating police corruption. This is a surprising conclusion, especially concerning telephone interceptions, and it certainly demands further investigation on a larger sample and a check of additional hypotheses. For instance, the measure, *record direct communication/record telephone conversations*, received significantly higher grades in Kazakhstan (M = 3.04) and in Serbia (M = 3.68). Perhaps the reasons can be explained by the fact that the criminals, corrupted police officers, know that the police monitors the electronic communication of the suspects, so the suspects are careful about what they speak over the phone and with whom they communicate. On the other hand, there are legal limitations and a complex procedure for receiving a permit for using these measures, which makes their use in the investigation of police corruption much more difficult.

The variable *targeted polygraph testing* (a6_2), which concerns the evaluation of the anticorruption potential of a proactive measure with the aim of revealing corrupted police officers, also showed surprising results. Serbian police officers rated this measure with a high score of 3.44 (50% of the respondents gave score points of 4 and 5). It can be seen from the previous table that this measure is most frequently applied in Serbia. Police officers from Kazakhstan rated this measure with an average score of 2.63, with a significant dispersion of responses (SD = 1.36). Interviewed police officers from Austria unanimously rated polygraph testing as an extremely efficient measure in fighting corruption (M = 4.7, and by far, the highest percentage of interviewed police officers [77.8%] rated this measure with score point 5, while the dispersion of responses was SD = 0.92). This result is especially surprising, knowing that Table 4.2 clearly shows that this measure is not applied in Austria (M = 1.17; 81.5% of respondents stated that this measure is never applied, nor is it planned to be introduced). Undoubtedly, the response of the Austrian police officers shows their attitude that they believe in the effectiveness of polygraph testing of the suspects, and according to their opinion, it should be introduced in the anticorruption potential of Austria.

Classic police measure *using internal informants* (a7_2), which is applied in each of the three states, was rated the highest by the police officers in Serbia (M = 3.26), followed by the police officers from Kazakhstan (M = 2.66), and finally the lowest score came from the police officers from Austria (M = 1.91). It would be interesting to conduct a research on the code of silence among the police officers in these three states and compare the results with the evaluation of the effectiveness of this measure.

The variable *targeted integrity testing* (a8_2), which concerns evaluation of the anticorruption potential of the proactive measure that is applied in the case of police officers suspected of corruption, also shows very interesting responses. As it can be seen in Table 4.2, no integrity testing is applied in Serbia, whatsoever (M = 1.52; see Table 4.2), or in Austria (M = 1.25; see Table 4.2); however, from the aspect of effectiveness, it is highly rated precisely by the police officers from Serbia (M = 3.37) and Austria (M = 4.28!). Even 44% of the interviewed police officers from Serbia rated this measure with highest score points of 4 and 5. Among the interviewed Austrian police officers, 66% of them rated this measure highly with scores of 4 and 5. The police officers from Kazakhstan rated integrity testing as an anticorruption measure with a pretty modest average score of M = 2.26.

The next variables (*random integrity testing, control polygraph testing, psychological and ethic testing*) concerned the evaluation of the effectiveness of three proactive measures (in the narrow sense of the word) in the control of police corruption, conducted on a random sample or as screening testing.

The anticorruption potential of *random integrity testing* (a9_2) as proactive and control measures were rated M = 3.53 by the police officers from Serbia; the police officers from Kazakhstan rated it M = 2.62, while the police officers from Austria rated it M = 3.21. Serbian and Austrian police officers rated this measure higher than reactive and proactive measures that are in standard use in these countries.

Control polygraph testing (a10_2), as a proactive measure (undertaken in situations when there is no doubt about the tested subject), was rated with an above average grade of M = 3.40 by the police officers from Serbia; the police officers from Kazakhstan rated it 2.26, and the police officers from Austria gave it the highest score of M = 4.88! (88, 9% of the interviewed police officers rated this measure with score point 5!; SD = 0.43!). Having in mind that control polygraph testing, as a rule, is not applied in Austria; interviewed police officers from this state clearly stated their opinion that it should be included in the array of anticorruption measures; that is to say, they rated its possible effectiveness as extremely high.

The application of the measure *psychological and ethic testing* (a11_2) in the police, applied with the aim to discover individuals who are prone to corruption and also prone to other misuse of the orders, was rated M = 3.42 by the police officers from Serbia; the police officers from Kazakhstan, M = 2.62; and the Austrian police officers rated it M = 2.8.

Finally, the application of the measure *unhidden video–acoustic recording of certain official activities in the police* (a12_2) was rated as the most effective by the police officers from Serbia (M = 4.8; that is to say, 70% of the interviewed police officers gave the highest score points of 4 and 5; SD = 0.96). Such a high evaluation of the effectiveness can be explained by the fact that in the last year or two, this measure started being introduced in the police of Serbia as an anticorruption control measure, so the expectations about it are still high. Police officers from Kazakhstan rated this measure as 2.86, and the police officers from Austria rated it with a below average score of M = 2.65.

The results of the means of the responses from Kazakhstan concerning the evaluation of the effectiveness of these anticorruption measures in the control of police corruption are different from the responses of the police officers from the two other countries, which is reflected by the fact that there are no deviations and peaks in their responses. All the responses have a mean value of around 3 or slightly below. Regarding such responses, it is possible to set up more hypotheses and test them in further research. The following questions can be asked: Do these responses mean that the respondents from Kazakhstan do not believe in the anticorruption potential of the said measures; i.e., does this mean that they do not believe in the possibility of a successful control of police corruption? The possibility of the control of police corruption is limited with the overall state of corruption in the society, the political will, the (in)efficiency of the courts in sentencing the cases of corruption, as it is the case in Serbia. One of the biggest problems of the control of corruption is reconciliation (living) with it.

The statistical analysis of the significance of the differences in the distribution of the responses to the questions about measures implementation of particular anticorruption measures, among the interviewed police officers from different countries using *t*-test for equality of means for independent samples, showed significant differences which can be seen in Table 4.3.

Discussion

Theoretically, it is completely indisputable that the prevention of corruption begins at the top with strong leadership (Punch, 2000, p. 319). Effective leadership means zero tolerance for corruption in the police and equal treatment of all police officers with reasonable suspicion of being corrupted. This also means mandatory pronouncement of suspension until the finalization of the procedure for each police officer suspected of taking a bribe.

Our research conducted in three states shows that mandatory suspension for police officers suspected of corruption is consistently pronounced and without exception only in Austria, which is not the case in Serbia and Kazakhstan.

The results of this research for Serbia are in accordance with research conducted by the Ministry of Interior of the Republic of Serbia in 2011 within a Twinning project financed by the government of Holland. One of the main conclusions of that research was that the Ministry of Interior of Serbia does not enforce the strategy of zero tolerance for corruption in the police. This conclusion is supported by the results of a survey of citizens and police officers. A sample of 2224 surveyed citizens included a question, "Did the police act upon your denunciation of a police officer?" The results of the survey show that the citizens mostly do not know if their denunciation has been acted upon (80 respondents); while 101 citizens claimed that there was no action. Only 16 respondents had information that there have been criminal charges against corrupted the police officer they denounced, and the same number stated that their denouncements of corrupted police officers were not proven (Strategic and Intelligence Assessment of the Corruption, 2012).

The problem of lack of principle of police management when it comes to fighting corruption is not only present in Serbia and Kazakhstan. Research conducted in Bosnia and Herzegovina also observed a tolerant attitude of police management for corruption and other forms of misconduct in the police (Kutnjak Ivković and Shelley, 2005, p. 458). Not acting in accordance with the principle of zero tolerance for corruption has detrimental consequences and undermines the integrity system from the inside. With regard to the unwillingness of the police management of New York to tackle the corruption in their lines, a warning has been stated with a universal value for all police systems: "the reluctance to uncover and effectively investigate corruption infected the entire anti-corruption apparatus" (Mollen Commission Report, 1994, p. 12).

Implementing a program for improving the integrity in the policy stands no chance of success, unless the strategy of zero tolerance is applied in practice and corruptive behavior is unquestionably sanctioned. "Sanctions applied on a consistent basis form an important part of any integrity programme. Officers who commit integrity breaches and are allowed to remain in post or to resign without sanctions imposed upon them give contradictory messages to officer and staff as well as the public about the commitment of the service to countering corruption" (Benchmarking Police Integrity Programmes, 2013, pp. 11–12).

Corruption in the state authorities and in the police affects the increase in lack of confidence in the police (Kääriäinen, 2007, p. 410). The validity of this theoretical stance is confirmed by the mentioned research conducted in Serbia 2011. Within the researched sample, only 2.6% of the citizens denounced corrupted police officers to the police administration in charge. From the research, it can be concluded that the reasons why the citizens do not denounce lie in their lack of confidence in relevant authorities and their unwillingness to undertake adequate measures for sanctioning this kind of behavior (Strategic and Intelligence Assessment of the Corruption, 2012, p. 22).

The rigidness of corruption in the police is identified by our research as well, as it showed that Austria (unlike the two other countries) applies the strategy of zero tolerance for corruption in the police, but on the other hand, the same research shows the lack of confidence of interviewed police officers in the effectiveness of the measure—mandatory suspension. A similar thing occurs in the example of South Korea, where zero tolerance is rigorously applied in practice, yet it still does not guarantee the eradication of corruption in the police: "Taking bribery, would result in dismissal. The value of the item taken or accepted is not relevant; officers disciplined for bribe acceptance are fired automatically, even if the bribe amounts to a single dollar. There is a well-known case of a police officer who took a bribe worth the equivalent of 5 dollars for not issuing a ticket. Once officially processed, he was dismissed and arrested" (Kutnjak Ivković and Kang, 2012, p. 83).

The efficient fight against corruption in the police implies intensive and vigorous work on checking all allegations that indicate corruption, gathering evidence, and initiating a procedure (discipline and penal) against the suspects. In the stages of checking the initial allegations, whether a police officer is corrupted (e.g., there are rumors only), and gathering evidence, mistakes and oversights happen, which hinder the establishment of the truth and the prosecution of the suspects. Newburn (1999, p. 38) emphasizes that the literature on police corruption is full of sorry tales of the failure of police forces to properly investigate allegations of, or intelligence concerning, corrupt practices. There is no doubt that it is not easy to prove police corruption due to numerous reasons: police officers have a certain space for discretion in decision-making, they avoid the presence of witnesses during corrupt acts, victims of corruption can be intimidated or blackmailed, or the "victim" can have his/her own interest in the corrupt act and therefore lack motivation to denounce; this is so-called criminal without the victim (Zimring and Johnson, 2005, p. 799); police officers are familiar with the possibilities and the limitations of the police in the process of gathering evidence; they are, perfectly familiar with the weaknesses of their police management, etc.

Our research showed that a high percentage of police officers in Serbia and Kazakhstan considers that in their police systems, evidence is not always gathered, without exception and regardless of the position or the rank of the police officer against whom there are allegations of corruption. The mentioned research of Serbia's Ministry of Interior in 2011 shows that in the case when a police officer has filed an internal complaint about the corruptness of his colleague, 91.1% of the interviewed police officers chose the following responses to the question about the possible measures of the Ministry: "No measure has been undertaken." "I am not informed in this regard." "The allegations of corruption have not been proven." This leads to a conclusion of the research: "Statistical overview shows that less than 1 of 10 denouncements of corruption in the Ministry of Interior have a positive outcome" (Strategic and Intelligence Assessment of the Corruption, 2012, p. 38).

This definitely shows the inability or the unwillingness of the police management in Serbia to seriously tackle the problem of corruption. Nonaction or misaction (that is to say, not providing evidence) in the case of allegations about the corruptness of a person could be compared to complicity in corruption and sabotage of the internal defense system or, at best, to unacceptable incompetence and incapability. The collapse of the responsibility of the police chiefs for corruption in the units under their command is not only a typical problem of developing countries such as Serbia and Kazakhstan. On the other end of the globe, the same problem is seen by the Mollen Commission Report (1994, p. 3).

The response of the Austrian police officers indicates a different kind of the problem concerning the gathering of evidence of police corruption. On one hand, the Austrian police officers state that the police always gathers evidence about the corruptness of police officers (92.6%, M = 4.93), and on the other hand, they rate this measure very low on the scale of effectiveness (M = 1.24; 88.9% of the respondents rated this measure with the lowest score point—1). There is no doubt that these two responses concerning the measure of gathering evidence indicate serious weaknesses in the system (strategy and tactics) when it comes to gathering evidence of the corruption in the police of Austria.

Obtaining awkward first information about the corruption in the police, acting accordingly, and working on gathering evidence are some of the most critical stages of repressive action. Classic institutional methods in revealing and combating corruption are insufficient. Unless the focus is directed to proactive investigation; application of investigating methods; gathering information or intelligence collated from a number of sources (Criminal Justice Commission, 2001, p. 3); internal reporting; informants, anonymous or otherwise; specific intelligence gathering process, which gained information on the internal pattern of corruption and developed a profile of the corrupt officer (Moran, 2005, p. 65), the only possibility left is for the police management to dedicate more attention to petty misconduct than serious corruption (Mollen Commission Report, 1994, p. 3). In a part of the literature and in practice of some countries, there is an accepted attitude that treating corruption in the police demands employing the same methods as those applied against organized criminals: a concentration of intelligence; the use of informants, the use of covert listening, telephone intercepts and sting operation (Punch, 2000, p. 318). In that respect, it is important to mention a warning from an Australian committee that most of the complaints of the citizens concern less serious cases of corruption. Relying on citizens' complaints can be wrong, as the most serious cases of corruption are related to drugs, and they are out of public sight. Major corruption acts in the police happen outside of the sight and the knowledge of soft approaches, such as citizens' perception and their complaints. For this reason, the Australian research concludes that effective proactive measures should be applied (Criminal Justice Commission, 2001, p. 10). Covert high-technology surveillance can overcome the problems of lack of witnesses or lack of supervision capacity by secretly recording conversations and actions that may involve misconduct (e.g., Prenzler and Ronken [2003, p. 153]).

Covert investigation techniques directed toward the police officers suspected of corruption (the variables: simulated offering bribes, using undercover agents [a3_2], recording direct and telephone conversation [a4_2], and covert surveillance of space and cars [a5_2]) are being applied in all the three analyzed countries (this is also confirmed by our research). However, police officers from Kazakhstan and especially from Austria, unexpectedly, rated the effectiveness of these measures quite low. Such low evaluation of effectiveness of proactive measures, most certainly demands further research on a bigger sample. It is necessary to have in mind that covert investigation techniques in analyzed countries are applied as evidentiary actions since recently. The period of application of these measures and the experience of the police officers are much shorter than in the United States, for example. On the other hand, in the communist history of Serbian and Kazakhstan police, covert investigation techniques were applied as operative actions, and they were used and misused against political opponents. That is probably why there is a certain aloofness and mistrust among the police officers from these two states when it comes to these measures, which is particularly evident in the responses from Kazakhstan.

The application of integrity tests, as well as other covert investigation techniques applied in the treatment of suspects of police corruption, is highly rated in the literature that covers the problem of corruption in the police (Kutnjak Ivković and Kang, 2012, p. 79; Moran, 2005, p. 64; Prenzler and Ronken, 2001, p. 339; Punch, 2000, p. 318). Our research showed that the respondents highly rated the effectiveness of polygraph testing and integrity tests as proactive measures directed toward the police officers suspected of being corrupt (targeted using). It is especially evident in the responses of interviewed police officers from Austria. On the other hand, integrity tests and polygraph testing are not applied in Austria whatsoever. This fact can be explained by the fact that the police officers from Austria are not satisfied with the existing measures of control of the corruption in the police (which is also shown by this research), and they consider that new methods should be introduced.

Integrity testing is not applied in Serbia, but like in Austria, the effectiveness of this method received a high score (M = 3.37). This result too can be explained with the same reasons as in the case of the interviewed Austrian police officers. The polygraph testing of the suspect is in use in Serbia; however, in this country, the result of polygraph testing has no substantial value as evidence, so after a positive result of polygraph testing is obtained, police need to search for other evidence. Police officers from Kazakhstan gave quite low marks to the effectiveness of polygraph testing (M = 2.63) and integrity testing (M = 2.26) as measures targeted toward the suspects. Such response demands additional research for the purpose of giving a quality explanation. There is a possibility that the reason can be found in the fact that the theory of the application of integrity tests has a negative connotation in this part of the world (Konov, 2011); however, polygraph testing is applied in this region (see the study by Yuri and Akentiev [2004]).

In certain countries, especially those with Anglo-saxon legal systems, integrity tests are applied as control measures with a random sample of police or with police officers in a position with a higher risk of corruption than positions in routine police work (Newburn, 1999, p. 34). The aim of this type of integrity tests is intimidation and deterrence, since the tested subject cannot know whether it is an integrity test or a real offer for corruption scheme. The application of these measures on a random sample (random testing), i.e., for the purpose of control, is disputable in theory and in practice, first of all, from the ethical aspect (Konov, 2011; Moran, 2005, pp. 66–67; Newburn, 1999, p. 37; Police Integrity, England, Wales and Northern Ireland, 1999, p. 59; Prenzler and Ronken, 2001, p. 339; Prenzler and Ronken, 2003).

Apart from that, the polygraph testing of police officers (screening testing) is applied as a control proactive method in the departments that work on suppressing drugs or in other sensitive departments in different parts of the world, but not much is written about this topic (for American experience, see the works of Crawford [2002], Kraphol [2002], and Lersch [2001]. For screening polygraph testing in Russia, see the study by Yuri and Akentiev [2004]). This method does not involve delusion or provocation.

There is no developed practice of the application of these methods in the continental part of Europe; there are legal obstacles, as the law prohibits provocation and incitement of criminal acts by the police or state authorities. In the countries analyzed by this research, proactive covert investigation techniques are not applied (for example, in Austria). When it comes to Serbia, they are applied to a limited extent (on several occasions, police officers that work on combating organized crime or undercover agents were subjected to polygraph testing). The application of these measures is limited in Kazakhstan, which can be seen in Table 4.2. Regardless of the nonapplication of these measures (or extremely limited application), the interviewed police officers from Serbia and especially the ones from Austria rated these measures as very effective in fighting corruption in the police. This result can be interpreted as the attitude of the interviewed police officers that it is necessary to introduce new methods in the control of corruption in the police.

Having all this in mind, the authors of this chapter consider that this research has confirmed the hypothesis that the attitudes of police officers about the frequency of measure implementation and measure effectiveness in the control of police corruption are a significant factor and should be considered in the process of forming (definition, guidance, correction) anticorruption strategies.

Conclusions

Without implementing the strategy of zero tolerance for corruption in the police, all programs and attempts of building and strengthening the integrity of the profession of police officers stand no chance of success. The literature emphasizes the dominant responsibility of police management. Focuses on the quality of police agency's own methods of detection, investigation, and discipline of rule violations are very important (Kutnjak Ivković, 2005, p. 464), Newburn (1999, p. 33) underlines internal accountability, tight supervision, 'early warning' systems. However, a great obstacle in these attempts is the inefficiency of the courts and the judicial system, which is evident in the developing countries (this is an obvious problem in Serbia).

Legal systems should embrace the idea that police officers, especially the ones in positions that involve high risks, can and should be subjected to various tests of integrity. The privilege of police and state officers definitely deserves it. Research conducted in this chapter showed that the interviewed police officers in all three states are mostly in agreement with this idea.

Finally, one should be aware of the warning: "It is naive to assume that corruption will be completely eliminated with the implementation of new tactics. A lack of realism about the prospects of reform, will lead to the cycle beginning all over again" (Criminal Justice Commission, 2001, pp. 7–8).

References

Anti-Corruption Investigation and Trial Guide. 2005. *Tools and Techniques to Investigate and Try the Corruption Case*. Washington, DC: United States Agency for International Development.

Association of Chief Police Officers. 2013, January. Benchmarking police integrity programmes. London: Association of Chief Police Officers.

Bayley, D., and Perito, R. 2011, November 1–19. Police corruption. Special Report 294. Washington, DC: United States Institute of Peace.

Crawford, C. C. 2002. The polygraph in agent interrogation. *Polygraph*. 30: 28–32.

Criminal Justice Commission. 2001. Is the standing commission of inquiry a successful model for anti-corruption commissions? Canberra, Australia: Queensland Criminal Justice Commission. Retrieved from http://www.ethicsinstitute.com /pdf/Corruption%20commission%20report.pdf.

Fijnaut, C., and Huberts, L. 2002. *Corruption, Integrity and Law Enforcement*. Hague, The Netherlands: Kluwer Law International.

Huberts, L. W. J. C., Lamboo, T., and Punch, M. 2003. Police integrity in the Netherlands and the United States: Awareness and alertness. *Police Practice and Research*. 4(3): 217–32.

Jenks, D., Johnson, L. M., and Matthews, T. 2012, January. Examining police integrity: Categorizing corruption vignettes. Working Paper No. 40. Retrieved from http://www.IPES.info, http://www.dcaf.ch, and http://www.coginta.org.

Kääriäinen, J. T. 2007. Trust in the police in 16 European countries: A multilevel analysis. *European Journal of Criminology*. 4(4): 409–35.

Kolthoff, E. 2010, September 8–10. The relation between corruption and human rights in police work. 32nd European Group for Public Administration Conference, Toulouse. Retrieved from http://www.law.kuleuven.be/integriteit /egpa/egpa2010/kolthoff_corruption-and-human-rights-in-police.pdf.

Konov, A. 2011, June 2–4. Proactive investigations of corruption: (Un)Ethical aspects. Paper presented at the Public Management Research Conference, Syracuse, NY.

Kraphol, D. 2002. The polygraph in personnel screening. In *Handbook of Polygraph Testing*. Kleiner, M., ed. London: Academic Press: 217–46.

Kutnjak Ivković, S. 2005. The Croatian police, police integrity, and transition toward democratic policing. *Policing: An International Journal of Police Strategies & Management*. 32(3): 459–88.

Kutnjak Ivković, S. 2009. Rotten apples, rotten branches, and rotten orchards. *Criminology and Public Policy*. 8(4): 777–85.

Kutnjak Ivković, S., and Kang, W. 2012. Police integrity in South Korea. *Policing: An International Journal of Police Strategies & Management*. 35(1): 76–103.

Kutnjak Ivković, S., and Shelley, T. O. 2005. The Bosnian police and police integrity: A continuing story. *European Journal of Criminology*. 2(4): 428–64.

Lersch, K. M. 2001. Drug related police corruption: The Miami experience. In *Police Misconduct, A Reader for the 21st Century*. Palmiotto, M., ed. Upper Saddle River, NJ: Prentice Hall. 132–44.

Marché, G. E. 2009. Integrity, culture, and scale: An empirical test of the big bad police agency. *Crime Law Social Change*. 51(5): 463–86.

McCormack, R. 2001. Police perceptions and the norming of institutional corruption. In *Police Misconduct, A Reader for the 21st Century*. Palmiotto, M., ed. Upper Saddle River, NJ: Prentice Hall. 100–8.

Mollen Commission Report. 1994. New York City commission to investigate allegations of police corruption and the anti-corruption procedures of the police department. New York.

Moran, J. 2005. "Blue walls," "grey areas" and "cleanups": Issues in the control of police corruption in England and Wales. *Crime, Law & Social Change*. 43(1): 57–79.

Mutonyi, J. 2005. Fighting corruption: Is Kenya on the right track? In *Policing Corruption: International Perspectives*. Sarre, R., Das, D., and Albrecht, H. J., eds. Lanham, MD: Lexington Books. 69–84.

Newburn, T. 1999. Understanding and preventing police corruption: Lessons from the literature. Police Research Series Paper 110. London: Home Office.

Osse, A. 1997. Corruption prevention: A course for police officers fighting organised crime. *Crime, Law & Social Change*. 28: 53–71.

Police Integrity, England, Wales and Northern Ireland. 1999, June. Securing and maintaining public confidence 1999. London: Home Office Communication Directorate.

Prenzler, T., and Ronken, C., 2001. Police integrity testing in Australia. *Criminology and Criminal Justice*. 1(3): 319–42.

Prenzler, T., and Ronken, C. 2003. A survey of innovations in the development and maintenance of ethical standards by Australian police departments. *Police Practice and Research*. 4(2): 149–61.

Punch, M. 2000. Police corruption and its prevention. *European Journal on Criminal Policy and Research*. 8(3): 301–24.

Rothwell, G. R., and Baldwin, J. N. 2007. Whistle-blowing and the code of silence in police agencies. *Crime & Delinquency*. 53: 605–32.

Sellbom, M., Fischler, G., and Ben-Porath, Y. S. 2007. Identifying MMPI-2 predictors of police officer integrity and misconduct. *Criminal Justice and Behavior*. 34(8): 985–1004.

Skolnick, J. H. 2002. Corruption and the blue code of silence. *Police Practice and Research*. 3: 7–19.

Skolnick, J. H. 2005. *Corruption and the blue code of silence*. In *Policing Corruption: International Perspectives*. Sarre, R., Das, D. K., and Albrecht, H. J., eds. Lanham, MD: Lexington Books. 301–16.

Strategic and Intelligence Assessment of the Corruption. 2012. Twinning project. Belgrade: Ministry of Interior of the Republic of Serbia.

Tankebe, J. 2010. Public confidence in the police, testing the effects of public experiences of police corruption in Ghana. *British Journal of Criminology*. 50(2): 296–319.

Ward, R., and McCormack, R. 1987. *Managing Police Corruption: International Perspectives*. Chicago: University of Illinois at Chicago.

Weitzer, R. 2002. Incidents of police misconduct and public opinion. *Journal of Criminal Justice*. 30(5): 397–408.
Yuri I. K., and Akentiev, P. V. 2004. Criminalistics use of polygraph in Russia: Modern level and development prospects. *Polygraph*. 33: 65–69. Retrieved from http://www.ncjrs.gov/App/Publications/abstract.aspx?ID=206783.
Zimring, F., and Johnson, D. 2005. On the comparative study of corruption. *British Journal of Criminology*. 45(6): 793–809.

Analysis

II

Using Complaints against the Police to Improve Community– Police Relations

5

JANE GOODMAN-DELAHUNTY
MIRA TAITZ
CHANTAL SOWEMIMO-COKER
IDA NGUYEN

Contents

Abstract

Police are often resistant to critical feedback from the public and over-look opportunities to use this information to advantage. Drawing on an empirical analysis of the content of complaints lodged over a one-year period by the public against the largest police force in Australia, practical recommendations are made on the ways to use the findings as a resource to improve community–police relations. Core strategies are outlined to devise an accurate and comprehensive source for evidence-driven training, to integrate customer service training into core polic-ing tasks, and to focus training on the most significant or high-risk complaint issues. Examples drawn from the New South Wales Police Force (NSWPF) are used to support each recommendation. By explor-ing the issues that underlie complaints, police can reduce legal risk and transform the negative workplace culture toward the complainants.

Introduction

A vast body of research has explored the dynamics involved in conducting and maximizing successful law enforcement. The relationship between the com-munity and the police has repercussions for citizen acceptance and support of the police (Goodman-Delahunty, Taitz, and Verbrugge, 2013). Without cavil, the primary role of law enforcement is to monitor legal norms and val-ues, enforce and prevent citizens from crossing boundaries, apprehend those who do, and protect citizens from community members who break the law (Murphy, Hinds, and Fleming, 2008). Citizen compliance and cooperation have consistently emerged as necessary components of effective policing. The levels of cooperation and compliance appear to be mediated by public attitudes toward, and perceptions of, police (Bradley, 1998; Murphy, Hinds, and Fleming, 2008). Research has shown that by focusing on the interactions between police and community members, and the strategies to strengthen this relationship, public satisfaction with the police can be improved (Hinds and Murphy, 2007), police legitimacy can be enhanced, and, importantly, policing law enforcement objectives and outcomes can be achieved (Murphy, Hinds, and Fleming, 2008).

Police Focus on Customer Service

Many policing organizations, both in Australia and overseas, have adopted a new ethos of managerialism, in which they are accountable to the public as customers to whom they are providers of a service, with customer satisfaction as a key measure of police agency performance (Chan, 1999). The police adoption of the accountability model of customer–provider relations was accompanied by an increase in community policing (assigning police officers to particular communities so that they might form relationships with local residents), focusing on partnerships, consultative processes, and community–police relationships (Drummond et al., 2000). Examinations of the factors influencing customer service revealed that the two most critical components of a healthy customer–service provider relationship are delivery of high quality service and satisfied customers (Christopher, Payne, and Ballantyne, 1991; Shemwell, Yavas, and Bilgin, 1998). The police focus on customer service has highlighted the need for a more trustworthy and transparent complaint system to better inform service development (Bell and Luddington, 2006).

The New South Wales Police Force Customer Service Program

Late in 2007, the NSWPF adopted a transformative ethos through a change management program called the Customer Service Program (CSP) in order to enhance customer service and improve service delivery to victims of crime (Burn, 2010). The goal of the CSP, among other things, was to improve public confidence in and satisfaction with the police, enhance interactions with the community, and reduce the number of complaints about the NSWPF (Goodman-Delahunty, Taitz, and Verbrugge, 2013). The CSP operates within the legislation that governs customer complaints about the NSWPF. Complaints can be made anonymously and lodged directly with the NSWPF or with the commissioner, or indirectly with multiple other authorities in New South Wales (NSW). All written complaints about the NSWPF since 2001 have been recorded in the Customer Assistance Tracking System (C@TSI), the official electronic complaints database.

In 2010, the first author and a team of researchers at Charles Sturt University were invited to attend and observe training classes on the customer service program. These observations identified several training needs, and recommendations to meet them, as summarized in Table 5.1.

Thereafter, a 12-month sample of approximately 3000 citizen complaints lodged in C@TSI against the NSWPF was provided to the researchers for analysis (Goodman-Delahunty, Verbrugge, and Taitz, 2011). The recommendations outlined in this chapter are based on the outcomes of those analyses

Global Issues in Contemporary Policing

Table 5.1 Identified Customer Service Training Needs and Recommendations

Training Need	Recommendations
Low participant motivation: Customer service not a core duty	Use training examples to stimulate group discussion, encourage participants to provide examples from their own practical experience.
Fear repercussions of complaints	Create a workplace culture that values complaints as feedback.
Little discussion of role plays	Use training examples to stimulate group participation.
Neutrality underemphasized	Regularly share trends in complaint data with staff in and outside of customer service training.
Simplistic triple win goal	Incorporate more complex real-life case studies.
Few realistic policing vignettes	Incorporate real-life cases; use relevance to stimulate motivation.

and are illustrated by examples drawn from the sample, which have been anonymized to protect the identities of the officers and the complainants.

The Role of Complaints in Building Police–Community Relationships

The health of the relationship between customers and their service providers is of great importance in the private sector. Complaints from customers are viewed as an integral component of that relationship and an indicator of its well-being (Nyer, 2000; Prim and Pras, 1998). This is exemplified by the fact that the Society of Consumer Affairs Professionals (SOCAP) holds workshops with titles such as "A Complaint is a Gift" (SOCAP Australia, 2011). Research indicating that customers who felt comfortable about making a complaint and were encouraged to complain typically expressed higher levels of service satisfaction demonstrated that a complaint system can play an important role in the customer–service provider relationship (Nyer, 2000).

Using complaints as an evaluative tool for public perception is a method derived from organizational psychology and consumer research on customer service that has, in recent years, found its way into a number of other disciplines, such as policing (Goodman-Delahunty, 2010). Indeed the Council of Europe Commissioner for Human Rights recently argued that a fair and effective police complaint system is a signature component of democratic and accountable policing (Smith, 2010). Conversely, an ineffective complaint system is the mark of a society at risk of developing a culture of impunity, in which abuses of human rights go unchecked (Smith, 2010). For this reason, the commissioner advocated an approach to police complaints in which "every complaint matters," from serious violations of human rights to minor instances of police rudeness (Smith, 2010). Even if complaints are unsubstantiated, resources spent on investigating complaints to public sector organizations are not wasted, as complaints investigation builds confidence in a well-functioning and trustworthy system (Brewer, 2007).

Complaints are considered useful indicators of public (customer) perception, but the number of submitted complaints is presumed to under-report public dissatisfaction and represent only a small portion of a larger population of dissatisfied customers (Bell and Luddington, 2006). If received complaints are only the tip of the iceberg of true public dissatisfaction, the complaints of those customers who take the trouble to communicate their dissatisfaction are a valuable tool, a barometer of wider sentiment. Rather than have citizens complaining among themselves, creating a climate of negative word-of-mouth communication about the police, an effective complaint system encourages citizens to engage with the police, to communicate their concerns. Thus, customer complaints can be a valuable resource to police and offer a reliable estimate of public opinion (Bell and Luddington, 2006; Gorst, Kanji, and Wallace, 1998; Nyer and Gopinath, 2005). However, policing research has yet to realize the benefits arising from the concept of "complaints as information" (Goldsmith, 1995, p. 122). Relative to the private sector, where a great deal of importance is placed on eliciting and managing complaints as a means of increasing customer loyalty, less weight has been given to the potential for a healthy and highly utilized police customer complaint system to improve citizen connectedness and judgments of police legitimacy.

Previous researchers have emphasized that a simple reactive strategy to problems identified and officers named in specific complaints is insufficient. An intervention aimed at reducing the number of complaints and preventing future similar complaints requires policies targeted at the level of organizational culture and must address the underlying issues (Porter, Prenzler, and Fleming, 2011). The implementation of reforms within the police can only be effective if the police officers themselves are engaged with, and are allowed to make sense of, the reforms in their own way. This will enable the shift in police culture that is necessary for more enduring change.

Gap between Perceptions and Realities regarding Complaints

A common police perception about most complaints has been that the majority were nonmeritorious, brought by complainants who were mentally disordered or seeking revenge. To prevent complaints from being ignored, dissuaded or poorly received and investigated, complaints need to be valued as an outlet for citizen voice. The overriding presumption by some police that all complaints are nonmeritorious until proven otherwise needs to change in order to build a workplace culture that values complaints. Training sessions should counter these misconceptions by providing officers with research findings documenting that the majority of complainants are sincere and genuinely aggrieved (Maguire and Corbett, 1991) and that most people who feel violated by police never complain (Woods, 2006). By incorporating the examples of individual complaints into training sessions, and reading these from the complainant's point of view (Goldsmith, 1996), the staff will become aware of the gaps between their perceptions and the realities regarding vexatious and nonmeritorious complaints.

Examples of individual complainant narratives drawn from the NSWPF customer complaints sample that assist in making this point are provided as follows.

> The complainant has written a letter outlining the attendance of the involved officer at the Dillwynia C. C. to investigate a report of an indecent assault upon an inmate. The complainant outlines that Constable X was very professional and courteous to the alleged victim and wished for him to be commended. As a contrast Constable Y is reported to be unprofessional, overbearing and intimidating at the time. Constable Y also received and answered a personal telephone call during the interview process with the alleged victim (LMI1001415 Sustained).

> The complainant stated that on 17/12/09 he was stopped by the subject officer on [Street, Suburb] after committing an alleged traffic offence. The complainant was issued with a traffic infringement notice for the offence of "Part of body outside window." The complainant alleges that when the subject officer approached him, the subject officer was rude and swore at him. The complainant further alleges the subject officer slammed a car door on the complainant's thigh (LMI1000933 Sustained).

> About 8pm on Friday 15/1/2010 the complainant and her son Mr. X attended Penrith Police to seek advice in relation to a domestic violence incident. They were met at the front counter by a female police officer who spoke to the family. It is alleged Senior Constable Y spoke to the complaint from a seated position at the computer without taking his eyes of the screen. He allegedly told the complainant that she was "wasting their time" and at the end of the conversation he was texting on his mobile phone. It is alleged that Constable Y refused to give the complainant a business card and stated that they were for victims and that the complainant was not a victim and she should "just go away," before telling the complainant to get out (LMI1000893 Sustained).

Other common police misperceptions about complainants were identified in the course of this research project, including the notion that most complainants were women and that most complainants were disgruntled suspects seeking to retaliate against the police, rather than other members of the public with a genuine grievance to communicate. The awareness of these misperceptions can be effectively increased by sharing research findings with the staff which show these beliefs to be false. These findings can take the form of statistical data, such as the findings reported in this study and in other research on complaints against police in other jurisdictions (Independent Police Complaints Commission, 2015), showing that the majority of complainants were not suspects, and that complainants were mostly men. Officers should also review data in the form of case study complaint narratives, which illustrate what complainants want in the majority of cases (i.e., an explanation, an acknowledgement, or an apology) (Goodman-Delahunty, Beckley, and Martin, 2014a).

Effective Use of Complaints in Customer Service Training Programs

A series of recommendations is made on ways police managers can use complaints from community members to enhance the content and the delivery of training on police customer service programs and improve police–community relations.

The Value of Customer Complaints as Training Tools

In order to reduce everyday police behaviors that deflect, minimize, dissuade, or hide complaints—often in imperceptible ways—all officers across the organization need to recognize the value of customer complaints. While the statutory requirements of the Police Act 1990 are generally acknowledged, few officers understand the value of complaints. Research has indicated that across both public and private sector organizations, and within police complaints policy, complaints are increasingly acknowledged as a valuable form of communication (Brewer, 2007; Bell and Luddington, 2006; Goodman-Delahunty, 2010). By presenting officers with a vignette describing a hypothetical jurisdiction in which no police complaints are received, and asking them to reflect on why this may be problematic, training participants can begin to appreciate the value of complaints as a tool of communication between the community members and the police. This may involve taking a middle ground, which involves seeking an optimum number of complaints and measuring the quality of complaints, rather than focusing on counting complaints to determine whether there are too many or too few. In training sessions, officers should be encouraged to understand the complainant's point of view through role plays, enabling them to move from a simplistic view of complaints as sustained/unsustained, or verified/unverified, to one in which the complainant's point of view is recognized and valued, even if it does not result in a sustained finding.

Incorporate Training on Police Misconduct in Customer Service Training Programs

Familiarization with the most frequent complaint types can aid in changing the deficient behavior and result in complaint reduction. Training should provide officers with information showing the high proportion of complaints about police mistreatment and the specific officer behaviors outlined in these complaints (Goodman-Delahunty, Beckley and Martin, 2014b). Examples of these behaviors are displayed in Table 5.2, drawn from analyses of a 12-month sample of customer complaints (Goodman-Delahunty, Verbrugge, and Taitz, 2011).

The training materials should be accompanied by case studies that illustrate the problem of customer mistreatment, followed by a group discussion so that officers can meaningfully engage with the problem of mistreatment and how to avoid it in the context of stressful day-to-day realities of police work.

Training should also provide officers with information about the high proportion of complaints reporting police misconduct. For instance, almost

Table 5.2 Type and Frequency of Reported Mistreatment in Complaint Narratives

Types of Mistreatment	Police Behavior	Frequency (%)	No. of Behaviors
Undue Aggression		**30.6**	**891**
Physical force	Excessive force, assault	14.3	415
	Inappropriate OC spray	0.2	7
	Shot at	0.1	2
Malicious verbal action	Verbal intimidation or aggression	9.4	274
	Spread rumors/lies	0.2	7
Threats	Physical intimidation	3.8	112
	Threat (arrest, fine, etc.)	2.8	82
Excessive action	Unwarranted, extreme action	1.8	51
	Provoked complainant	1.0	30
	Overzealous behavior	0.3	8
Incivility, Rude and Abusive Conduct		**30.5**	**887**
Insults	Discourteous	23.4	682
	Disinterest	1.6	47
	Discredited complainant	1.4	42
	Ridiculed complainant	0.9	26
Absence of compassion	Insensitivity, lack of compassion	4.1	118
Fail to act	Unhelpful	1.6	48
	Wasted complainant's time	1.3	38
Disrespectful	Attended at inappropriate time/place	1.6	48
	Failure to respect request	1.0	30
	Provided false information	2.0	57
	Denied right (phone call, food, toilet)	1.4	41
	Rights violated (e.g., during arrest)	0.7	20

Note: Based on the content analysis of 2910 unique complaint narratives.

one-third of complaints in the NSWPF 12-month sample of customer complaints specified illegal or unlawful conduct (Goodman-Delahunty, Verbrugge, and Taitz, 2011). Examples of these individual behaviors are presented in Table 5.3.

Illustrative examples from customers should be accompanied by case studies that highlight the problem of misconduct, in order to illustrate the types of events and police responses that generate complaints about unlawful police behavior.

Table 5.3 Types of Police Misconduct Reported in Complaint Narratives

Types of Misconduct	Police Behavior	Frequency (%)	No. of Behaviors
Illegal/Unlawful Conduct		**31.0**	**887**
Abuse of procedure	False arrest, search, charge, accusation, detention	12.0	349
	Misinformation recorded	3.0	88
	Unreasonable error	0.7	20
Misuse of power	Corruption (general)	5.6	163
	Protected criminals	3.0	88
	Protected family/friends	1.9	54
Violation of civil statutes	Breaking law	3.4	99
	Sexual harassment or assault	1.5	45
Interfering with justice	Give false information (e.g., in court)	3.1	90
	Withhold, suppress, or destroy evidence	1.9	55
	Pressure person (to sign statement/plead guilty)	1.5	43
	Unlawful associates	0.9	26
	Interfere with justice process	0.5	14
Unprofessional Conduct		**15.8**	**459**
Unprofessional conduct	Breached procedure	4.0	117
	Released confidential information	3.5	102
	Failed to provide identification	2.1	61
	Inappropriate use of COPS database	1.5	43
	Inappropriate (nonsexual) behavior	1.3	37
	Negative comment about police force	0.7	20
	Lost items (report, statement, property)	0.7	19
	Inflamed situation	0.2	5
Abuse of position	Personal use of police property (vehicle, internet)	2.3	67
	Private business while on duty	1.4	40
	Unlawful second job	0.4	13
Reckless conduct	Endanger public (e.g., reckless driving)	1.9	56

Note: Based on the content analysis of 2910 unique complaint narratives.

Target Police Behaviors That Produce Higher-Risk Consequences

In the training materials used to acquaint NSWPF with the CSP, the examples of police conduct included in the materials depicted behaviors such as incivility, rudeness, and failures to engage or reciprocate, all of which would be classified as low risk. As a consequence, the content tended to reinforce the common misperception that customer service obligations are separate and distinct from core policing tasks and high-risk performance. Conversely, the findings in our analysis of customer complaints against the NSWPF revealed that a substantial proportion of the complaints arose from police mistreatment and misconduct rated moderate to high in severity and directly related to core policing tasks; thus, there is a considerable exposure to legal risks (Goodman-Delahunty, Beckley, and Martin, 2014b). This finding mandates that effective future training should focus on police behaviors such as mistreatment and misconduct that not only generated the vast majority of complaints, but also entailed conduct with more severe- or high-risk consequences. Examples of high-risk behaviors are provided as follows.

Target Highly Visible Behaviors That Are Risk Prone, e.g., New Technologies (Facebook)

The risk of damage to police corporate image and reputation is heightened by the use of new technologies to record instances of unprofessional behavior or police misconduct, and these are records that are easily transmitted to the media. Training to increase the awareness of risks associated with technologies, such as Facebook, mobile phones, video cameras, etc., can assist in mitigating public incidents or damage to corporate image and in reducing these risks. Examples of illustrative complaints are presented as follows.

> The complainant has expressed concerns in relation to the interpretation of Domestic Violence Legislation and interactions by police over a domestic situation involving his nephew and his former partner. A provisional order has been granted on behalf of the nephew and the complainant alleges that this order has been breached by comments made on Facebook. The complainant also alleges that the subject officer showed him "complete disrespect" when he attended the police station (LMI1001788 Sustained).

This complainant objected that comments made on Facebook were not accepted by police as evidence of breach of an order and that he was not treated with respect by officers. Training should include direction on the significance of online communications in relation to domestic violence matters.

> The complainant alleges she contacted Mt Druitt Police Station at 4pm on 31 July 2009 expressing concern for her children who were on an access visit with their father. When she had heard nothing by 6pm, she again contacted the station and was advised no job had been created. By 9.16pm, she still had

not heard from Police and contacted for a third time, where she alleges she overheard W, "this job is a nightmare." As of 3 August, 2009, the complainant alleges she had still not been contacted by police (LMI0903621 Sustained).

This case illustrated a breakdown of trust through (1) police inaction, (2) failure to communicate, and (3) failure to be taken seriously inferred from overhearing an officer make a disparaging comment about her case. Officers should be aware that communication devices, including telephones and newer technologies such as e-mail, social networking sites, and mobile recording technologies (mobile phones with cameras) have increased the visibility of police actions and comments. Information that might be intended as a private interaction can be easily overheard, forwarded, recorded, and permanently preserved.

Target Behaviors That Involve Public and Media Exposure

Damage to the corporate image and reputation of a police force is most likely to follow after a negative exposure from public incidents of misconduct or inappropriate behavior, whether the witnesses are third parties, complainants, or fellow officers. By paying more attention to conduct that is highly visible to the members of the general public, the police can reduce complaints about public incidents and use these opportunities to build more positive relationships with the community instead. Several complaints demonstrated how public incidents resulted in increased legal risk. Examples of cases that can be used in training on this topic ranged from reckless driving to instances of police brutality and corruption and are presented as follows.

> An intoxicated man was yelling and stepped in front of the car driven by Ms. X and her friend Mr. Y. They stopped and persuaded him to get off the road and managed to calm him down. Several police then arrived and yelled at the man. She alleges two officers seized him and threw him bodily over a brick wall then three other officers allegedly attacked him by pushing, shoving and head butting. She states they dragged him to his feet and repeatedly knocked him down again. She claims a police officer told her "you have seen nothing tonight—is that clear" and was told to leave. She felt threatened by this. She and Mr. Y then attended Glebe Police Station and reported what she had seen (LMI0902215 Sustained).

The foregoing complaint indicated that passers-by who observed the police physically abuse and intimidate a third party were ordered to leave. This implied that the officers were aware that what was witnessed had corporate significance, and this exposed the police to legal risk.

> About 6.25pm on Friday 16 April 2010, the complainant states that he witnessed a police officer be unnecessarily aggressive towards a taxi driver on Goodlet Street, Surry Hills. The complainant states that the officer yelled, was rude and pushed/twisted the driver's wrist (LMI1001842 Sustained).

In this case, a bystander reported police mistreatment and disrespect for a taxi driver in a public location. This case showed that, sometimes, a bystander was motivated to complain after witnessing an incident of apparent misconduct.

Incorporate Real-Life Case Studies in Training to Increase Motivation

The findings in this study demonstrated that police behaviors indicating problems with police trustworthiness and lack of respectful treatment were the most significant concerns expressed by complainants (Goodman-Delahunty et al., 2013). The research observations of training sessions revealed that some police officers already recognized the importance of respectful treatment, a key tenet of good customer service, to improve suspect compliance. Training sessions with group-based discussions that tap into officers' preexisting commitments to elements of procedural justice, such as respectful treatment, will improve the motivation in training and the responses of participants to the content. Real examples taken from the field clearly showed that failures to adhere to those principles resulted in customer dissatisfaction and complaints (Goodman-Delahunty, Beckley, and Martin, 2014a,b). By providing real-world case examples, issues that arise in day-to-day core policing tasks can be integrated into a customer service training program.

Use Examples Showing How Core Policing Tasks Lead to Complaints

Framing customer service training through a more serious lens by incorporating real-life case studies of complex policing events may increase motivation and present the complexity of real-life police encounters that lead to complaints (Rowe, 2006). Case studies and complaint narratives can be used to stimulate discussion in training sessions and improve motivation by countering the misconception that customer service issues are of minor importance in core policing work. Reframing the content and anchoring the training in examples that officers regard as core policing business will assist in changing the workplace culture and motivation regarding customer service and the content of the training. Useful case examples highlighting the trajectory of policing failures leading to customer dissatisfaction and complaints are presented as follows.

- Illegal/unlawful conduct

    Police have unlawfully entered the complainant's home on the 06 October 2009 and that the complainant has been assaulted by police (LMI0904760).

    Anonymous complaint raises a general proposition that subject officer inappropriately uses his position as a weapons trainer when dealing with female recruits/officers. Secondly, an inference that subject officer had a sexual liaison with a student, R, and further, that this liaison may not have been consensual (LMI1000791).

Complainant alleges police have destroyed video and audio evidence relating to his arrest at Pitt Street, Redfern and subsequent custody at Redfern Police Station. He alleges this evidence is a crucial part of his legal defense (LMI0902242).

- Unprofessional conduct

It is alleged by the complainant that police failed to properly identify themselves during a motor vehicle stop where firearms were drawn, the improper recording of her vehicle as being stolen and the failure by police to rectify the identified problem (P0902776).

Members of the W family had met at their mother's residence in Deniliquin for a family meeting. An argument broke out and police officers attended. It is alleged that three officers were rude and fuelled the situation, and spoke to them like dogs (LMI1001297).

Complainant described being or referred to feeling in danger of harm due to police action. Erratic driving by highway patrol at scene of fatal MVA (LMI0904357).

- Police inaction

On 15 September 2009 the complainants daughters' house was firebombed E7 relates. On 17 Sept. 2009 she attended police station to report she had received a threatening text message stating "next one goes boom. It's not over until you are dead." It is alleged that the SO refused to take a report and was rude allegedly stating "It was not worth writing down" (LMI0904349).

Complaint by Mr. X. alleging that Holroyd Police failed to properly investigate a motor vehicle accident at Merrylands West on 13 May 2008 (LMI1001030).

Alleged complaint regarding a delay in the investigation into an assault matter concerning her and her neighbor (LMI0904401).

- Discriminatory treatment

Complainant alleges both he and his male partner were stopped and searched by Csts P and Q and treated to 50 minutes of intimidation and humiliation on the suspicion of drug dealing. Also alleges Cst P was aggressive, harsh and abrasive in her tone and attitude. Complainant also raised concern at both he and his partner being body searched by both officers and their wallets checked. Complainant alleges he and his partner were targeted by police because they are gay (LMI0904133).

Member of public observed male of African appearance in an agitated and frightened state attend Waratah Station to report an incident. Male observed to speak with broken English, however was understandable to observer to be reporting a robbery or break and enter. It is alleged that the subject officer was intolerant of the communication barrier, failing to provide assistance and failing to take a report or investigate report (LMI0904277).

Complainant alleges that the subject officer has pulled her son up on a number of times and threatening to "lock him up" and accusing him (on another occasion) of being responsible for fights between Wee Waa and Narrabri boys. Complaint believes that these accusations have no basis (LMI0904838).

Use Examples of Core Policing Tasks Involving Customer Service Skills

The NSW Ombudsman's 2011 (p. 25) audit of domestic violence-related complaints revealed that customer service was the most frequent complaint issue, occurring with "other substantive issues." This illustrated that customer service complaints cannot be construed as separate from core policing tasks, yet the current customer service training materials are framed to emphasize customer service as a distinct area of police practice. This approach is at odds with the findings from the current study showing that customer service issues are intermingled with core policing tasks such as responding to domestic violence cases, neighborhood disputes, and fatal motor vehicle accidents. Case examples that can be used in developing awareness of ways to integrate customer service skills in complex and challenging core policing tasks, such as domestic violence cases, neighborhood disputes, and fatal motor vehicle accidents, etc., are presented next.

Motor vehicle accidents, domestic violence incidents, and neighborhood disputes that led to complaints are typically complex and stressful situations. The importance of maintaining a professional demeanor and providing high quality customer service in these circumstances is heightened. Many of these cases illustrated the difficulties and the risks in labeling individuals as either suspects or nonsuspects to determine who is entitled to customer service, as is shown in the following examples.

> Complainant was in the vicinity of a fatal motor vehicle collision involving a pedestrian. Complainant required to walk beyond police barriers to gain access to his residence. Whilst being allowed past barriers, made comment to officer who is alleged to have told him to f' off and pushed him. Complainant ex-officer concerned for the overall demeanor and unprovoked actions of the officer notwithstanding the stressful situation (LMI0902273 Sustained).

This complainant objected to the disrespectful treatment of officers through both verbal and physical abuses. While he made a concession for the stressful situation faced by the officer, indicating a willingness to be understanding about a difficult situation, he nonetheless objected to the unprovoked physical and verbal attacks on a bystander.

> As a result of a report of domestic violence police attended the property of K and O. On entering the premises the victim hit police on the shoulder with a fire poker. Police delivered a short burst of Oleoresin capsicum spray disarmed the victim and placed her under arrest (LMI0903025 Sustained).

Use Examples of Customer Service in Challenging Tasks such as Domestic Violence Cases

Case examples drawn from complaint databases can be used in developing the awareness of the complexity of roles that make it challenging to distinguish victims from suspects in the midst of core policing tasks, such as domestic violence cases and neighborhood disputes. Yet police responses in these cases result in numerous complaints (Goodman-Delahunty and Corbo Crehan, 2016). A risk-averse approach in these situations is to treat all members of the public as customers (Goodman-Delahunty, Taitz, and Verbrugge, 2013).

Use Examples Showing the Complexity of Victim and Suspect Roles in Real Policing Tasks

Complaint narratives highlighted that in the midst of performing law enforcement duties, it can be difficult to definitively discern community members who are either victims or suspects. Other cases demonstrated that within a single incident, these roles could shift. For instance, the victims of domestic violence incidents themselves became suspects within the course of a complaint narrative. Training sessions, which include discussion of real-life situations such as these, will highlight that officers may have multiple responsibilities and duties toward a single community member and that suspect identity is often uncertain, complex, and changeable. By providing customer service to as many community members as possible, the risks can be obviated and the number of complaints from people with shifting suspect status reduced.

Offer Training on Active Listening to Reduce Dissatisfaction and Complaints

Research on what motivates complainants indicated that most customers were motivated by a desire to communicate a genuine grievance, while procedural justice research indicated the importance of citizen voice in police–community relations (Goodman-Delahunty, 2010; Tyler and Huo, 2002). Officer training in communication should include a specific focus on the importance of voice and the importance of listening to citizens and allowing them to explain their point of view. This will reduce the number of complaints by customers who feel that their point of view was not taken into account in the policing encounter and who may therefore be seeking to voice their point of view through the complaint system. Our review of the police training materials showed that active listening was covered in detail. This message should be strengthened. If citizens feel that they are genuinely listened to, the desire for both voice and trustworthiness will be fulfilled during the policing encounter, minimizing citizen desire to have these fulfilled in the complaints process. Training for all officers—and complaint handlers—should emphasize techniques such as this, which allow the staff to convey genuine concern and empathy to citizens. The training sections on communication for respectful treatment, and active listening, should therefore be retained and strengthened.

Fostering a Police Culture That Values Complaints

A number of recommendations are aimed at transforming police culture to increase the appreciation and the value of customer service complaints as useful feedback from the community. For instance, the use of examples in training that are drawn from practical experience, which is relevant to and recognizable to officers attending the training, will enhance the value of the training. Similarly, the value of the principles outlined in the customer service charter will be better appreciated if the trainees are exposed to the consequences of violating these principles. The examples of each of the procedural justice principles as they apply in community–police interactions are provided below.

Provide Examples from Practical Experience

The motivation to participate in and attend to the customer service training may be improved by engaging officers more directly in training sessions that make the content more relevant to their own practice. By increasing the number of group exercises, participants will have more opportunities to engage with the materials, and to offer their own input and interpretations. Group exercises are recognized as a key tool in adult learning and stimulate motivation by requiring active participation (Felder and Brent, 2005; Slavin, 1995). The training will be more effective if it is grounded in the everyday experiences of working officers, and their insights may assist the trainers in refining the training program.

Connect Complaints to Procedural Justice and Community Policing Models

The customer service training program materials and training sessions observed presented the target customer service behaviors as a series of dos and don'ts rather than as principles derived from any meaningful theory about the customer–provider relationship. Although the customer service charter was mentioned, its content was not well integrated into the training materials to convey a fundamental shift in approach to the core policing business. In the observed sessions, no illustrations of the customer service charter were provided. By drawing on a well-founded theoretical framework, such as the group value relational model (GVRM) and the principles of procedural justice, a more integrated and cohesive training program can be devised (Sunshine and Tyler, 2003). Implementing the GRVM as a framework for customer service training will ensure that all four elements of procedural justice (trustworthiness, neutrality, respectful treatment, and voice; Goodman-Delahunty, 2010; Goodman-Delahunty et al., 2013) are covered appropriately.

For training to be effective, both the content of the materials and the delivery need to give weight to the importance of customer service as a core element of policing duties, as procedural justice research indicated that how citizens perceived police treatment and trustworthiness was central to the confidence in police and police legitimacy. Training recipients are less likely to regard the program and the training as superficial and incidental to their work if they better appreciate these underpinnings.

Case examples selected to demonstrate the connection between the NSWPF customer service charter and the principles of procedural justice are presented as follows.

- Respectful treatment
    A man in custody was not informed why his clothing was removed, and his dignity was affronted when he was observed and ridiculed by police. The training should emphasize the devastating effects of humiliation and ridicule on some citizens, including suspects.

    Alleges that he was traumatized after being apprehended and when held in police custody he was stripped of his clothing and had to sleep naked all night. Further he was humiliated during the removal of his clothing by officers watching this occurrence and laughing at him (LMI0904060 Sustained).

    Further examples of complaints that arose because of lack of respectful treatment by police are provided in Table 5.4.
- Trustworthiness
    The following example illustrated an instance of neglect of duty to a vulnerable victim:

    Complainant's daughter reported to police a disgusting and life threatening letter received via "Facebook." Complainant alleges

Table 5.4   Examples of Complaints about a Lack of Respectful Treatment by Police

Officer Conduct	Case Examples
Rude and abusive	Complainant "felt bullied by the conversation" with officer attending the matter. Officer attitude "rude, arrogant, and derogatory and totally unprofessional" (LMI1001687).
Mistreatment	After issuing complainant with Traffic Infringement Notice, officer "rude and swore at him." Officer "slammed a car door on the complainant's thigh" (LMI1000933).
Failure to engage and rudeness	Complainant reported that "subject officer inappropriately belched," also "failed to listen to her and failed to respond to subsequent messages left by her" (LMI0902532).
Undue physical force	Complainant witnessed mistreatment of a taxi driver: "Officer yelled, was rude and pushed/twisted the driver's wrist" (LMI1001842).
Failure to respond	Failed to respond to parking complaint call: Complainant had to wait "outside in the cold for over five hours despite numerous requests for assistance" (LMI0903925).

the suspect has committed the offence of "intimidation" and police should have taken out an interim AVO. Complainant attended Casino Station on 7/10/09 and relayed his concerns to A/Sgt X who is alleged to have indicated he would contact him after 9/10/09. However the complainant and his daughter have not been contacted since. Complainant claims that due to the inaction of police the offender is going to continue to harass and intimidate members of his family (LMI0904785 Sustained).

The failure to take action and to "keep me informed," two of the core principles of the charter, led to ongoing risks, which could have been prevented had the officer made contact and taken appropriate action.

A high proportion of complaints reflected incidents that diminished police trustworthiness in the eyes of the community. Several examples are provided in Table 5.5.

• Neutrality

This case example illustrated an instance of victimization and retaliation by police:

About 8.15am on Wednesday 17 November 2009 the complainant was driving to work along Penshurst Street, Penshurst. A marked police car pulled out of a side street into lane 2 of stationary traffic. This blocked lane 1 and the complainant and other traffic were delayed for a brief time. The complainant then stopped beside the police car at a set of traffic lights and calmly made comment about the poor display of driving by police. Immediately upon traffic

Table 5.5   Examples of Complaints about Conduct Diminishing Police Trustworthiness

Police Behavior	Case Examples
Police inaction and negligence; assault	Complainant attended to assist at a street brawl. 000 calls were only responded to after 40 minutes. Officers "took no control of the situation" and officer called complainant "a 'dickhead'" several times. Complains that "all police just stood around like stunned mullets whilst the offenders left." Complainant observed "one male who was trying to explain what was happening get punched in the head and slapped in the face by the officer because the officer stated he failed to move on." Complainant typed this information after a severe panic and anxiety attack and breaking down in tears (LMI1001163).
Citizen mistreatment	While in police custody complainant "stripped of his clothing and had to sleep naked all night." Complainant "humiliated during the removal of his clothing by officers watching this occurrence and laughing at him." Complainant "traumatized" (LMI0904060).
Unlawful conduct	Complainant alleges that officer conversation on Facebook said "Mate... save yourself a court matter. Do what I use to do. Turn the ICV [in Car Video] off...get $50 off them and send them on their way. Is that wrong of me? I hope no-one can read this? ... ha" (P0905591).
Undue physical force	Complainant reported "that Blacktown Police do not treat her with respect and are rude to her. She further states that Blacktown Police caused bruising by throwing her into the back of a police van" (LMI0904342).
Unlawful conduct	Off duty officer "lied to the insurance company by giving an untrue version of the collision (that the car he was driving was stationary when it happened)" (P0905274).
Failure to provide care	Complainant reported "police searched the complainant's vehicle, made her four children stand by the side of the road at night, in the rain. Did not tell them the reason for searching the vehicle" (LMI0902050).
Failure to provide care; belittling	Police took a phone call relating to the 13 y/old son of the complainant being plied with alcohol and exposed to drugs. The officer allegedly showed contempt for the complainant, her concern and even laughed at her and hung up (LMI0905284).

moving, police pulled the complainant over. The subject officer demanded the complainant's license and conducted a breath test before subjecting the complainant to a string of questions about car ownership etc. delaying him a further 10 minutes. The complainant believes his treatment by the subject officer was an act of retribution for his comment, and obviously designed to inconvenience and denigrate him (LMI0905220 Sustained).

The complainant was singled out for investigation because he voiced his criticism of this officer's driving. The harassment was experienced as both an inconvenience and an act of humiliation or denigration.

- Voice

    Most complainants did not seek apologies or compensation but were seeking an opportunity to voice their concerns to the police, as was illustrated in this example both during the random breath test (RBT) and in making the subsequent complaint.

> On the 27th of November 2009 the complainant was stopped for the purpose of random breath testing in Chantry Street, Goulburn. The complainant states that as soon as the officer approached her window he was immediately aggressive and condescending toward her, tried to goad her into arguing with him, that he was rude and obnoxious and would not listen to her. The complainant has been spoken to and indicates that her treatment by the subject officer made her feel very stressed and nervous but she does not wish for any formal action against the subject officer other than for him to be reminded of his customer service obligations (LMI0905222 Sustained).

A Comprehensive Source for Data-Driven Training

To generate a more comprehensive and reliable source for data-driven training based on feedback received in the form of complaints, the three following steps are recommended: (1) neutral and objective procedures to record incoming complaints; (2) identify and record what customers want; and (3) conduct regular evaluations of the customer service training program. These steps are described in more detail as follows.

Train Data Entry Staff to Ensure Complaint Information Is Recorded Neutrally

Complaints have been recorded in ways that did not preserve the complainant's own words or undermined the validity of the complaint. In these cases, the recorder's knowledge or point of view colored the complaint record, and it was difficult to identify the complainant's own voice or words. Events were sometimes shaped by the person receiving and documenting the complaint. Staff training is recommended regarding the importance of avoiding coloring complaint records with their own knowledge, comments, or point of view, especially in such a way where it is difficult to distinguish this information from the complainant's own words. To some degree, whoever defines the problem has control over the resolution. If the procedural justice principle of the voice is to be respected, the complainants' words must be faithfully and neutrally recorded.

Record What Customers Want When They Lodge a Complaint

Numerous complainants specified that their objective in making a complaint was simply to report a procedural failure so that this problem could be addressed and would not recur in the future to the detriment of someone else in the community. Other complainants sought an acknowledgement, an apology, or some specific form of redress. When complaints are received, the staff should identify and separate the customer goal from the description of the events leading to the complaint and ensure that their own comments about the potential outcomes are separately recorded from those of the complainant. By tracking the complainants' objectives, appropriate triage and follow-up can be arranged.

Systematic Evaluations of the Customer Service Training Program

Ideally, some systematic and periodic assessment should be conducted to measure behavioral changes, and cultural change, and to find out from the participants and the consumers of the training what recommendations they can make for improvements.

Conclusion

Based on observations of customer service training program sessions and the analysis of a 12-month sample of complaints lodged against a major police agency in Australia, several training needs to improve police–community relations were identified. Recommendations to addresses each of the identified training needs were provided and elaborated.

In addition, a series of key practical recommendations were outlined for police agencies to improve the handling of customer complaints, illustrated by examples drawn from actual complaints against police by citizens in NSW. By implementing these recommendations, managers can increase their capacity to achieve the following goals:

- Create a more accurate complaint database as a tool for data-driven training.
- Enhance motivation and create a workplace culture that values complaints.
- Integrate customer service training into core policing tasks.
- Deliver evidence-based training about the most significant complaint issues.
- Achieve a more optimal number of complaints and reduce legal risk.

References

Bell, S. J., and Luddington, J. A. 2006. Coping with customer complaints. *Journal of Service Research*. 8: 221–33.

Bradley, R. 1998. Public expectations and perceptions of policing. Police Research Series, Paper 96. London: Policing and Reducing Crime Unit. Retrieved from http://rds.homeoffice.gov.uk/rds/prgpdfs/fprs96.pdf.

Brewer, B. 2007. Citizen or customer? Complaints handling in the public sector. *International Review of Administrative Sciences*. 73(4): 549–56.

Burn, C. 2010. The NSW Police Force Customer Service Programme. *Policing: A Journal of Policy and Practice*. 4(3): 249–57.

Chan, J. B. L. 1999. Governing police practice: Limits of the new accountability. *British Journal of Sociology*. 50(2): 251–70.

Christopher, M., Payne, A., and Ballantyne, D. 1991. *Relationship Marketing: Bringing Quality, Customer Service and Marketing Together*. London: Butterworth-Heineman.

Drummond, G., Ensor, J., Laing, A., and Richardson, N. 2000. Market orientation applied to police service strategies. *The International Journal of Public Sector Management*. 13(7): 571–87.

Felder, R. M., and Brent, R. 2005. Understanding student differences. *Journal of Engineering Education*. 94(1): 57–72.

Goldsmith, A. J. 1995. Necessary but not sufficient: The role of public complaints procedures in police accountability. In *Accountability for Criminal Justice: Selected Essays*. Stenning, P. C., ed. Toronto, ON: University of Toronto Press.

Goldsmith, A. J. 1996. What's wrong with complaint investigations? Dealing with difference differently in complaints against police. *Criminal Justice Ethics*. 15(1): 36–55.

Goodman-Delahunty, J. 2010. Four ingredients: New recipes for procedural justice in Australian policing. *Policing: A Journal of Policing and Practice*. 4: 403–10.

Goodman-Delahunty, J., and Corbo Crehan, A. 2016. Enhancing police responses to domestic violence incidents: Reports from client advocates in New South Wales. *Violence Against Women*. 22(8): 1007–1026.

Goodman-Delahunty, J., Beckley, A., and Martin, M. 2014a. Resolving or escalating disputes? Experiences of the NSW Police Force complaints process. *Australasian Dispute Resolution Journal*. 25(2): 79–90.

Goodman-Delahunty, J., Beckley, A., Martin, M. 2014b. Complaints against the New South Wales Police Force: Analysis of risks and rights in reported police conduct. *Australian Journal of Human Rights*. 20(2): 81–105.

Goodman-Delahunty, J., Taitz, M., and Verbrugge, 2013. Complaining to the police: Insights from a psychological analysis. *Policing: A Journal of Policy and Practice*. 7(3): 280–8.

Goodman-Delahunty, J., Verbrugge, H., Sowemimo-Coker, C.R., Kingsford, J., and Taitz, M. 2013. The centrality of procedural justice in citizen complaints about police. *The Journal of the Institute of Justice & International Studies*. 13: 83–98.

Goodman-Delahunty, J., Verbrugge, H., and Taitz, M. 2011. New South Wales Police Force Customer Service Program evaluation and analysis. Unpublished research report to the New South Wales Police Force. Manly, Australia: Charles Sturt University.

Gorst, J., Kanji, G., and Wallace, W. 1998. Providing customer satisfaction. *Total Quality Management*. 9: 100–3.

Hinds, L., and Murphy, K. 2007. Public satisfaction with police: Using procedural justice to improve police legitimacy. *The Australian and New Zealand Journal of Criminology*. 40: 27–42.

Independent Police Complaints Commission. 2015. *Police complaints: Statistics for England and Wales 2014/15*. London: Author. Retrieved from https://www.ipcc.gov.uk/sites/default/files/Documents/research_stats/complaints_statistics_2014_15.pdf.

Maguire, M., and Corbett, C. 1991. *A Study of the Police Complaints System*. London: Her Majesty's Stationary Office (HMSO).

Murphy, K., Hinds, L., and Fleming, J. 2008. Encouraging public cooperation and support for police. *Policing and Society*. 18: 136–55.

Nyer, P. U. 2000. An investigation into whether complaining can cause increased consumer satisfaction. *Journal of Consumer Marketing*. 17: 9–19.

Nyer, P. U., and Gopinath, M. 2005. Effects of complaining versus negative word of mouth on subsequent changes in satisfaction: The role of public commitment. *Psychology and Marketing*. 22: 937–53.

Porter, L., Prenzler, T., and Fleming, J. 2011. Complaint reduction in the Tasmania police. *Policing and Society*. 22(4): 426–47.

Prim, I., and Pras, B. 1998. "Friendly" complaining behaviours: Toward a relational approach. *Journal of Market Focused Management*. 3(3–4): 333–52.

Rowe, M. 2006. Following the leader: Front-line narratives on police leadership *Policing: An International Journal of Police Strategies & Management*. 29(4): 757–67.

Shemwell, D. J., Yavas, U., and Bilgin, Z. 1998. Customer-service provider relationships: An empirical test of a model of service quality, satisfaction and relationship-oriented outcomes. *International Journal of Service Industry Management*. 9(2): 155–68.

Slavin, R. E. 1995. Research on cooperative learning and achievement: What we know, what we need to know. *Contemporary Educational Psychology*. 21(1): 43–69.

Smith, G. 2010. Every complaint matters: Human Rights Commissioner's opinion concerning independent and effective determination of complaints against the police. *International Journal of Law, Crime and Justice*. 38: 59–74.

Society of Consumer Affairs Professionals Australia. 2011, March. A complaint is a gift: Creating opportunities to repair and strengthen your customer relationships. Sydney: Workshop. Retrieved from http://www.socap.org.au.

Sunshine, J., and Tyler, T. 2003. Moral solidarity, identification with the community, and the importance of procedural justice: The police as prototypical representatives of a group's moral values. *Social Psychology Quarterly*. 66: 153–65.

Tyler, T. R., and Huo, Y. 2002. *Trust in the Law: Encouraging Public Cooperation with the Police and Courts*. New York: Russell Sage Foundation.

Woods, T. 2006. *Oakland Police Survey*. Oakland, CA: People United for a Better Oakland (PUEBLO). Retrieved from PUEBLO website: http://www.peopleunited.org/.

Cybercrime, Cyberattacks, and Problems of Implementing Organizational Cybersecurity

6

ANTHONY MINNAAR

Contents

Abstract

Given modern societies' increased reliance on borderless and decentralized information technologies (ITs), cyberspace has been identified as an easy target for organized criminals, criminal hackers (crackers), hacktivists, governments themselves, or even terrorist networks and for the perpetration of a number of wide-ranging illegal activities. Gone are the days when encryption was foolproof, e-commerce was safe, gaming was just for fun, war was fought by actual people, and the Internet was safely in the hands of responsible entities. The control over the Internet has become free for all, and nothing is hack-proof with old cybersecurity models collapsing. Information security has become an increasingly critical concern for organizations of all kinds. Trends, such as device mobility (of smartphones, tablets/iPads, and notebooks), cloud computing, consumerization (online shopping), and flexi-work or bring your own device (BYOD) to work, mean that more people are accessing an organization's applications and data from more places and in more ways than ever before. This chapter examines the cybercrime basics, the anatomy of cyberattacks as launched against networks by professional hackers/crackers, and then turns to looking at the enormous problems of implementing cybersecurity in an ordinary organization and finally the current threats and vulnerabilities of mobile devices and the growing practice of BYOD to work.

Introduction

To perpetrate various cybercrimes, cybercriminals make use of a number of stratagems ranging from e-mail scams (to get your personal details and steal your identification [ID] and maybe also bank account details) to phishing spam expeditions. But the increasing use is made of cyberattacks by professional hackers to access databases and steal information, which is then fraudulently used to obtain some sort of advantage or financial benefits (e.g., cyberransom, denial-of-service attack, cybercoercion, cyberwarfare, cyberespionage, cyberfraud, theft of intellectual property, cyberblackmail/extortion—a favorite of porn sites—and hacktivism). Furthermore, with the increasing sophistication of technologies, as well as the proliferation of Internet connection devices like smartphones and iPads, the recourse to unsecured social media sites, and the implementation of BYOD to work, has led to an increase in cybersecurity vulnerabilities. A further vulnerability to information security systems has been that posed by the so-called insider threat. All these trends have created even more opportunities for cybercriminals to exploit.

The international challenge for many governments, organizations, and businesses has been to adequately provide preventative and protective cybersecurity measures for all kinds of information and services. Some of the proposed measures infringe on other rights such as privacy, freedom of expression, consumer and commercial rights, etc. A further problem has been those around international prosecutions and obtaining adequate evidence of cybercrime to convict criminals. Nevertheless, the digital environment has no international boundaries, and increasingly, governments are looking to a coordinated international approach to regulating, controlling, combating, and prosecuting cybercriminals. However, the needed measures are all in the realm of cybersecurity, and the very essence of cyberspace* is its unfettered and open nature that essentially is uncontrollable.

But with the exponential expansion of cyberspace with increased broadband capabilities (the rate of data transference with ever more powerful communication technologies) and improved Wi-Fi connectivity, the proliferation of mobile and handheld devices—smartphones, tablets/iPads, and notebooks—has also increased vulnerabilities to information databases and methods of storage (e.g., in the so-called cloud).

Faced with increasingly sophisticated attacks from gangs of cybercriminals and foreign governments probing systems for sensitive data, threats frequently go undetected for days, weeks, and even months. It is not just financial data being stolen. Terrorists and rogue governments may steal confidential data, including intelligence information, which can expose a country and its citizens to potential harm.

Unfortunately, the traditional fortress approach no longer suffices. Firewalls, intrusion detection systems, and other security devices can stop the average hacker, but new threats use stealth techniques that these defenses cannot detect on their own.

Entry-Level Risks and Vulnerabilities

Mobile Device Vulnerabilities

There are also electronic information storage database vulnerabilities linked to mobile devices and the growing practice of BYOD to work. Mobile devices (notebooks, smartphones, and tablets/iPads) are small and valuable. Increasingly, they are becoming a target of theft, not just for the device itself but also for the information stored on them.

---

* Almost anything that relies on software programming code and has a link to a network could be a part of cyberspace. Included then are smartphones, home computers and laptops, tablets, and the Internet. The development of ever smaller and more sophisticated devices is also linked in to cyberspace. For example, security cameras, elevators, scanning machines (like credit card readers); global positioning systems and satellites; jet fighters and global banking networks; commuter trains; and computers that control power grids, rail transport networks, and water systems (O'Harrow, 2012a).

Mobile applications—in cell phones, smartphones, iPhones, iPads, and tablets—increasingly rely on a browser function, which in itself presents unique challenges to security in terms of usability and scale. Keyboards are also hard to use or nonexistent on phones and tablets. This often results in the owner/user autosaving their passwords for e-mail and virtual private network access passwords. If the device got into the hands of a cybercriminal, it could open up an organization's or a company's information and other resources to anyone who takes possession of such mobile device.

Mobile devices, as information storage devices, allow cyberattackers to use short message service, e-mail, and mobile web browsers to launch an attack, then silently record and steal data. Mobile phones can facilitate attacks on otherwise protected systems, i.e., when downloading data to a company network or office personal computer (PC)/laptop. Mobile browsers are more susceptible to attacks launched just by touching the display or the pop-up when connecting to the Internet web. Furthermore, unlike network computer systems, mobile devices do not commonly receive patches and security updates.

For these reasons, the security techniques that work for desktops and PCs are not enough for mobile devices—a major vulnerability these days in protecting and securing stored organizational information.

Industrial Control Computers and Indirect Data Connections

In 2009, John Matherly released a search engine program called *Shodan*, which initially only set out to map and capture the specifications of everything from desktop computers, network printers to web servers linked to the Internet and the intranets worldwide. But this program soon found an astonishingly high number of industrial or so-called control computers that could be accessed and hacked into by even moderately talented hackers through unintended links via the Internet. Basically, these control computers on-site are used for the remote control of industrial machinery, but those links have remained largely unsecured since controllers never realized their vulnerabilities since they were reckoned to be safe within the facilities, protected by obscurity, and disconnected from outside networks. However, these stand-alone control computers can become linked to external networks often through indirect connections. Because of the nature of cyberspace and the web, an employee walking through a facility or a plant with a wireless connection on a laptop can create a temporary data link that can expose the control computer systems to intruders, (e.g., a cyberterrorist in a nuclear power plant) (O'Harrow, 2012b).

Insider Threat

A further vulnerability to information security systems has been that posed by the so-called insider threat. For example, WikiLeaks—the so-called whistle-blower or antisecrecy website—is largely dependent on information provided by organization insiders like U.S. Marine Private Bradley Manning and Edward Snowden—a data and systems analyst contracted to the U.S. National Security Agency with security clearance—both of whom supplied WikiLeaks founder, Julian Assange, with confidential U.S. government information. Manning provided 700,000 government files (Savage, 2013), and Snowden, more recently, details regarding the extent of the PRISM e-Surveillance and Monitoring Program, i.e., data mining, of the United States (Poplak, 2013), whereas the group known as Anonymous hacks and defaces or destroys (corrupts) information databases of targeted organizations or government departments. These are the so-called hacktivists.

It is every organization's nightmare that a young hacker will infiltrate a computer network from the outside and crash it or gain access to valuable classified information like trade secrets and publicize it. Although there has been much publicity on hacking and destroying computer systems, it is usually not an outside job. Hackers are more commonly known to be an employee or a disgruntled ex-employee who has a grudge against the organization. The company/organization's computer system is then infiltrated from the inside and then destroyed or valuable information is sold to a syndicate (for criminal purposes) or even sold to a competitor for possible market advantage (industrial espionage) or used for cyberblackmail/cyberransom (Workplace Staff, 2006).

Other attacks on a company's information systems could include deleting company address books or client lists, the deliberate deletion or destruction of information, which can all have far reaching economic consequences for any company. Whole databases containing sensitive customer information are also stolen and sometimes offered for sale to a competitor, or the thief sets up a business for himself/herself, using this information to get his or her business off the ground.

Minimalist Definition as an Offshoot of White-Collar Crime and New Typologies

As a starting point, only the minimalist definition of cybercrime (also known as *hi-tech*** or electronic crime) is provided here. Cybercrime broadly refers to a criminal activity where a computer or a computer network is the source, the tool, the target, or the place of a crime. Initially, cybercrime was merely

---

* High-technology crime specifically refers to the use of advanced technology and equipment in the perpetration of cybercrime, including not only devices such as, besides a base computer or a PC, telephones, cell phones, smartphones, and tablets (iPads) but also such devices as cheque-reading machines, credit card machines, and even biometric (fingerprint, iris, or facial recognition)-reading machines (see the study by Moore [2011]).

seen as an offshoot of the so-called white-collar crime, which itself has been defined as a financially motivated nonviolent crime committed for illegal monetary gain (cf. Sutherland, 1949). Like a white-collar crime, the two foundational crimes of fraud and theft underpin cybercrime. In other words, using online Internet as the medium in order to obtain money or some other benefit by means of deliberate deception. Cybercrime has itself spawned a growing number of more detailed typologies ranging from initial foundational ones, such as cyberactivism, cybertrespass (as related to the activity of hacking), cybertheft, cyberobscenity and cyberpornography, cyberfraud, cyberstalking, cyberhoaxing, cyberbullying, cybervigilantism, cybermanipulation, and cyberransom, to more recent additional typologies, namely, cybersecurity, cyberattack and cyberthreats, cyberwarfare and cyberdefense, cyberterrorism and cyberespionage.

As can be seen from the list, not all are strictly financial crimes or overtly criminal but remain nevertheless illegal. For instance, cyberwarfare, cyberterrorism, and cyberoffensive operations have a huge potential to disrupt and cripple whole economies. For instance, the impact of an attack on critical infrastructure or strategic installations, such as railways, electricity grids, airlines, nuclear power stations, and even large irrigation reservoirs that depend on so-called control computer systems for their effective and efficient operations, could be major. For example, a terrorist hacker could manipulate a large dam to release a flood of water downstream and thereby destroying valuable farmland and urban areas alongside the river. Cyberterrorists could also use its access to a nation's critical infrastructures to blackmail a government.

Cybercrime itself can be categorized into three basic categories, namely, white-collar crimes such as fraud/theft (via online phishing scams), social fabric crime (e.g., sexual offences or pornographic exploitation largely using social media platforms), and lastly, the broad category of security or state crime (e.g., cyberwarfare, cyberespionage, hacker activists, and cyberterrorism), whose main thrust is via hacking cyberattacks.

Basic Stratagem: Electronic Online Approach to a Potential Victim

The E-Mail Phishing Scam

This is designed to lead a recipient/s to counterfeit websites that aim to trick them into divulging financial data such as account usernames and passwords or credit card details. These e-mails look like they come from trusted sources, such as banks or legitimate companies. Phishing e-mails typically request that users click on a link (hyperlink) in the e-mail, which will direct users to a spoofed website, where they need to confirm login and other account security information, etc.

Theft of Digital Certificates

Linked to phishing scams is the theft of digital certificates (DCs). DCs are a system intended to verify the authenticity of a particular website—to ensure, in effect, that a website is genuine/authentic, i.e., by verifying a site's identity and that the connection to the site is encrypted and difficult for an outsider to monitor. By stealing digital certificates, hackers can create fake credentials that could allow someone to snoop on Internet connections that appear to be secure. Armed with certificates stolen from companies that have the power to issue the DCs that the whole Internet system relies upon to verify a site's identity; someone with control over an Internet service provider (ISP), could trick Internet users into thinking that they were safely connected to a familiar site, while eavesdropping on their online activity and/or stealing information for fraudulent use, blackmail, ransom, industrial espionage, etc.

Hacking and Hackers

Central to cybercriminals' modus operandi has been the technological advances in the science of hacking. Increasing use is being made of cyberattacks by professional hackers or as legitimate system engineers label criminal hackers, *crackers*—to access databases and steal information. A so-called hacker/cracker is someone who seeks and exploits weaknesses in a computer system or a computer network and can bring a computer system to a grinding halt or will make copies of sensitive information for use in an unlawful manner. Hackers log into a computer network and gain entry to it without having the necessary authority to do so, i.e., cybermanipulation. An example of this would be where a perpetrator logs onto a government network by means of their own personal computer and modem, in order to look at classified documents. Alternatively, the hacker might copy a file with all the company's customers' credit card information, planning to use it to buy goods on credit. Accordingly, there are a number of different types of hackers, depending on their motivation and occupation. For example, hacktivists are hackers who hack into secure databases to make a social, an ideological, a religious, or a political point. In general, most hacktivism involves website defacement or denial-of-service attacks. However, the art of hacking and the techniques used to access information databases is the cornerstone of all cybercrime and allied illegal cyberactivities.

Hacker Methods

According to the U.S. FBI, terrorists, transnational criminals, and intelligence services worldwide make use of cyberinformation exploitation tools known as computer viruses—so-called Trojan horses, worms, logic bombs, and eavesdropping sniffers—that can destroy, intercept, and degrade the integrity of, or deny access to, data. In addition, an insider poses a significant threat to an organization, a government department, or a company's network security (Kouri, 2005).

These methods typically involve the deliberate planting of viruses, hacking into databases and stealing sensitive information, or disrupting and destroying network systems. They do this by bypassing the technical systems (upgrades, security kits, and high-end encryption of firewalls) via so-called system backdoors. However, gaining network access often means tricking someone into helping an unauthorized person to gain access to IT systems and networks. Criminal hackers therefore prey on the weakest link in a security system—the human being—by exploiting human vulnerabilities such as ignorance, naiveté, and possibly an individual's own greed, i.e., through bribery and corruption.

Besides gaining access by manipulating or exploiting an insider, hackers make use of cyberattacks using so-called malware—a malicious software program—to disrupt a network service, a website, or an information database. These days, a common form of such a computer-based attack is the hiding of spyware in an innocent e-mail message or where an employee may encounter a pop-up informing them that they have lost their connection to the server. The user is advised to type in his/her username and password and to press enter. This information is then automatically e-mailed to the perpetrator, and the user ends up being unaware that any breach of security has occurred. Besides this basic entry mode, a malware typically takes advantage of system vulnerabilities and software bugs or hacker-installed backdoors that allow a malicious code to be installed on computers without the owners' consent or knowledge. They then load themselves into such computers, often for criminal intent purposes. Bots*—individual computers infected with bot malware—are then turned into so-called zombies. These can then be used as remote attack tools or to form part of a botnet under the control of the botnet controller. In other words, the zombie computer has a sleeper cell waiting to be activated on their command. If such an attacker can install the malware on a series of computers, a botnet is formed, i.e., a network of linked bot-controlled computers. In this way, a bot computer program allows

---

* The term *bot* is short for robot, while a *botnet* is a collection of Internet-connected programs communicating with other similar programs on captive computers, in order to perform a variety of tasks.

a net attacker (hacker) to remotely control vulnerable computers. In this way, the attacker/controller can establish and form a virtual network of so-called zombies or botnets (see the study by Choo [2007]). Once such botnets have been set up, they are then used and manipulated (leveraged) in order to orchestrate a concerted attack against other computing resources—the so-called distributed denial-of-service (DDoS) attack.

Once the malware has been installed on a target computer, it is a small step for criminal-minded hackers to manipulate their use for criminal ends. In other words, the original bot or malware programs were redesigned as either spyware or crimeware, i.e., often, the two were combined in the theft of information off a computer. Crimeware is software that performs illegal actions unanticipated by a user running the software and which aims to yield financial benefits to the installer of such software. Essentially, this method uses technical subterfuge schemes to plant the crimeware program onto PCs to directly steal credentials. This is where spyware comes into the equation. The spyware typically uses viruses and/or Trojans* to install programs called *key loggers* on a computer. Keystroke logging can be done through either hardware or software. Key loggers can be installed as simply as running an e-mail attachment that installs the software on a computer. This spyware then uses the installed key logging system to intercept consumers' keystrokes and capture and send out information—this collected information can include online account usernames and passwords and other information including credit card numbers and bank account details (if you do Internet banking, for instance)—back to the phisher and to corrupt local and remote navigational infrastructures to misdirect consumers to counterfeit websites and to authentic websites through phisher-controlled proxies (i.e., the zombies) (see the study by Minnaar [2008] for more details on this aspect of cybercrime).

What hackers also look for is a so-called zero day—a vulnerability or a flaw in the software that has never been made public and for which there is no known fix, i.e., a door through a network security is found that can be exploited to break into a system and to take 'control' of a computer and then use it to penetrate further into an organization's networks. Their existence has been known to hackers and security specialists since the early days of hacking. Zero days have proliferated along with the growth in software. Those who found them often had no incentive to share their finds with the

---

* *Trojans* refer to the Trojan horse of Greek mythology where attackers hid inside a wooden horse left at the gates of the besieged city of Troy—the wooden horse was taken inside the city, and the hidden attackers only emerging late at night to open the gates to the rest of the Greek army (that had sailed away convincing the Trojans that the siege had been ended). When referring to cybercrime, a Trojan (horse) is a computer program concealed on a computer (hard drive) that is meant to disrupt, undermine, subvert, or destroy; i.e., it contains a hidden function (concealed stratagem) that causes damage to other programs while appearing to perform a valid function.

affected users and client companies. Sometimes the vulnerabilities would be publicly released on the Internet to warn the public at large of their existence. According to security specialists, a number of government agencies, particularly in the United States, have secretly engaged in hacking operations, over the years,* along with some affected software makers, making use of zero-day information bought from a thriving underground market to engage in such clandestine operations (O'Harrow, 2012a).

Cyberattacks and DDoS Attacks

A cyberattack has been defined as a hostile act using a computer (or any computer-like device such as a smartphone, a tablet, or a notebook) via networks or systems. Such an attack is intended to disrupt, deny access, and/or destroy or degrade an adversary's critical cybersystems, assets, or functions. The intended effects of a cyberattack are not only necessarily limited to the targeted computer systems or information databases themselves, but also in manipulating or destroying information on the target information system itself or even destroying a target's communication and logistic channels. Some individuals use cyberspace for their own devious actions, targeting unsuspecting individuals for their own enjoyment, nefarious purposes, exploitation, or simply for profit (cybercrime). When governments or military establishments are attacked through cybermethods, it is a whole new kind of attack known as cyberwarfare or cyberterrorism.

Central to current cyberattacks are the so-called DDoS cyberattack. A DDoS attack is a method an attacker uses to deny access for legitimate users of an online service. This service could be a bank website, an e-commerce site, or any other type of network service. An attacker having built themselves a botnet of zombies—i.e., compromised vulnerable PCs around the world—sends bogus traffic to a site. If the attacker sends enough traffic, legitimate users of a site cannot be serviced, i.e., a denial of service occurs. The most common form of a DDoS attack is a buffer overflow attack, which involves the delivery of traffic to a target network address that is greater in volume than its data buffers are able to handle. DDoS attacks vary in both sophistication and size. If the attackers have enough computing resources at their disposal, they can direct enough traffic to overwhelm the target's bandwidth. These simply flood the network and the servers to such an extent that they can no longer process legitimate network traffic because the attacks

---

* The resumé of the U.S. National Security Agency security consultant, in reference to these hacking activities by a government agency simply states the following: "Performed computer network scanning and reconnaissance. Identified weaknesses and vulnerabilities in computer networks. Executed numerous computer network exploitations against foreign targets" (O'Harrow, 2012a).

have saturated the network connectivity of the target. Such an attack then simulates a real user trying to use a web application by searching for content on the site and then cracks open the access to sensitive and confidential information databases of an organization. In other words, DDoS attack is often a mask for other information-stealing activities and designed to crash or damage the attacked website (Leach, 2013, pp. 1–2).

Hacking Data Breaches

According to Verizon's* Data Breach Investigations Report for 2011, more than 174 million data/information records were compromised in a total of 855 data breaches in what was called "an all-time low" for protection against data hacking breaches. Their report outlined that 96% of firms that were required to comply with the payment card industry data security standard and that fell victim to data breaches and as recorded in Verizon's own caseload from 2011, were "not compliant with the security standards." For its 2012 report, Verizon had analyzed[†] more than 47,000 reported security breach incidents and found that in 621 "confirmed data disclosures," at least 44 million records had been "compromised." Hacking was involved in more than half of these data disclosures. Furthermore, Verizon found that malware was present in 40% of the data disclosure cases, while 76% of all the investigated cases from 2012, "weak or stolen credentials" facilitated the network hacking intrusions. Moreover, criminal financial motives[‡] were the predominant single driver behind the data breaches, while 71% of cases involved the targeting of user devices (not only desktop computers but also mobile devices such as laptops, tablets, and smartphones—see the following for more details on mobile device vulnerabilities). With the growth and the proliferation of these mobile devices, Verizon expected the 2013 report on data breaches to show a similar exponential growth in their targeting. The 2012 report was also Verizon's first report to contain information on breaches resulting from state-affiliated cyberespionage[§] attacks. It was found that these types of cyberattacks had accounted for 20% of all of the reported data breaches covered by the report. What was even more worrying from a cybersecurity perspective was the fact

---

* Verizon is a computer software cybersecurity company.
† The analysis of these was not only based on the investigations done by Verizon's own RISK Team but also an amalgamation of the investigation reports by 18 other organizations from all over the world, including national computer emergency response teams and law enforcement agencies.
‡ Targets of this cybercrime were typically retail organizations, restaurants, food service-type firms, banks and financial institutions.
§ This kind of attack targets intellectual property, industrial and manufacturing information, as well as any military secret information the cyberspies can access and steal.

that in most cases (69%), the network intrusions and the data breaches were identified by external parties, such as ISPs, rather than the target organization experiencing the breach. In addition, Verizon found that in two-thirds of the cases, the breaches had taken months to be discovered and revealed to the organization's management (Anon., 2012, 2013).

Preventing and Combating Cybercrime

Insider Prevention

A key aspect of computer-related crime is the malicious tampering with computer data by disgruntled or dishonest employees. A virus can be manually entered onto a company's system and, for instance, spread through a retail chain's group of stores across the country, thereby damaging the company's computer network.

But because there is virtually no foolproof way of stopping a determined employee who wants to do harm to his/her employer, it is essential that a range of IT systems be put in place to track the electronic movement of each and every employee. This includes having access to their e-mail and keeping a watchful eye on their activities on the Internet (Workplace Staff, 2006).

How are these cybercrime practices combated? A company can install their own spyware on all computers on the company network, i.e., they can track the keystrokes of all employees and any activity via company networks, e.g., the source of viruses generated via company e-mail. Secondly, employing so-called cybersleuths who undertake periodic forensic investigations in the company for which they work. Once the cybersleuths have detected some cyberfraud or other cybercrime, a company should then immediately get in the experts who know exactly how to correctly (technically) download from a computer, a laptop, or a server digital evidence as well as within the parameters of the law requirements (legally) so that such digital evidence can be used in court to prosecute cybercriminals, i.e., use cyberforensics investigative methods to build a cybercase against a cybercriminal.

An additional security measure is the hardening of network and information security systems with the securing of networks and individual computers by means of sophisticated firewalls and antivirus software. Furthermore, security can be increased by the frequent (compulsory) changing of passwords by employees and IT administrators and allowing access to sensitive information only to selected individuals who have been background and integrity checked. A further security measure is the formulation of an effective company whistle-blowing policy, which needs to be in place (implemented other than just being a policy in a manual) so that honest employees can blow the whistle on their crooked colleagues.

However, the biggest weapon against cybercriminals who try to fraudulently obtain your banking, other financial, or ID details by e-mail or more recently via your cell phone, is your awareness. You would not give your ATM pin number to a stranger, so why would you share your private details with an unknown source on the Internet or cell phone? The same principle applies to all e-mails—deal only with credible and known sources. If you receive any e-mail from a retailer you have never heard of or agreed to receive mail from, delete it immediately. Whatever you do, do not click on any links in the e-mail message. Always be suspicious of e-mails with puzzling origins. Accordingly, it is important for employers to implement e-security awareness program for all employees especially on the use of the Internet and e-mails and the protocols to observe when surfing websites, i.e., not to click on and go to the website link in an e-mail, and to be wary of pop-ups.

Combating Cyberattacks

Cybersecurity

Cybersecurity typically refers to all organizational actions required to ensure protection from online danger of attacks, threats, and risk to the security of information in all its digital electronic forms and the security of the computer equipment, systems, and networks where information is stored, accessed, processed, and transmitted, including precautions taken to guard against crime, attack, sabotage, espionage, accidents, and failures.

Cyberdefense or what is now being termed *proactive cyberdefense* means acting in anticipation to oppose an attack against computers (and electronic devices such as smartphones, tablets, and iPads) and networks. Proactive cyberdefense will most often require additional cybersecurity from ISPs (see the study by the Department of Defense [DoD] [2013a]).

Cybersecurity also includes countermeasures against cyberattacks of all kinds. Some of these defensive or preventative measures include such techniques and information protection software as intrusion protection systems, preemptive blocks, and blacklisting; hunting within networks (actively searching for insiders and other adversaries or malware); passive and active intelligence (including law enforcement) employed to detect cyberthreats; and/or actions to temporarily isolate a system engaged in hostile cyberactivities. The so-called offensive countermeasures (as opposed to purely defensive strategies) might include electronic jamming or other negation measures intended to disrupt an adversary's cybercapabilities during the execution of the latter's cyberattack (DoD, 2013b).

In terms of DDoS attacks, according to the U.S. Department of Defense Cyber Command Unit, at least 85% of targeted cyberattacks could be prevented by organizations implementing four simple strategies:

1. Implementing so-called application whitelisting—the opposite of blacklisting—by creating a list of approved programs for running on all networked devices. This will prevent malicious software, malware, and other nonapproved programs from running on their network systems.
2. Regular network installation of so-called patches to all applications. These are designed to fix programs or update a computer system or software to prevent bugs and viruses by patching applications, operating systems, and web browsers. Patches are routinely provided by software developers for the secure running of their licensed programs.
3. Finally, minimize the number of users with administrative login privileges and implement strict accountabilities at each access level (Leathley, 2013).

But it is not as simple as that.

Difficulties of Stopping Hacker Cyberattacks

Installation of Specialized On-Premises Equipment

Instead of relying on existing firewalls (which cannot resist a powerful DDoS), individual organizations/companies need to purchase dedicated DDoS mitigation appliances and deploy them in their IT/data center. These are specialized hardware devices that are connected in front of their normal servers and routers and are specifically built to detect and filter the malicious traffic. But there are some fundamental problems with these devices.

1. They are very expensive and may sit around doing nothing until the organization's network is attacked. Not only that; they are expensive to operate. You need very skilled network and security specialists to work these devices.
2. They must be constantly updated with the latest threat analysis and detection programs. DDoS tactics change almost daily, and the mutations of attack modes are merely a reflection of how skilled professional cyberattackers have become. An organization's IT security team of specialists must be prepared to constantly update these devices to the latest threats. But that action is also dependent on

whether the vendor has also been active in patching and updating the system to keep up with the attacks.

3. These detection devices cannot also handle huge volume attacks. This is to do with an organization's existing bandwidth, so these hardware appliances do not do any good when a cyberattack exceeds the organization's network capacity (Leach, 2013, p. 2).

Cybersecurity Provision by Your Internet Service Provider

The next level up of cybersecurity is that provided by—and the responsibility of—ISPs. Some organizations and businesses use their ISP (i.e., the same network provider they get their bandwidth from) to provide network security against DDoS attacks. These ISPs usually have access to much more bandwidth than the organization itself and as such could then deal or deflect the big attack volumes of Internet traffic. But again, there are three key problems with these services, namely,

1. Lack of core competency: ISPs are in the business of selling bandwidth so are not in the habit of investing unnecessarily (in opposition to the maxim of maximizing their profit bottom line) the required capital and resources to stay ahead of the latest DDoS threats. Such cybersecurity funding outlays can become a nonreturn-on-investment cost center, i.e., something they have to provide to obtain or increase their business growth by selling more bandwidth time to users. In the provision of DDoS mitigation measures, ISPs, to be security effective in protecting their clients' information databases, have to be constantly aware, researching the latest threats, developing countermeasures, etc. This is *not* a service to do on the cheap, which unfortunately a lot of ISPs try to do as cheaply as possible, if at all.

2. Single- versus multiple-provider protection: Most enterprises today make use of two or more network providers in tandem in order to remove the single point of failure of one provider going down and taking the organization's/company's site with it. Having two or more providers is a best practice so that uptime, i.e., always being available to service clients, is maximized. But ISP network security measures against DDoS cyberattacks only protect the network links for which they are responsible for, not the other network provider links a company might be using (multiple networks is also the principle now being applied to multiple storage sites in the cloud). For decades, the cloud symbol has represented a network without divulging technical details. The symbol is used when only the points of entry and exit need to be identified. Inside the Internet cloud, there may be

any number of cables, routers, switches, and servers that handle the forwarding of data from one point to another, as well as the required data processing. In other words, cloud computing is a synonym for distributed computing over a network and means the ability to run a program on many connected computers at the same time. So now, the organization will need two or more DDoS prevention services, from two or more different network providers, thus doubling or tripling the costs of securing your network connections against cyberattacks.

3. No cloud protection: Similar to single-provider protection, a lot of web applications these days are split between enterprise-owned data centers and cloud services (so-called big data like Amazon AWS, GoGrid, Rackspace, etc.). ISPs simply cannot protect an organization's traffic to and from these cloud services (Leach, 2013, pp. 2–3).

Security Provision by Cloud Security Providers

The final level of cybersecurity is that provided by cloud service providers. These are the experts at providing network protection from the cloud against DDoS cyberattacks. This means that they have developed massive amounts of network bandwidth and DDoS mitigation capacity at multiple sites all over the Internet. This huge network/bandwidth capacity can take in any type of network traffic (whether the use is made of multiple ISPs, own data center, any number of cloud information storage service providers, etc.). Such cloud security providers typically scrub the Internet traffic for a client and send the clean traffic back toward an organization's information hub or data center.

Such cloud network security providers have the following benefits:

1. Expertise: Generally, these providers have any number of network and security engineers and researchers who are constantly monitoring for the latest DDoS tactics to better protect their customers (as a core service provision of a basket of cloud services).
2. Large amount of bandwidth: These providers have much more bandwidth than a single organization or business could provide on their own to stop the very big by volume cyberattacks.
3. Use of multiple types of DDoS mitigation hardware: DDoS attacks are extremely complex. There is a need for multiple layers of filtering to be able to keep up with the latest threats. Cloud providers essentially need to take advantage of multiple technologies, utilizing both commercial off-the-shelf and their own proprietary technology to defend against attacks (again, research and development

costs are a factor in making use of these advanced cybersecurity measures).

4. Border gateway protocol (BGP) or domain name service (DNS): In defending organizations against cyberattacks, such cloud cybersecurity providers take on the rerouted cyberattack Internet traffic initially destined for a customer's website either via the BGP, the protocol that manages all the routing on the Internet, or by the customer simply making a DNS change to point to the cloud service network provider. (The DNS translates Internet domain and host names to Internet protocol [IP] addresses. DNS automatically converts the names we type in our web browser address bar to the IP addresses of Web servers hosting those sites.) Once the Internet traffic hits a cloud-scrubbing center, it filters out the bad DDoS traffic and passes on the good traffic to clients—no matter where their site is hosted (Leach, 2013, pp. 2–3).

Cloud mitigation service providers have become the logical choice for organizations for their DDoS protection needs. They are the most cost-effective and scalable solution to keep up with the rapid advances in DDoS attacker tools and techniques (Leach, 2013, p. 3).

Concluding Remarks

It should be noted earlier the use of the term *mitigation*—one can never prevent a cyberattack but can only mitigate (lessen) its impact. One of the ways to do that is to be constantly alert and utilize intrusion detection software. In other words, the software program will alert the security center that a cyberattack (network intrusion) is underway. The scale of the impact is therefore lessened by the speed of the response or the counterattack measures taken. This speed factor again requires expensive services such as 24/7 live or real-time monitoring. Often, to break up or deflect a cyberattack, a network security provider can instruct an organization to immediately shutdown their server.

The bottom line is that any network cybersecurity system is only as good as its weakest link. Simple passwords for a PC or a mobile device for gaining access to an organization's network, local area network, or intranet are simply no longer sufficient. There is a need for the implementation and the use of additional cybersecurity measures. For example, utilizing biometrics, such as fingerprint, voice, or even iris and/or facial recognition software on a computing device. But mobile devices (and of course human beings on the inside) remain the most vulnerable routes for hacker intrusions.

References

Anon. 2012. *Data Breach Investigation Report 2011*. New York: Verizon. Accessed July 6, 2013. Retrieved from http://www.verizon.com./enterprise/2012dbir/us.

Anon. 2013. *Data Breach Investigation Report 2012*. New York: Verizon. Accessed July 6, 2013. Retrieved from http://www.verizon.com./enterprise/2013dbir/us.

Choo, K.-K. R. 2007, March. Zombies and botnets. *Trends & Issues in Crime and Criminal Justice*. No. 333. Canberra, Australia: Australian Institute for Criminology (AIC).

Kouri, J. 2005, December 15. Combating cyber crime and cyber terrorism. *World Security Network*. Accessed March 20, 2013. Retrieved from http://www.worldsecuritynet work.com/Other/Kouri-Jim-1/Combating-Cyber-Crime-and-Cyber-Terrorism.

Leach, S. 2013, June 12. DDoS Blog Series 1: Four Approaches to DDoS Protection. *Between the Dots*. [Sl]: Verisign. Accessed on June 20, 2013. Retrieved from http://blogs.verisign.com/blog/entry/ddos_blog_series_1_4.

Leathley, S. 2013, August. Fighting back against cybercrime. *Risk Management*. Accessed August 13, 2013. Retrieved from http://www.riskmanagementmagazine .com.au/article/fighting-back-against-cyber-crime-178046.aspx.

Minnaar, A. 2008. "You've received a greeting e-card from....": The changing face of cybercrime e-mail spam scams. *Acta Criminologica: South African Journal of Criminology*. CRIMSA 2007 Conference Special Edition No. 2: 92–116.

Moore, R. 2011. *Cybercrime: Investigating high technology computer crime*. Second edition. Burlington, MA: Elsevier/Anderson Publishing.

O'Harrow, R. 2012a, June 2. Zero day: The threat in Cyberspace—Digital universe riddled with holes. *The Washington Post* (Special Report). Accessed June 5, 2012. Retrieved from http://www.washingtonpost.com/investigations/understanding-cyberspace -is-key-to-defending-against-digital-attacks/2012/06/02/gJQAsIr19U_story.html.

O'Harrow, R. 2012b, June 3. Zero day: The threat in cyberspace—Cyber search engine Shodan exposes industrial control systems to new risks. *The Washington Post* (Special Report). Accessed June 5, 2012. Retrieved from http://www.washington post.com/investigations/cyber-search-engine-exposes-vulnerabilities/2012 /06/03/gJQAIK9KCV_story_1.html.

Poplak, R. 2013, June 12. Edward Snowden prism and the privacy we never had. *Mail & Guardian*. Accessed June 14, 2012. Retrieved from http://mg.co.za/article /2013-06-12-edward-snowden-prism-and-the-privacy-we-never-had.

Savage, C. 2013, August 15. Manning, facing prison for leaks, apologizes at court-martial trial. *New York Times*. Accessed August 18, 2013. Retrieved from http:// www.nytimes.com/2013/08/15/us/manning-apologizes-for-leaks-my-actions -hurt-people.html?nl=todaysheadlines&emc=edit_th_20130815&_r=0.

Sutherland, E. H. 1949. *White Collar Crime*. New York: Dryden Press.

U.S. Department of Defense (DOD). 2013a. Department of Defense Dictionary of Military and Associated Terms. JP 1-02. Washington, DC: U.S. Department of Defence. Accessed July 27, 2013. Retrieved from http://www.dtic.mil/doctrine /new_pubs/jp1_02.pdf.

U.S. Department of Defense. 2013b. The cyberdomain: Security and operations. Washington, DC: U.S. Department of Defence. Accessed July 27, 2013. Retrieved from http://www.defense.gov/home/features/2013/0713_cyberdomain/.

Workplace Staff. 2006, August 28. Compu-crime costs SA economy R40bn. *Independent Online*. Accessed October 6, 2006. Retrieved from http://www.iol.co.za.

Intelligence Analysis: A Key Tool for Modern Police Management
The Romanian Perspective

7

SORINA-MARIA COFAN
AUREL-MIHAIL BĂLOI

Contents

Abstract

Intelligence analyst, as a properly defined occupation, has enriched the Romanian labor market since early 2012. Following a one-year scientific-based research, a consortium of governmental agencies, private companies, and academic institutions, hosted by the Institute for Studies on Public Order, established the intelligence analyst's National Occupational Standard (NOS), which defines needed skills and abilities, professional key requests, quality benchmarks, and evaluation tools. The partnership built around the new occupation has generated a strong synergy between professionals from police, army, intelligence services, private sectors, and the education field. Romanian crime intelligence analysts belong now to a socioprofessional area with their own identity and statute on the labor market. This chapter describes the philosophy setting behind the new intelligence analyst NOS, as well as useful experiences and lessons to learn that may inspire other similar initiatives.

Decision-Making Process in the Police and the Relationship with Crime Intelligence Analysis

> Commander, our request for additional police forces in the public safety area no. 23 was rejected! Latest drafts on events reported by the citizens in this area continue to validate the rising crime trend. What are your orders? ...

Fifteen years ago, in the Romanian public order forces context, it might have been likely for the management to take a decision based on personal experience. Operational solutions were built mostly on a commander's professional experience and sometimes on his closest advisers' experience. Occasionally, it worked, but there were good managers and less good managers and the same were their professional decisions.

We like to believe that nowadays' answer to the mentioned question is "ask intelligence analysis unit to submit for the following management meeting, a tactical assessment for public safety area no. 23, to understand better the phenomenon, identify possible targets (key suspects) and establish action priorities."

Both good managers and less good managers are likely to be found in the police, as they were 15 years ago. But today, they all have intelligence analysis units at their hand, to substantiate their decisions. These specialists have implemented operational and professional standards that provide managers with additional guarantees for the effectiveness and the increased quality of the police public safety services offered to the citizens.

Although the situation described earlier gives only one common picture that is multiplied at the operational management level, we believe that the change should occur in this specific component of the public order forces, willing to become part of the intelligence-led policing era.

In our days and 15 years ago, the managerial process consisted of decision—action—monitoring and evaluation—analysis (DAMA) (see Figure 7.1). What makes the difference today is the institutionalization of the management process, once it appeared professionalized departments to achieve each mentioned step. From the DAMA process perspective in the modern police era, the main focus is on the relationship between decision and action. There are some institutional improvements that increase police efficiency in the action stage: professionalization of the police investigation units, investments in the crime scene forensic research instruments,

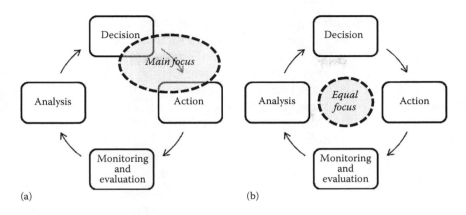

Figure 7.1 Focus in the modern police era (a) and intelligence-led policing era (b).

or special operations performance (catch in the act, electronic operative surveillance, rapid response, etc.).

Each police officer or manager in their daily activity takes decisions, acts to put them into practice, assesses their results and then, through simple analysis of processes, documents their future decisions. This DAMA process exists in the police from the simple street cop to the highest levels in an organization. The quality of the process differs. How can a police officer or a manager (at any level) make decisions quickly and correctly?

Under the impact of the information age and the Gordon E. Moore's* law of technology development, intelligence analysis units take on a key role in the decision-making process of the policing managerial process by providing professional services in order to obtain knowledge concerning the criminal phenomena, the suspects, the institutional capabilities, and the community served by the police.

A balanced approach is needed on each DAMA stage. Monitoring and evaluation play a decisive role in ensuring institutional health. In our days, police have specialized institutional performance assessment units to identify the organization alignment with the objectives set by the strategies. For the analysis stage, intelligence analysis units were developed.

Looking Back on the Historical Evolution of the Romanian Police Intelligence Analysis

The Romanian police system evolved similarly to most police evolutionary models around the world. It requires continuous adaptation and response

---

* Moore's law is the observation that, over the history of computing hardware, the number of transistors on integrated circuits doubles approximately every two years (Wikipedia, 2013).

to the challenges of criminal phenomenon, which is closely related to socio-cultural, political, and technological development of society. With an institutional tradition of more than half a millennium, the Romanian police system has diversified over time, according to the Romanian society, and has evolved from a coercive instrument of the state to a public service, with multiple functions. Romanian police responsibilities cover a wide range of activities, from checking of identity and ensuring public order and public safety to investigating economic crimes, cybercrimes, and most complex forms of organized and transborder crimes.

The year 1903 is a significant milestone in the development of modern Romanian police. At that time, it adopted the first police organic law, the law on the Organization of the General State Police (Cârjan, 2000), drafted by the interior minister of that time, Vasile Lascăr—the organizer of the Romanian police. At that time, information exchanges were not common for law enforcement; police were documenting criminal activities in the competence area and using information with immediate possibilities of exploitation.

Information processing began to be used in policing after the Second World War (Şinca, 2006), especially on serious crimes committed by criminal groups. This early process of intelligence analysis contributes to the police investigation by obtaining information and clues that could be converted into evidence. In the current police activities, the first manual records in card indexes related to identity, fingerprints, and convictions were created and used.

In the communist era, the boundary between illegal and against state security was almost nonexistent. Militia conducted intrusive* activities not always obeying the constitutional rights of the citizens. What we would call today *intelligence*† was nothing but a pile of folders containing a collection of raw information, recorded in reports, about people who were believed to be criminals or their associates or individuals considered to be a threat to national security or to the communist system of that time. All these activities investigated in these files were suspected and not yet proved. Beyond the normative acts of the time, early information initiatives lacked explicit direction and were shrouded in a mystery aura. State secret was exacerbated, and it was proceeding to excessive classification of documents.

After the 1990s, informative police actions were directed against serious crime, crimes committed with violence, and organized crime. The lessons learned during the communist period have led to significant care related to recorded intelligence activities. Intelligence is now collected, stored,

* Wiretaps, surveillance, investigations (after the Soviet model), interrogations and searches, violation of the correspondence secret, etc.
† With the meaning generally accepted, given by the definition "information (knowledge) for action," (*Strategic Intelligence Analysis Course*, 2002).

analyzed, and disseminated in a manner that corresponds to international legal corpus.*

Today's police are facing huge amounts of data that require processing and analysis to provide a useful situational picture to support the decision-making process. In this context, storing, processing, and analyzing information is an intrinsic necessity for the police.

The emergence of large urban areas facilitates anonymity for offenders. The free movement of people, goods, and cash has brought increased mobility of perpetrators. New modus operandi appeared, and individuals can be harmed from thousands of miles away, the contact between offenders and victims no longer being required. Highly specialized, hierarchical criminal organizations have developed that require the establishment of new police structures with interdisciplinary skills, flexible and able to investigate their activities. At this juncture, international police cooperation even on intercontinental space, intelligence analysis, and information exchange become essential in ensuring crime control. An individual state approach in combating organized crime, continually expanding and diversifying, would not make any sense.

We witness substantial growth and diversification of crime, and volume crime concept occurs. A one-to-one investigation for each offense committed is no longer possible, but proactive approaches to undermine the criminal enterprises and targeted interventions in hot spot areas. Intelligence analysis plays a decisive role. As a result, a new professional community appeared, intelligence analysts, consisting of experts with special skills and training (Richards, 1999), able to develop meanings and understandings from raw information. This supports investigative activities and the decision-making process by applying a specialized body of methods and techniques. Intelligence analysts support the police to prioritize all activities on special action directions, undertaken to institutionally assumed goals.

By using the latest technology in crime intelligence analysis, these departments can help police units maintain and improve the role they have taken in the society. Recent technological breakthroughs in global

---

* Stockholm Programme: An open and secure Europe serving and protecting citizens (2010/C 115/01) (EUR-Lex) (European Council, 2010); Hague Programme: Strengthening freedom, security and justice in the European Union (2005/C 53/01) (EUR-Lex) (European Council, 03.03.2005); Prüm Convention (Council of the European Union, 07.07.2005); "The European Code of Police Ethics," Recommendation Rec(2001)10 adopted by the Ministers Committee of the European Council on 19.01.2001 (The Ministers Committee of the European Council, 19.01.2001); Council Framework Decision 2008/977/JHA of 27.11.2008 on the protection of personal data processed in the framework of police and judicial cooperation in criminal matters (EUR-Lex) (European Council, 27.11.2008); Council Framework Decision 2006/960/JHA on simplifying the exchange of information and intelligence between law enforcement authorities of the Member States of the European Union (The Swedish Initiative) (EUR-Lex) (European Council, 18.12.2006).

communications are a challenge to every segment of the society to become part of a wider culture, which eventually includes the whole world. Intelligence analysis is only a small wheel in the huge machinery, and the results it brings can affect extensive areas of activity, as all parts of the whole being increasingly interconnected.

Intelligence analysis is developing as an interdisciplinary domain, using techniques and tools from sciences (mathematics, statistics, topography, social sciences, etc.), information technology, banking, finance, etc., all in response to the diversification challenges of today's complex crime, itself multidisciplinary (cybercrime, human and drugs trafficking, dual-use* military goods and technology trafficking, financial engineering and refined forms of corruption, copyright infringement and economic espionage, terrorism, etc.). The principal need to share becomes top priority and shows its superior benefits to the need to know one, with a long tradition in the policing activity.

In order to have a viable development, law enforcement intelligence analysts community should evolve in close relations and as part of the Romanian intelligence analysts' community, and connected to the European and the international ones.

International Framework of Intelligence Analysis on the Labor Market

First works on the conceptualization of intelligence analysis have existed since the first half of the twentieth century, having Sherman Kent as the protagonist, often called the father of intelligence analysis (Wikipedia, 27.02.2016). Sherman Kent was the first person to show the importance of establishing standards and best practices for both defining the concepts in intelligence analysis and setting up professional relationships between analysts and beneficiaries.

Kent also highlighted the importance of the valorization of the senior analysts' experience and the need to study the changes in intelligence as a result of technological, social, and conceptual evolution in the field (Davis, 2002).

Occupations† practiced on the labor market are recorded in national classifications of occupations, according to the International Standard Classification of Occupations (ISCO).

---

* Civil and military.
† The meaning of this term, and all the technical ones concerning the labor market regulations, is in accordance with the following normative: ISCO-08: Recommendations 2008/C111/01/CE of European Parliament and Council (23.04.2008); Law no. 1/2011 of National Education (10.01.2011) and Common Order of the Ministry of Labor and Social Solidarity and National Institute of Statistics no. 270/273/12.06.2002 regarding the procedure for updating COR Nomenclature (12.06.2002/18.06.2002).

ISCO organizes occupations into groups and subgroups by the activities undertaken within the occupation. The reasons for developing this classification are common international standards for reporting, comparing, and data exchanging in occupational area, national/regional development model for the classification of occupations, and a system that can be used by countries that have not developed their own classification system of occupations. ISCO also facilitates and manages workforce migration between states, according to the international labor market needs and the development of training programs for adults.

Without claiming an exhaustive description, we present the following situational setting picture in the field of intelligence analysis, within a few representative states:

1. Australia and New Zealand—Australian and New Zealand Standard Classification of Occupations (ANZSCO, 2008)

   ANZSCO contains eight major groups: 1 Managers, 2 Professionals, 3 Technicians and Trades Workers, 4 Community and Personal Service Workers, 5 Clerical and Administrative Workers, 6 Sales Workers, 7 Machinery Operators and Drivers, and 8 Laborers.

   In the second major group, Professionals, in the sub-major group 22 (business, human resource, and marketing professionals groups), the minor group 224, information and organization professionals, can be found and is described in Table 7.1.

2. Canada—The National Occupational Classification 2011 (NOC, 2011)

   NOC contains 10 major groups: 0 Management Occupations, 1 Business, Finance, and Administration Occupations, 2 Natural and Applied Sciences and Related Occupations, 3 Health Occupations, 4 Occupations in Education, Law and Social, Community and Government Services, 5 Occupations in Art, Culture, Recreation, and Sport, 6 Sales and Service Occupations, 7 Trades, Transport, and Equipment Operators and Related Occupations, 8 Natural Resources, Agriculture Production, and Related Occupations, and 9 Occupations in Manufacturing and Utilities.

   By searching the NOC, you can find no less than 277 occupations containing the word *analyst* in the title, but none of it is *intelligence analyst*. Among this occupations we mention those listed in Table 7.2.

3. United States—Standard Occupational Classification (SOC, 2010)

   SOC has 23 major groups (for example, 11-0000 Management Occupations, 13-0000 Business and Financial Operations Occupations, 15-0000 Computer and Mathematical Occupations, 17-0000 Architecture and Engineering Occupations, 19-0000 Life,

Table 7.1 **Detailed Description of Minor Group 224 "Information and Organization Professionals"**

Minor Group	Main Group	Occupations	Specializations	Skill Level[a]
224 Information and Organization Professionals	2244 Intelligence and Policy Analysts	224411 Intelligence Officer	Criminal Intelligence Analyst	1
			Defense Intelligence Analyst	
		224412 Policy Analyst/ Policy Adviser	Research and Evaluation Analyst	1
	2247 Management and Organization Analysts	224711 Management Consultant/ Business Consultant	Business Analyst	1
		224712 Organization and Methods Analyst/ Procedures Analyst	Change Management Facilitator	1
			Industry Analyst	1
			Quality Auditor	1
			Skills Auditor	1

[a] ANZSCO skill level 1—Qualification of a bachelor's degree or higher; at least five years of relevant experience may substitute for the formal qualification. In some instances, relevant experience and/or on-the-job training may be required in addition to the formal qualification.

Physical, and Social Science Occupations, 21-0000 Community and Social Services Occupations, and 23-0000 Legal Occupations).

In the SOC, one can find 34 types of analysts as listed in Table 7.3.

4. United Kingdom—Standard Occupational Classification 2010 (SOC, 2010)

SOC 2010 consists of nine major groups: 1 Managers, Directors, and Senior Officials, 2 Professional Occupations, 3 Associate Professional and Technical Occupations, 4 Administrative and Secretarial Occupations, 5 Skilled Trades Occupations, 6 Caring, Leisure, and Other Service Occupations, 7 Sales and Customer Service Occupations, 8 Process, Plant, and Machine Operatives, 9 Elementary Occupations.

In the second major group, sub-major group 24 Business, Media, and Public Service Professionals, sub-major group 242 Business, Research, and Administrative Professionals are the following unit groups and related occupations (Table 7.4).

Various field analysis specialists expressed the need of setting quality benchmarks for their work and some training criteria, minimum knowledge needed to practice the occupation, all included in the curricula of initial and specialization training.

Table 7.2   Few Types of Analysts According to Canadian NOC

Unit Group	Occupations
• 1112 Financial and investment analysts	• Financial analyst • Investment analyst • Securities analyst
• 1221 Administrative officers	• Administration analyst • Records analyst—Access to information
• 2161 Mathematicians, statisticians, and actuaries	• Statistical analyst • Artificial intelligence analyst
• 2172 Database analysts and data administrators	• Data mining analyst • Data warehouse analyst • Database analyst • Information resource analyst
• 4162 Economists and economic policy researchers and analysts	• Economic analyst • Risk management analyst
• 4164 Social policy researchers, consultants, and program officers	• Immigration policy analyst
• 4169 Other professional occupations in social science, not elsewhere classified	• Handwriting analyst
• 5123 Journalists	• News analyst • Political analyst—Radio or television
• 6561 Image, social, and other personal consultants	• Color analyst, fashion

In this circumstance, during the period 2003–2004, the International Association of Law Enforcement Intelligence Analysts (IALEIA), at the request of the Global Justice Information Sharing Initiative (Global), the Global Intelligence Working Group (GIWG) initiated and coordinated the drafting of the "Law Enforcement Analytic Standards" (IALEIA, November 2004). These working sessions brought together numerous contributors from the United States, Canada, and the UK law enforcement agencies, as follows: IALEIA members, International Association of Chiefs of Police members, representatives of the US Drug Enforcement Administration, National Drug Intelligence Center, Central Intelligence Agency, FBI, and other volunteers interested in the field.

At the end of 2004, GIWG approved the "Law Enforcement Analytic Standards" under the Global Advisory Council. In April 2012, these standards were updated (IALEIA, April 2012) and include recommendations for analyst managers, standards for analysts (analytic attributes, education, basic training, continuing education and advanced training, professional development, certification, professional liaison, leadership), standards for analytical processes (standards for each stage of the information cycle), standards

Table 7.3   Few Types on Analysts According to United States SOC

Major Group	Occupations
13-0000 Business and Financial Operations Occupations	131081 Analysts, Logistics
	131111 Analysts, Business Management
	131111 Analysts, Industrial
	131111 Analysts, Management
	131111 Analysts, Program
	131141 Analysts, Job
	131161 Analysts, Market Research
	132031 Analysts, Budget
	132031 Analysts, Cost
	132041 Analysts, Credit
	132041 Analysts, Credit Assessment
	132041 Analysts, Credit Risk
	132051 Analysts, Corporate Financial
	132051 Analysts, Corporate Securities Research
	132051 Analysts, Financial
	132051 Analysts, Institutional Commodity
	132053 Analysts, Insurance
	132072 Analysts, Collection
15-0000 Computer and Mathematical Occupations	151121 Analysts, Applications
	151121 Analysts, Computer Systems
	151121 Analysts, Data Processing Systems
	151121 Analysts, Information Systems
	151122 Analysts, Information Security
	151122 Analysts, Network Security
	152021 Analysts, Cryptographic Vulnerability
	152031 Analysts, Operations
	152031 Analysts, Operations Research
	152031 Analysts, Procedure
	152031 Analysts, Process
	152041 Analysts, Statistical
	152099 Analysts, Harmonic
19-0000 Life, Physical, and Social Science Occupations	193011 Analysts, Economic Research
	194011 Analysts, Seed
27-0000 Arts, Design, Entertainment, Sports, and Media Occupations	273021 Analysts, Broadcast News

for analytical products (analytic accuracy, analytic product content, analytic product format, analytic report, data source attribution, analytic feedback, and product evaluation, presentations, and testimony).

Based on the law enforcement analytic standards, the U.S. Department Enforcement Analyst Certification Standards" (January 2010). The same institution has developed the "Minimum Criminal Intelligence Training Standards for Law Enforcement and Other Criminal Justice Agencies in the United States" (October 2007) that sets benchmarks of the initial training of specialists in criminal intelligence (intelligence analyst, intelligence

Table 7.4   Unit Groups and Related Occupation According to UK SOC 2010

Unit Group	Occupations
2135 IT business analysts, architects, and systems designers	Analyst, Business, IT
	Analyst, Business
	Analyst, Comms, data
	Analyst, Comms, technical
	Analyst, Communications, data
	Analyst, Computer
	Analyst, Maintenance
	Analyst, Operations
	Analyst, System
	Analyst, Systems
	Analyst, Technical
	Analyst, Telecommunications
	Analyst, Voice, Communications
	Analyst, Warehouse, data
2136 Programmers and Software Development Professionals	Analyst, Data
	Analyst, Database
	Analyst, Implementation
	Analyst, Information
	Analyst, Project, IT
	Analyst, Software
	Analyst, Technology, Information
	Analyst
	Analyst, Programmer
2423 Management Consultants and Business Analysts	Analyst, Business
	Analyst, Commercial
	Analyst, Risk, Financial
	Analyst, Risk
	Analyst, Trading
2425 Actuaries, Economists, and Statisticians	Analyst, Economic
	Analyst, Political
	Analyst, Quantitative
	Analyst, Statistical
2426 Business and Related Research Professionals	Analyst, Computer, forensic
	Analyst, Crime
	Analyst, Information
	Analyst, Intelligence, criminal

manager/commander, law enforcement executive, general law enforcement officers—basic refresher criminal intelligence and criminal intelligence, criminal intelligence officer, train-the-trainer).

Another institutional regulatory initiative, in intelligence analysis, belongs to the Commission on Accreditation for Law Enforcement Agencies (CALEA, July 2006), the only internationally recognized body for the accreditation of law enforcement agencies. Chapter 15 of the "Standards for Law Enforcement Agencies," issued by CALEA, provides the guidelines for the development of institutional policies in intelligence analysis within law enforcement agencies.

In the United Kingdom, Skills for Justice has developed in 2006 the occupational standard for intelligence analyst occupation that defines and describes 10 professional competences (from CM1: Discuss and Develop terms of reference for an intelligence analysis product to CM10: Review the role of an intelligence analysis technique in the organization [Skills for Justice, April 2006]).

This standard applies to intelligence analysts within law enforcement institutions in the United Kingdom.

In the European Union, Frontex has developed the Common Integrated Risk Analysis model with the view of providing support to their own and a Member States analysts activity. This standard establishes the conceptual and methodological frameworks for the development of risk analysis in Frontex and the European Union Member States border police, in order to ensure the effectiveness of the European border security.

Bernard Besson (27.10.2006) posted an article on the *Economic Intelligence* blog, entitled "The New Jobs List Created by the Economic Intelligence," where the author identifies on the French labor market the emergence of several new jobs, including an analyst in the field of economic intelligence. The analyst is defined as a "person or entity acting at the request or by its own initiative, full or part time, doing a validation, interpretation and analysis activities in the private or public sector, in one or more areas of expertise. The analyst contributes to the performance, innovation, prevention of risks and threats and to protect the organization."

Standardization initiatives for intelligence analysts' activity, mentioned earlier, are addressed to the analysts' communities from certain activity areas, and they are most often targeted at law enforcement agencies.

Intelligence Analyst Occupation in the Context of the Romanian Labor Market

Legal Framework of Qualifications

The Romanian labor market is governed by a legislative body internationally harmonized with the specific legislation in this field. The occupations practiced on the labor market are registered by the Ministry of Labor, Family, Social Protection and Elderly People and coded in the Romanian Occupations Classification (COR) Nomenclature divided into nine major groups, sub-major group, minor groups, and basic groups, depending on the level of education required for practicing the profession and the level of competence (Ministry of Labor and Social Solidarity and the National Statistics

Institute, 12.06.2002/18.06.2002, article). Every occupation receives a unique code of six digits.

The use of the COR code is mandatory (Ministry of Labor and Social Solidarity and the National Statistics Institute, 12.06.2002/18.06.2002, article 3) for all state institutions, businesses companies, trade unions, professional and political organizations, nongovernment organizations, individuals, and legal persons. The COR's updating (Ministry of Labor and Social Solidarity and the National Statistics Institute, 12.06.2002/18.06.2002, article 5) is made by the Ministry of Labor by the user organizations' request, in accordance with the changes in the structure of the national economy, the national and international laws in force concerning the regulation of new functions, and the professions and occupations on the labor market.

In order to perform an occupation on the labor market, a person must prove the qualification in a particular field.

The National Qualifications Authority (ANC) (Romanian Parliament 05.01.2011, article 340) is the state authority entitled to develop, implement, and update the National Qualifications Framework (CNC). In this purpose ANC manages the National Qualifications Registry and the National Adult Training Providers Registry.

CNC is a tool used for the classification of qualifications according to a set of criteria associated to the specified levels of learning achieved. CNC aims to integrate and coordinate national qualifications subsystems and improve transparency, access, progression, and quality of qualifications in relation to the labor market and the civil society.

CNC implements in Romania the provisions of Recommendation 2008/C111/01/CE of European Parliament and Council on the establishment of the European Qualifications Framework (EQF) for lifelong learning. CNC lays down the acquisition, the development, and the recognition of knowledge, skill, and competence conditions for Romanian citizens, thus facilitating their access to employment and equal opportunities for employment. The harmonization of CNC with the EQF ensures labor mobility, not only on the Romanian labor market but also on the European one, the qualifications obtained in Romania becoming comparable and equivalent to those existent in all other European countries.

Occupational standards and/or training standards are developed for the existing occupations in the COR Nomenclature. They establish the units of competence and achievement criteria associated with the outcome of the activities described by the elements of competency and how to fulfill them, the contexts of activities, and the necessary knowledge to accomplish them.

In order to exercise an occupation, one can gain professional competencies by participating in an authorized training program based on occupational/training standards, delivered by a certified training provider. The professional competencies validation is achieved by passing the final/

qualification examination in front of an ANC-authorized commission. Approved occupational/training standards become valuable tools for training and evaluation of providers. The training curricula as well as a series of tests to be applied to the applicants to prove the possession of the given competences are currently being developed on these standards.

Depending on the training program and the training forms, authorized training providers will issue (Romanian Government, 31.08.2000, article 31, paragraph 1) professional qualification certificates at the end of the qualification or requalification courses and graduation certificates for initial, improving, and specialization training. After the assessment of professional competences acquired in nonformal and informal ways (Romanian Government, 31.08.2000, article 5; paragraph 2), authorized skills assessment centers will issue certificates of professional competence. The effects resulting from owning a certificate are similar and provide the holder with a formal recognition of the professional competences required for the performance of existing occupations on the Romanian and European labor markets.

The Recognition of Intelligence Analyst Occupation on Labor Market and the Drafting of the Occupational Standard

The intelligence analyst occupation has been recognized on the Romanian labor market and is registered in the COR (Ministry of Labor and Social Solidarity and the National Statistics Institute, 25.01.2013/01.02.2013), through a process initiated in the spring of 2012 by the Ministry of Home Affairs, a process that was brought together in a working group of leading experts from main law enforcement institutions, national security and defense, education, and Romanian private sector. A year later, the group has managed to developed and get ANC approval* for the "Intelligence Analyst Occupational Standard" (Ministry of Home Affairs, 04.04.2013), for which two qualifications are associated: Intelligence Analyst (COR code 242224) and Intelligence Assistant Analyst (COR code 413207).

What is unique about this approach of defining intelligence analyst occupation in Romania is the interinstitutional approach, which integrates different perspectives of home affairs stakeholders, as well as from intelligence, defense, money laundering-combating, business, and education. For many years, they all have been challenged with the conceptual definition of *intelligence analysis*. Each of the institutions involved have lived in the last 10 years of internal transformations in information management (Matei and Nițu, 2012), aiming to achieve high performance and to develop coherent politics on medium and long terms.

---

* ANC Decision no. 122/04.12.2013.

In the context of accelerating and diversifying global information exchange, facilitated by the technological and economic booms of the recent decades, and the free movement of people, goods, and cash, the activity of intelligence analysts, both in the state and business sectors, has evolved and adapted to the latest challenges. Thus, the emerging national and international needs for cooperation between analysts from various public and private entities and bringing the means of expression used to a common standard are now topics of interest.

In this way, the need to express a unitary vision in the field of intelligence analysis, including the definition of a conceptual corpus in the domain, valid in all sectors of the labor market where intelligence analysts work, and the development of a coherent training system and recruitment criteria of these specialists were outlined.

According to this, intelligence analyst represents* the employee with bachelor degrees, in charged with duties like collection, evaluation, collation, and analysis of information from various sources, which provide their beneficiaries[†] with conclusions, assumptions, estimations, and predictions required for the fulfillment of organizational goals and objectives.

The requirements to carry out the intelligence analyst occupation[‡] tasks are as follows:

1. Long-term higher education attested by a diploma or equivalent
2. Specialized training in national[§] and international specialized courses in the field or postuniversity courses in the domain
3. Knowledge in areas such as computer operating, foreign languages, statistics, etc.
4. Skills of assessment capability, analysis and synthesis, flexibility in thinking, responsiveness, forecasting, analytical and conceptual thinking, cleverness, foresight, self-control, ability to use large amounts of data/information, focus, autodidact; good oral and written expression; exigency, objectivity, critical thinking, self-critical, consistency, dedication, observation spirit, communication skills, ability to plan working activities, opportunity and efficiency; and skills to perform research and investigations

---

* Explanatory Memorandum to introduce intelligence analyst occupation in COR, page 3, submitted to the Ministry of Labor, Family, Social Protection and Elderly People.
† *Beneficiary* is a concept that includes both the client that have asked for the analytical product and the people that will use its results. An important criterion on accepting a certain category of analysis (strategic) is to have more than one beneficiary.
‡ Intelligence analyst occupation description, page 4, submitted to the Ministry of Labor, Family, Social Protection and Elderly People to approve the introduction of this occupation in COR.
§ ANC-approved training programs for intelligence analyst occupation.

5. Attitudes of willingness to work in teams, sociability, discretion, ability to work under time pressure and stress, strength and mental stability, timeliness and accountability in the performance of assigned tasks; irreproachable moral conduct, responsibility, initiative, innovation of activity (consistent guidance on what should be changed in order to improve the accomplishment of the tasks), and availability to change; perseverance.

The development of the "Intelligence Analysts Occupational Standard" has focused on the analytical process, which is the common issue for all participant institutions. Even though the institutions use different types of specific information (financial, banking and national security, social, political, policing, statistics, etc.), they all have not been the subject of the debate.

In the first stage, data were collected from occupational area through the following methods, as established in the working group: focus group, job description study, existing international* standards study, and expert roundtable. The "Occupational Analysis," a document subject of verification and validation by the Administration and Public Services Sectoral† Committee experts, was afterwards developed.

In the second stage, based on the "Occupational Analysis," the "Occupational Standard" and its associated qualifications were drafted, which then became a subject of verification and validation by the aforementioned sectoral committee and approved by the ANC.

The "Occupational Standard" identifies 10 competences for intelligence analysts, as follows:

General:
    Unit 1: Apply quality procedures
Specific:
    Unit 1: Planning analysis-circumscribed activities
    Unit 2: Documenting the jurisdiction issues
    Unit 3: Creating an information database necessary to perform analysis
    Unit 4: Processing data and information
    Unit 5: Applying analytical methods and techniques
    Unit 6: Developing analytical products
    Unit 7: Evaluating analytical product

---

* The United States and the United Kingdom.
† Sectoral committees are institutions of social dialogue, public utility, with legal personality, organized under Law no. 132/1999 (Romanian Parliament, 20.07.1999) with subsequent amendments, the industries defined by the collective bargaining agreement. At an industry level, it can be a single sectoral committee.

Unit 8: Establishing the ways of using the analytical product
Unit 9: Providing expertise

Benefits of the Conceptualization
of Intelligence Analyst Occupation

The registration of intelligence analyst in the COR and the setting-up of the "Occupational Standard" represent the first and one of the most important step on the way to its nationwide conceptualization. From now on, the professional identity of this specialists and their belongingness to a well-defined socioprofessional community are tangible.

Over the time, Romanian institutions have adopted different models and concepts of intelligence analysis. Consequently, confusion has often appeared when bringing together interinstitutional working groups. A sort of cold distance kept the institutions away from each other, as a result.

Besides the recognition of the intelligence analyst occupation and the development of the "Occupational Standard," all stakeholders involved found a good opportunity to meet, negotiate, and harmonize their position around a so-called Romanian model, which has then been validated by well-known international experts.

The existence of an occupational standard for intelligence analyst set up a new beginning in the training area, by defining the milestones a professional must reach in order to perform a good job. Quality standards, practical skills, theoretical knowledge, and attitudes desirable for these professionals* are also highlighted. It should be emphasized, however, that the simple existence of suitable, updated training curricula cannot guarantee by itself the high performance of intelligence analysts. The way the recruitment of these specialists is done is equally responsible for that. Certain native skills, along with professional ethics and loyalty are essential when these specialists step on the way of training in intelligence analysis. A sound knowledge about institutional activities, policies, goals and objectives, information, and working flows are paramount for specialized well-tailored training. Quite often located in the close proximity of the decision making process, the analyst needs to develop the ability to see both the overview and the detailed picture. Readiness for innovative approaches and flexibility of thought must be constantly maintained.

Moreover, the official recognition on the labor market of this occupation helps intelligence analysts to find themselves as parts of a new professional community, which opens windows toward individual growth by idea exchanges

---

* Methodology for development and revision of occupational standards and qualifications is available at http://www.cnfpa.ro/Files/phare/Metodologia%20M2.pdf.

during conferences, roundtables, workshops, and other scientific events. A nationwide network facilitates the practice exchanges among people who understand the power of a common approach and agree to put an end to professional isolation by establishing professional contacts and providing mutual support. Such a support was offered by Intergraph Computer Services (INGR)* to the Ministry of Home Affairs with the view of setting up the Geospatial Laboratory in ISOP—a common effort together with the American consortium Intergraph. The lab is planning to conduct training and research activities, using the latest geographic information system technology. Activities are carried out together with INGR specialists, both institutions supporting each other through experience exchanges and knowledge transfer.

At the same time, a group of more than 40 national intelligence analysts, from almost all fields of activity, contributes to the first compendium-like volume published in Romania (Maior and Nitu, 2013).

Nevertheless, the analysts from police, border police, intelligence department, anticorruption general directorate, and ISOP designed and piloted the first integrated course on intelligence analysis based on the "Occupational Standard." The course was received enthusiastically by both the analysts and the top management of the beneficiary institutions.

Training-provider institutions can evolve as scientific environments in which high expertise specialists are included. Research outcomes could then be tested and validated in daily basis activities, while knowledge obtained could be disseminated to the entire professional community to increase their efficiency.

The legitimacy on labor market for practitioners in this field, the mobility of labor force from a region to another in accordance with the social–economic needs, and a common language for the analysts, are all additional benefits of this approach.

Perspectives—A Community of Specialists

Although the process started as a working group of colleagues from various institutions, motivated to give recognition to their occupation, it is now growing to a professional association, which aims to extend the cooperation toward similar international associations (IALEIA, IACA, IPES, etc.)—a way to promote professional interests of analysts, an opportunity to access specialized training programs in the field, a platform to support idea exchanges and career development. This associative framework may support partnerships for projects, organize meetings/conferences, roundtables, seminars,

* Member of the Intelligence Analyst Working Group.

workshops on specialized topics, issue publications and newsletters, and conduct research projects.

It may also initiate lobby activities on the labor market to increase the visibility of the professional area they represent. It will invest its resources to establish a testing professional skills center, to certify senior intelligence analysts, to increase the quality of work by sharing best practices and research findings. Such an association should polarize field innovation and idea synergy, not just facilitating exchange channels between professionals, but also developing the consciousness of belonging to a community of experts.

There are premises for drafting a code of ethics and professional conduct, stating explicitly the values shared by this community, regardless of affiliation, whether independent, or from the national security system, business, and law enforcement. The existence of such a code will increase cohesion, professional identity, and belongingness to a professional group.

Intelligence analysts that identify themselves as a community will improve the adaptability to social and technological changes, as well as to the challenges brought by global trends. They are often promoters of institutional changes, optimizers of internal workflows, performance innovators, state-of-the-art technology promoters, and exploiters of institutional growth opportunities. Institution performances and quality of their services will significantly increase once interoperable databases develop.

Last but not least, once getting membership in a community where senior analysts are the pillars, the young analysts would receive positive professional legitimacy along with their first steps. They will have the opportunity to evolve in a stimulating professional environment, being in contact with most experienced analysts.

Acknowledgments

I would like to express my deep gratitude to the staff of Intergraph Computer Services for making possible my participation in the IPES annual meeting and the existence of this article.

Very great appreciation to Aurel Vlădulescu, PhD, and Dumitru Licsandru, PhD, for their valuable and constructive suggestions during the planning and the development of this research work. Their willingness to give their time so generously has been of very much help.

I would also like to thank to my colleagues, Lucian Ivan, Anca Cios, Mihaela Savin, Victor-Wili Apreutesei, Mihai Dascălu, and Ioan Năstase, for their enthusiastic encouragement and useful critiques of this research work.

References

Australian and New Zealand Standard Classification of Occupations (ANZCSO). 2008. Retrieved from http://www.abs.gov.au/ausstats/abs@.nsf/Latestproducts /5BEF0CD9B86A053ECA2575DF002DA5C7?opendocument.

Besson, B. 2006. La liste des nouveaux métiers créés par l'intelligence économique. Retrieved from http://blogs.lesechos.fr/intelligence-economique/la-liste-des -nouveaux-metiers-a707.html.

Cârjan, L. 2002. *Romanian Police History from Its Origins to 1949*. Vestala, Bucharest.

Commission on Accreditation for Law Enforcement Agencies (CALEA) Standards, Chapter 15, July 2006. Retrieved from http://www.iaca.net/CAUDC/CALEA /CALEAChapter15.pdf.

Common Order of the Ministry of Labor and Social Solidarity and the National Statistics Institute no. 270/273/12.06.2002 on the approval of the procedure for updating the COR Nomenclature. Official Monitor no. 531/22.07.2002. Retrieved from http://www.mmuncii.ro/pub/imagemanager/images/file/Legislatie /ORDINE/O270-2002.pdf.

Council Framework Decision 2006/960/JHA on simplifying the exchange of information and intelligence between law enforcement authorities of the Member States of the European Union (The Swedish Initiative). Retrieved from http://eur-lex .europa.eu/LexUriServ/LexUriServ.do?uri=OJ:L:2006:386:0089:0100:EN:PDF.

Council Framework Decision 2008/977/JHA/27.11.2008 on the protection of personal data processed in the framework of police and judicial cooperation in criminal matters. Retrieved from http://eur-lex.europa.eu/LexUriServ/LexUriServ.do?ur i=OJ:L:2008:350:0060:0071:en:PDF.

Davis, J. 2002, November. Sherman Kent and the profession of intelligence analysis, *The Sherman Kent Center for Intelligence Analysis, Occasional Papers*. 1(5) p. 8. Retrieved from https://www.cia.gov/library/kent-center-occasional-papers/vol1 no5.htm.

Government Ordinance no. 129/2000 on adult training Romanian Government, 31.08.2000. Official Monitor no. 711/30.09.2002 (republished). Retrieved from http://www.dreptonline.ro/legislatie/og_129_2000_formarea_profesionala _adultilor_republicata.php.

Government Decision no. 1.352/2010 regarding the COR structure—ISCO 08. Retrieved from http://www.mmuncii.ro/pub/imagemanager/images/file/Legislatie /HOTARARI-DE-GUVERN/H1352_2010.pdf.

Hague Programme: Strengthening freedom, security and justice in the European Union (2005/C 53/01). http://ec.europa.eu/home-affairs/doc_centre/docs/hague _programme_en.pdf.

Intelligence Analyst Occupational Standard, Ministry of Home Affairs, 2013. Retrieved from http://www.conta-conta.ro/miscellaneous/601_miscellaneous_contabilitate _files%20601_pdf.

Licsandru, D., Cofan, S.-M., Minjina, B., Ristea, A.-G., Savin, M., Dascălu, M., Gighileanu, F., Petculescu, R., Cios, A., Buda, I., Condrea, C., Costea, C., Harmanescu, I., Nitu, I., Dumitru, I., Seceleanu, F., Parlog, A., Baloi, A.-M., Ganea, V., Bumbac, A., and Ivan, V. Intelligence Analyst Occupational Standard. Ministry of Home Affairs, 2013. Retrieved from http://www.conta-conta.ro /miscellaneous/601_miscellaneous_contabilitate_files%20601_.pdf.

Law Enforcement Analytic Standards 2004. Retrieved from https://members.ialeia
.org/files/other/law_enforcement_analytic_standards.pdf.

Law Enforcement Analytic Standards 2012. Retrieved from https://www.it.ojp.gov
/documents/d/Law%20Enforcement%20Analytic%20Standards%2004202
_combined_compliant.pdf.

Law Enforcement Analyst Certification Standards, US Department of Justice's
Global Justice Information Sharing initiative, Jan. 2010. Retrieved from
https://it.ojp.gov/documents/d/Law%20Enforcement%20Analyst%20certifi
cation.pdf.

Law no. 1/05.01.2011 of National Education. Roman Parliament, 05.01.2011. Official
Monitor no. 18/10.01.2011. Retrieved from http://www.unibuc.ro/n/organizare
/biro-perf/docs/2013/mar/20_15_03_49Legea_Educatiei_Nationale.pdf.

Law no. 132/1999 regarding the organization and functioning of the National
Council for Adult Training. Romanian Parliament, 20.07.1999. Official Monitor
no. 68/27.01.2004. Retrieved from http://www.mmuncii.ro/pub/imagemanager
/images/file/Legislatie/LEGI/L132_1999.pdf.

Maior, G. C., and Nitu, I. (Coordinators). 2013. *Ars Analytica: Challenges and Trends
in Intelligence Analysis*. Rao Publishing House, Bucharest.

Matei, M. and Niţu, I. 2012. Intelligence analysis in Romania's SRI: The critical
"Ps"—People, Processes, Products. *International Journal of Intelligence and
Counterintelligence*. 25:4, 700–26. Retrieved from http://dx.doi.org/10.1080/08
850607.2012.678714.

Minimum Criminal Intelligence Training Standards for Law Enforcement and Other
Criminal Justice Agencies in the United States. US Department of Justice's
Global Justice Information sharing Initiative, Oct. 2007. Retrieved from
http://www.ncirc.gov/documents/public/Minimum_Criminal_Intel_Training
_Standards.pdf.

Ministry of Labor, Family, Social Protection and Elderly People. Order no. 150/2013,
respectively National Statistics Institute Order no. 132/2013, 25.01.2013/
01.02.2013. Retrieved from http://www.rubinian.com/cor_5_ocupatia.php
?id=2422.

National Occupational Classification (NOC). 2011. Retrieved from http://www5
.hrsdc.gc.ca/NOC/English/NOC/2011/Welcome.aspx.

Prüm Convention. Retrieved from http://register.consilium.europa.eu/pdf/en/05
/st10/st10900.en05.pdf.

Recommendations 2008/C111/01/CE of European Parliament and Council.
Retrieved from http://eur-lex.europa.eu/legal-content/EN/TXT/?uri=uriserv:
OJ.C_.2008.111.01.0001.01.ENG&toc=OJ:C:2008:111:FULL.

Richards, H. 1999. *Psychology of Intelligence Analysis*. Washington, DC: Center for the
Study of Intelligence, Washington.

Şinca, F. 2006. From the history of the Romanian Police. In *Between Honor and
Obedience*, vol. 1. Bucharest, Printing House RCR Print.

Standard Occupational Classification (SOC). 2010. Retrieved from http://www.bls
.gov/soc/classification.htm.

Standard Occupational Classification 2010 (SOC2010). Retrieved from http://www
.ons.gov.uk/ons/guide-method/classifications/current-standard-classifications
/soc2010/soc2010-volume-1-structure-and-descriptions-of-unit-groups/index
.html.

Stockholm Programme—An open and secure Europe serving and protecting citizens (2012/C 115/01). Retrieved from https://ec.europa.eu/anti-trafficking /sites/antitrafficking/files/the_stockholm_programme_-_an_open_and_secure _europe_en_1.pdf.

Strategic Intelligence Analysis Course. 2002. Den Haag, Europol.

The European Code of Police Ethics: Recommendation Rec(2001)10 adopted by Ministers Committee of the European Council on 19.01.2001. Retrieved from http://polis.osce.org/library/f/2687/500/CoE-FRA-RPT-2687-EN-European %20Code%20of%20Police%20Ethics.pdf.

UK Intelligence Analyst Occupational Standards: CM1 to CM10. Retrieved from www.skillsforjustice-nosfinder.com/get_nos.php?id=446.

Wikipedia. Gordon E. Moore law. Retrieved from http://en.wikipedia.org/wiki /Moore's_law.

Wikipedia. 27.02.2016. Sherman Kent biography. Retrieved from http://en.wikipedia .org/wiki/Sherman_Kent.

Satisfaction and Community Connections

Paradigm Shift in Hong Kong Public Order Policing

8

WING KWONG YUNG
SANDY CHAU

Contents

Abstract

In this chapter, we analyze a paradigm shift in public order policing
in Hong Kong. During most of its colonial history, the police force
adopted a more classical theory of crowd control that could be called
the *command and control model* of public order policing. This model
emphasizes that a crowd is often irrational and could therefore be easily influenced by disruptive elements. This classical model permeated
almost every aspect of public order policing before the 1980s. During
that period, the police force was preoccupied with controlling political
opposition in order to maintain public order as reflected by the Public
Order Ordinance (Law of Hong Kong Chapter 245, November 17,
1967). In the years leading to the transfer of sovereignty in 1997 and

later, a paradigm shift has taken place in that the police force now adopts a theory that can be referred to as the *service-oriented model*. This approach focuses more on differentiation and facilitation in order to manage crowd control in the context of a rapidly changing society. The reasons for such a paradigm shift are also discussed in this chapter.

Introduction

The main argument in this chapter is that there was a paradigm shift in Hong Kong public order policing at around the time the sovereignty was transferred in 1997. The public order in this chapter is understood as an absence of disorder where ordinary people are able to carry out their business in a quiet and orderly fashion in the public domain and with people behaving sensibly, rationally, and respecting each other.

The exercise of public order policing in Hong Kong is governed by relevant legislation, which was enacted and revised in response to the underlying societal–polity transformations before and after the change of sovereignty. In this chapter, we shall first explain the legislative changes relating to public order as subject to the sociopolitical pressures developing in Hong Kong. Next, we interpret the paradigm shift in public order policing as a reflection of the changes within Hong Kong's internal population composition as well as the influence of relevant external legislation. These changes have caused the Hong Kong Police Force to adopt a different crowd theory in interpreting and managing public order situations.

Refugee Town

The concept of public order policing is best understood in Hong Kong from a historical perspective. From a city of immigrants in the 1950s to a city of emigrants in the run-up to 1997, the refugee mentality has diffused into the political, economic, and social lives of Hong Kong Chinese.

Politically, the prevalence of the refugee mentality meant that there was a sort of a priori acceptance, or better, tolerance, during the British colonial rule (Wong and Lui, 1992). As outlined by Lau (1997), a substantial proportion of Hong Kong Chinese came to Hong Kong either to flee political persecution and turmoil or to seek economic opportunities. This meant that there was a strong sentiment against the Communist regime in China in Hong Kong, which naturally became a core element of the Hong Kong Chinese identity. Besides this mentality, people in Hong Kong also had a very strong work ethic and placed a high value on education. As a city of immigrants, it is generally regarded that before the 1970s, the *don't rock the boat* mentality prevailed among the mainland refugees living in Hong Kong.

Sociologist Lau Siu Kai (1997) explained that the civil society in Hong Kong was very much separated from its polity. Ordinary people were more interested in improving their livelihood rather than participating in politics, which was divorced from the everyday life of most of the populace.

Before the 1970s, the administrative absorption of politics or the boundary politics of the political structure was well maintained. The colonial government adhered to a positive nonintervention policy and left the industrial sector to develop (Chiu, 1994). From the 1970s, there was a relative openness and fairness in terms of the social mobility of Hong Kong society (Wong and Lui, 1993; Lui, 1997). As the local economy took off, a more educated middle class emerged who were able to climb the social ladder (Lui, 1997).

Command and Control Model

The classic model of crowd control, which can be referred to as a *command and control model*, permeated almost every aspect of public order policing in the days of Hong Kong as a British colony. This command and control model was used in many British colonies throughout the world and in other entities as well, in a more conservative era.

A basic pattern can be identified whereby public order policing emphasized this classic theory of the crowd. Before the 1980s, public order policing reflected a concept of the crowd as irrational and therefore easily influenced by undesirable elements. This in turn was associated with a strategic emphasis on the removal, the containment, or the disruption of agitators through the use of force, lest they manifest their ability to hijack the crowd. When it was not possible to achieve this, then a strategic and tactical shift toward the use of force against crowds as a whole was evident.

The classical view of crowds is probably best expressed by Gustave Le Bon, a French psychologist whose book *The Crowd* was first published in 1895. It is still widely cited today and has been called the most influential psychology text of all time. Le Bon argues that when people become anonymous within the mass, they lose their individual identity and forget their normal values and standards, and their ability to think, reason, and judge is impaired.

One of the most familiar assumptions of classical crowd psychology is what one might call *the agitator view.* According to classical crowd psychology, crowd members are mindless and, thus, easily influenced by unscrupulous individuals to cause disorder.

Before the 1970s, Hong Kong was governed by a very authoritarian style of colonial rule. In 1967, at the height of the Cultural Revolution in China, the revolutionary furore spilled over into Hong Kong. Left-wing worke instigated a long period of bloody riots in Hong Kong. The Hong Kong Police lost 10 men during the turmoil but used an iron hand in suppressing the riots after it was known that Beijing had no intention of resuming sovereignty over Hong Kong. For its efforts in suppressing the riots in 1967, the Hong Kong Police were granted the *Royal* prefix in 1969; this made the Royal Hong Kong Police one of only five forces in the Commonwealth that received this honor.

The Public Order Ordinance (POO) was first enacted as a result of the 1967 riots. From then on until the 1980s, there was a high degree of restriction on public assembly. For any public assembly with three or more persons, an application for a public procession license was required or the gathering would be considered unlawful under the POO.

The POO required the organizers of public gatherings in Hong Kong to issue a seven-day prior notification to the commissioner of police. The POO also placed restrictions on noise control during public meetings and limited meetings on private premises to not more than 500 people.

Traditionally, in Hong Kong, public event organizers were willing to negotiate with police and other related stakeholders to make concessions. However, the post-1980s groups who insist in fighting for their human rights would frequently refuse to compromise, making the chance of peaceful resolution impossible.

Rapidly Emerging Political Identity

In Hong Kong, earlier immigrants were mostly penniless refugees from southern China. Only a handful of Chinese from places such as Shanghai were wealthier industrialists. There was basically no middle class in Hong Kong in the 1950s and the 1960s. However, by the 1970s, a new locally born generation was slowly growing up in Hong Kong to fill the middle class vacuum.

Before the emergence of a social and political identity, public order was quite easily controlled in Hong Kong as the police force was not shy to use force on the one hand, and on the other hand, most people in Hong Kong were just busy making money and not involved in the political process.

Social unrest became more common from the 1970s. For instance, the Chinese Movement in 1970, the Protection of Diaoyu Islands Movement in 1971, the Anti-Corruption Movement in 1973, the Golden Jubilee Incident in 1977, and the Yau Ma Tei Boat People Incident in 1978 all gave rise to a group of social leaders (contenders). They became the social activists and opinion leaders striving for the parochial interests of specific communities.

Stepping into the 1980s, the Sino-British negotiations over the sovereignty of Hong Kong triggered a decade-long politicization and mobilization process (Ma, 2002). By 1984, the British might have thought that they could run Hong Kong and have a free hand to change the political system before 1997. China certainly disliked the idea of any form of rapid democratic development being implanted in Hong Kong. Xu Jiatun (director of the Xinhua News Agency at that time) stated on November 21, 1985, that all political reform during the transition period must adhere to and be in tune with the constitutional structure as laid down in the Basic Law. The British later generally agreed that the political development in Hong Kong before 1997 had to comply with the Basic Law.

The social movements in the 1970s and the 1980s were spearheaded by the local middle class and professionals; these groups later formed the backbone of the prodemocracy movements. This new generation, described by Ma (2002), as a locally born, better educated elite, had a stronger Hong Kong identity and were more sympathetic to western values such as democracy, social equality, freedom, and human rights. Their social mobility signified the relative openness and fairness of the Hong Kong society in the 1970s (Wong and Lui, 1992, 1993; Leung, 1996).

This new middle class, who took for granted China's relative openness in the 1980s, has a perception of China that is greatly different from their parents. They have vocally challenged China's concept of convergence and disliked what they perceived China's unnecessary interference during the transition. Thus, instead of seeing the Hong Kong middle class as a particular group of people, it is more appropriate to regard them as the symbol of certain societal values and worldview, which prevails in Hong Kong society (Lui, 1997).

Initiated in 2001, the ministerial system was launched to strengthen the accountability of the principal officials to the public and to ensure better responses to the demands of the people and better coordination of government policies (Hong Kong Special Administrative Region Government, 2001). Yet political accountability is not a convention and government legitimacy remains low.

Even though the ministerial system is modeled upon the Western democracies, the critical difference lies in the election of the executive head not being by popular election. With the election of the second-term chief executive by an 800-member election committee, the so-called accountability system was viewed as actually another form of authoritarianism (Ma, 2002).

The Emergence of Political Groups in the 1980s

In 1982–1984, there was the Sino-British negotiation on Hong Kong's future post-1997. During that time, the middle class in Hong Kong realized that it should take part in politics more actively to lobby for a democratic self-governed Hong Kong after the handover in 1997.

In 1982, different political groups, such as Meeting Point, the New Hong Kong Society, the Hong Kong Affairs Society, and the Hong Kong Forum, were formed and call for the democratization in modern Hong Kong.

The political participation of middle class liberals inevitably led to a reaction from conservative groups in Hong Kong, such as leaders of business and industry, who had long sought to depoliticize Hong Kong, thinking that democratization would harm the economy. They, too, started to get involved in politics. Political polarization occurred as liberals and conservatives became embroiled in a controversy over local political reform. However, these political groups, which usually lacked grassroots support, did not develop into political parties.

Emergence of More Political Groups after the Tiananmen Square Incident

The 1989 Tiananmen Square incident marked another turning point in popular attitudes toward political participation. Against a background of rising aspirations for democracy and support for political parties as institutions, the final version of the Basic Law provided that only 20 of the 60 seats in the legislature would be directly elected in 1997 instead of half, as proposed by the Office of Members of Executive and Legislative Councils. This led to the formation of three political parties in 1990—the United Democrats of Hong Kong (UDHK), the Hong Kong Democratic Foundation, and the Liberal Democratic Federation. In the legislative council (Legco) of 1991, prodemocracy forces won the majority of directly elected seats.

With the encouragement of the Chinese authorities, pro-China forces, too, began to organize political parties in the early 1990s to counter the prodemocracy forces. The Democratic Alliance for the Betterment of Hong Kong was formed in 1992. In 1993, the Liberal Party was formed by business people led by Allen Lee. The Hong Kong Progressive Alliance was formed in 1994. While Hong Kong witnessed the emergence of several new political groups in the early 1990s, two old political groups, i.e., Meeting Point and the UDHK, decided to merge in 1994 to form the Hong Kong Democratic Party.

Governor Chris Patten's reform proposals in the 1992–1994 period led to a more obvious political polarization. There was growing party identification among the electorate with either the pro-China or prodemocracy forces. The prodemocracy forces claimed to be "the moral mirror image of the Chinese government" and pro-China forces were usually seen as more conservative and realized the need to deal with China in a more pragmatic way by at least communicating, if not cooperating with, China. In the 1995 Legco election, the prodemocracy forces again won a victory against the pro-China forces.

The Tiananmen Square incident accelerated the birth of various political groups. However, the number of political groups has remained constant, as no formal political party has been formed since the handover. Despite the fact that the number of political groups in Hong Kong is small, they have been guiding the debate on Hong Kong's political development. The prodemocracy camp has called for universal suffrage of the chief executive by 2017, while the pro-China forces claimed that Hong Kong has to observe the Basic Law with regard to the pace of democratization. Political polarization, in terms of the pace of democratization, still exists.

Legislative Changes That Govern Public Order Policing in Hong Kong

Before the handover of the sovereignty of Hong Kong from the British government to the Chinese government, the Sino-British Joint Declaration (1984) was signed and stated that the Hong Kong Special Administrative Region Government was to protect and maintain the rights and the freedoms of its inhabitants as provided for by the laws previously in force. In the drafting of the Basic Law, the constitutional document of Hong Kong Special Administrative Region, the International Covenant on Civil and Political Rights (ICCPR) was incorporated.

After the handover of the sovereignty in 1997, the landscape of law enforcement in public order changed dramatically. On one hand, the political awareness grew among Hong Kong citizens, and on the other hand, the crux of public order policing in Hong Kong has changed from "the restriction on public gathering" to "the right of peaceful assembly." The right of peaceful assembly took effect in Hong Kong as ICCPR was applied. As part of the International Bill of Human Rights, ICCPR commits its parties to respect the civil and political rights of individuals, which includes freedom of assembly.

The application of the ICCPR is found in Article 39 of the Basic Law (1990), which states that "The provisions of the ICCPR as applied to Hong Kong shall remain in force and shall be implemented through the laws of the Hong Kong Special Administrative Region. The rights and freedoms enjoyed by Hong Kong residents shall not be restricted unless as prescribed by law. Such restrictions shall not contravene the provisions of the preceding paragraph of this Article."

In addition, the Bill of Rights Ordinance (1991) stipulated that "everyone shall have the right to hold opinions without interference and shall have the right to freedom of expression; this right shall include freedom to seek, receive and impart information and ideas of all kinds, regardless of frontiers, either orally, in writing or in print, in the form of art, or through any other media of his choice."

Thus in post-1997, the legality of civil liberties and human rights in Hong Kong rooted the Basic Law (Appendix I) and the Bill of Rights (Appendix II). The freedom or the right of peaceful assembly and procession is enshrined in Article 27 of the Basic Law and Article 17 of the Hong Kong Bill of Rights Ordinance (Cap. 383).

Paradigm Shift in Public Order Policing as Adoptions of Different Crowd Theories

Since the handover of sovereignty in 1997, the number of public order events has increased tremendously. In 2010, the police managed a total of 5656 notified or nonnotified public order events. These included 1137 public processions and 4519 public meetings.

Balancing the rights of protesters and other citizens with the duty to protect people and property from the threat of harm or injury defines the policing dilemma in relation to public protest. In a democratic society policed by consent, planning and action at every level must be seen to reconcile all these factors, particularly when a minority of people may be determined to cause disorder or worse. The law is an important consideration in public order events.

It is necessary to recognize peaceful protest as legitimate activity and as the everyday business of a democratic and open society. This is a sound starting point for the police when planning public order operations relating to protests. Having considered the essential nature of the freedom of association and its close relationship with a democratic movement, there must be convincing reasons to justify police intervention in the freedom of peaceful assembly. There are particular challenges of policing a capital city and competing demands of multifaceted policing operations, such as the G20 operation, Consequent operational choices must be made by police, including constraints imposed because of police resources, which are legitimate factors influencing police decision making.

In 2004, the Hong Kong Police Force adopted a three-tier structure with each tier to provide resources for internal security and public order capability to the commissioner, the regional commanders, and the district commanders. According to the Police Tactical Unit (PTU) training aide-mémoire (2010), the unit undergoes weeks training, which covers internal security, crowd management, anticrime, use of weapons, and physical force. The main objective of the PTU is to provide internal security coverage during riot situations. In addition, the PTU is also responsible for dealing with major crowd control and public order events. Over the past decade, there have been great changes in policing public order events as the level of transparency of the government expected by the members of the public is increasing. Police officers always have to be prepared to justify the actions they have taken, in particular those involving the use of force, when being queried by the press, members of the public, and public organizations.

In modern policing, the social identity theory of crowds has replaced the classical view on crowds (mass irrationality) in the training for crowd management. The social identity theory, which was developed from the psychology of group processes, proposes that individuals do not lose identity in the crowd. Rather, a member of the crowd experiences a shift from personal identity (what makes me as an individual distinctive from other individuals) to social identity (what makes my group distinctive compared to other groups). In this regard, individuals do not lose values and standards in the crowd but rather shift to act in terms of the values and the standards associated with the relevant group.

What social identity theory says about the agitator model is that crowd members will only listen to those they see as sharing their standards and will follow suggestions that fit with those standards. Therefore, a physical mass of people is not one psychological crowd. Most physical crowds or gatherings contain many different psychological groups with different social identities. Hence, a single demonstration will characteristically contain groups with widely diverging goals, widely diverging relationships with outside groups (notably the police), and widely diverging orientations to conflict and violence. More often than not, only some groups, often a small minority, have goals that are illegal and start out with an intention of pursuing their goals with violence.

The social identity theory of crowd management leads to the strategies of facilitation and differentiation in crowd policing as now practiced in Hong Kong. The approach to treating crowd members is not *how can we frustrate them?* but *how can we facilitate them?* Facilitation is paramount at all stages of the police operation. In planning for an event, the police need to identify the legitimate aims of crowd members in order to consider how best to organize policing so as to enable the members of the group. Similar to public order policing in the United States and the United Kingdom over the last few decades, the Hong Kong Police has witnessed a shift from a focus on force, to a focus on escalating force, and then to a focus on negotiation.

Moreover, the Hong Kong Police recognized the need to treat different sections of the crowd in different ways. The pitfall of treating all crowd members as the same, and as potentially dangerous, is rectified by the differentiation in crowd policing. Aided by strategies of intelligence-led policing, the Hong Kong Police is trained to be aware that not all crowd members are the same and that different identities, different ways of acting and of reacting, coexist in the public order events.

On occasions of public order events, Hong Kong police officers seek to enable crowds and give them an opportunity to express their dissent. In doing so, there is a distinctive shift in managing public order by the police force in Hong Kong. This new paradigm is referred to as the *service-oriented model* in public order policing.

According to the service-oriented model, public order policing means that the Hong Kong Police should enable the expressions of right of peaceful assembly as lawful assemblies. The measures to be taken by the Hong Kong police include issuing verbal warnings or orders, collection of evidence for subsequent investigation and consideration of prosecution, and peaceful dispersal of the crowd or other law enforcement including arrest actions in order to regulate public meetings and processions.

The emphasis is on facilitating lawful and peaceful public meetings and processions. Therefore, in carrying out their duties, the Hong Kong Police has to strike a balance between maintaining public order and ensuring the rights and the safety of those who participate in public order events.

At present, the Hong Kong Police positions itself as service oriented. Even though there are clear guidelines and standards of use of force during public order event, the use of only minimum force necessary for public order policing is called for. Various crowd control tactics such as pressure point control and strike attack are utilized with great discretion for fear of criticism concerning misuse of force and police power.

Conclusion

Over the past decade, the Hong Kong Police Force has had to face the challenge of the changing nature of the public order events where tremendous pressures have been placed on the frontline units. The policing of public order events has become a major issue for the Hong Kong Police Force on an almost daily basis. The paradigm shift in Hong Kong public order policing has been caused first by an inherent political identity development within the population composition in Hong Kong. Second, it has also been caused by the external development of legislation that has also inevitably affected the laws of Hong Kong. In response to these changes, the Hong Kong Police Force has shifted from a command and control model to a service-oriented model in managing public order events.

In view of the trend toward globalization and democratization, Hong Kong is not the only place facing this changing nature of public order events. Like other entities such as Taiwan, Korea, and even mainland China, confrontations arising from public order events frequently occur between the participants and the law enforcement agencies. More research efforts are needed in this area in order for all of us to better understand the phenomenon of public order policing.

Appendix

Appendix I

Basic Law

- Under Article 25, "All Hong Kong residents shall be equal before the law."
- Under Article 27, "Hong Kong residents shall have freedom of speech ...; freedom of association, of assembly, of procession and of demonstration...."
- Under Article 28, "The freedom of the person of Hong Kong residents shall be inviolable."
- Under Article 35, "Hong Kong residents shall have the right to confidential legal advice, ... choice of lawyers for timely protection of their lawful rights and interest...."
- Under Article 38, "Hong Kong residents shall enjoy the other rights and freedoms safeguarded by the laws of Hong Kong Special Administrative Region (HKSAR)."
- Under Article 39, constitutional protection is also given to freedom of opinion, of expression, and of peaceful assembly as provided for in Articles 16 and 17 of the Hong Kong Bill of Rights, those articles being the equivalents of Articles 19 and 21 of the International Covenant on Civil and Political Rights and representing part of the ICCPR as applied to Hong Kong.

Appendix II

Bill of Rights

- Article 1—Hong Kong Bill of Rights ensures the rights granted are applied in a nondiscriminatory way irrespective of race, color, sex, language, religion, national. Men and women shall have an equal right to the enjoyment of all civil and political rights.
- Article 3—Torture and cruel, inhuman, or degrading punishment and treatment are prohibited.
- Article 11—Right of persons charged with or convicted or criminal offense.

- Article 16—Everyone shall have the right to hold opinions without interference and the right to freedom of expression.
- Article 17—No restrictions may be placed on the exercise of the right of peaceful assembly other than those imposed in conformity with the law and that are necessary in a democratic society in the interests of national security or public safety and public order.

References

Aide Memoire: Police Tactical Unit (PTU) Training, Duties and Standards Required of Personnel. 2010. Hong Kong: Hong Kong Police Force.

Basic Law. 1990. Retrieved from http://www.basiclaw.gov.hk/en/index.

Bill of Rights Ordinance. 1991. Retrieved from http://hkhrm.org.hk/english/law/eng _boro1.html.

Chiu, W. K. 1994. *The Politics of Laissez-faire Hong Kong's Strategy of Industrialization in Historical Perspective* Hong Kong: Hong Kong Institute of Asia-Pacific Studies, Chinese University of Hong Kong.

Lau, S. K. 1997. *Hongkongese or Chinese: The Problem of Identity on the Eve of Resumption of Chinese Sovereignty Over Hong Kong*. Hong Kong: Hong Kong Institute of Asia-Pacific Studies, Chinese University of Hong Kong.

Le Bon, G. 1895. *The Crowd: A Study of the Popular Mind*. London: Ernest Benn.

Leung, B. K. P. 1996. *Perspectives on Hong Kong Society*. Hong Kong: Oxford University Press.

Lui, T. L. 1997, August 9. What are the middle class thinking? (Authors' translation) *Ming Pao Newspapers Limited*, Hong Kong.

Ma, N. 2002. Changing political cleavages in post-1997 Hong Kong: A study of the changes through the electoral arena. In *Crisis and Transformation in China's Hong Kong*. Chan, M. K., and So, A., eds. Hong Kong: Hong Kong University Press.

Sino-British Joint Declaration. 1984. Retrieved http://www.cmab.gov.hk/en/issues /joint3.htm.

Wong, T. W. P., and Lui, T. L. 1992. *From One Brand Politics to One Brand of Political Culture*. Occasional Paper No. 10. Hong Kong: Hong Kong Institute of Asia-Pacific Studies, Chinese University of Hong Kong.

Wong, T. W. P., and Lui, T. L. 1993. *Morality, Class and the Hong Kong Way of Life*. Occasional Paper No. 30. Hong Kong: Hong Kong Institute of Asia-Pacific Studies, Chinese University of Hong Kong.

Citizen Satisfaction with Police

9

The Effects of Income Level and Prior Victimization Experiences on Citizen Perceptions of Police

ROBERT D. HANSER
CREEL S. GALLAGHER
ATTAPOL KUANLIANG

Contents

Abstract

This chapter analyzed data from a citizen satisfaction survey disseminated by researchers and community volunteers, on behalf of a medium-
sized municipal police agency. Citizen perceptions of their local police
department were analyzed. The analysis examined two primary
research questions. The first research question sought to determine
whether socioeconomic status was a significant variable for predicting

citizen perceptions of police. The second research question was related to whether the classification as a crime victim was a significant variable for predicting citizen perceptions. Statistically significant results were found to be related to both research questions. Recommendations for agencies and future researchers are provided.

Introduction

In this chapter, we contend that assessment is fundamental to gauging the relationship between the police agencies and the surrounding community. Even when a program has been implemented and presumed to be successful, continued assessment and evaluation is needed. Evaluations can confirm successes, identify discrepancies in philosophy and practice, recognize any changes occurring that could affect the process in the near future, and acknowledge areas where improvements can be made (Davis and Ford, 2002; Hanser et al., 2012). Many tools can be used to gather information for the evaluation of police–community relations, including police self-assessments, crime data, and community surveys.

In assessing police–community relations in this chapter, surveys were used as the primary assessment tool to evaluate citizen views of municipal police in a small-to-midsize town in the United States. This study surveyed citizens throughout the city's jurisdiction to learn their attitudes and perceptions pertaining to their community and their local police agency. The agency examined in this chapter has placed community relations as a priority since 1993, when community policing ideals were implemented, with intermittent surveys throughout that time to record and evaluate their efforts to building effective community partnerships.

Specifically, this study sought to determine two key issues of interest. First, it was a priority to determine whether socioeconomic status is a factor in determining satisfaction with police activity in this jurisdiction. Second, this study examined differences between prior crime victims and nonvictims in citizen satisfaction with police response. These areas of interest have been cited in prior literature as being sources of disparate satisfaction, and it was the desire of police administrators in this municipal jurisdiction to determine if the same was true for their own community. Our study was designed to provide an answer to these research questions posed by these administrators.

Literature Review

The use of partnerships that bring the police and the surrounding community together serves to establish positive relationships and trust (Diamond and

Weiss, 2009a). Increased trust in police can lead to greater community coop-eration (Community-Oriented Policing Services, 2009). Furthermore, the community is an essential source of information for not only incidents but also specific community concerns (Community Policing Consortium [CPC], 1994). Challenges engaging the community in the effort must be addressed, and efforts to encourage community participation should be promoted. The community needs to be involved in the effort to define problems, develop solutions, and promote safety.

Providing service is one connecting point for police to develop good relationships with the community. Service-oriented efforts include not only responses to calls but also interaction with community residents in non-emergency matters. Relationships can be built through a service-oriented cycle of policing. First, police serve and, over time, trust are developed. With that trust comes access to valuable information. That information can lead to solutions to community problems or specific criminal incidents. Upon those positive results, individuals may be more willing to support crime-control measures in their community (Diamond and Weiss, 2009a; Vito, Walsh, and Kunselman, 2005). This gives the community and the police the opportunity to strengthen current partnerships and establish new ones (CPC, 1994). This idea of ongoing efforts to develop community partnerships is something that can be built upon to increase support for the community policing efforts over time.

The two major factors that shape community involvement are atti-tudes toward police and neighborhood attachment (Garcia et al., 2003). As it turns out, these two factors tend to be interconnected with one another. "Individuals' feelings about the state of the neighborhood are associated with their level of satisfaction with police" (Reisig and Parks, 2002, p. 4). The neighborhood quality of life is a strong determinate of citizen satisfac-tion with police, and the satisfaction levels help shape the citizens' attitudes toward police (Reisig and Parks, 2002).

Another strong determinant of citizens' satisfaction with the police is first-hand experience interacting with officers. The officers' attitudes toward citizens affect the citizens' attitudes toward the police. Encounters with police, both direct and vicarious experiences, develop individuals' percep-tions and attitudes toward the police. Having direct contact with the police influences a person's perception of the police as a whole. Therefore, if the experience was negative, then that person's attitude toward the police will likely be negative. A person's perception of how an officer treats him or her during the interaction, and that experience shared with others such as fam-ily, friends, or media, helps shape the vicarious experiences that ultimately affect perceptions of police (Schuck, Rosenbaum, and Hawkins, 2008).

The degree of satisfaction or dissatisfaction with police during a direct experience is dependent on the nature of the encounter, whether or not it was initiated by police or citizen, and the perception of how the officer treated the person during the course of the encounter (Schuck, Rosenbaum, and Hawkins, 2008; Skogan, 2005). How an officer treats a citizen during the encounter is very important in shaping that person's satisfaction. It can extend beyond the individual as well. A relative or an acquaintance may use the second-hand knowledge of the experience to decide on their own level of satisfaction with police. Some factors that shape a person's perception of police during an interaction include officers' politeness, attentiveness, patience, and helpfulness (Skogan, 2005).

Therefore, it can be concluded that the quality of police encounters affects citizens' satisfaction with the police. Reisig and Parks (2002) found that encounters with the police are a significant determinant of resident satisfaction. They affirm that individuals dissatisfied with a specific encounter rated their overall satisfaction with the police lower than those without a similar experience with the police and vice versa. A favorable encounter is better than no encounter in the overall satisfaction levels, but an unfavorable encounter can significantly lower citizens' level of satisfaction (Reisig and Parks, 2002; Skogan, 2005). This is significant because persons satisfied with the police may be more likely to support efforts to reduce crime and social disorder. "Favorable views of the police influence how readily people step forward to help the police by reporting crimes, identifying offenders, and serving as witnesses" (Skogan, 2005, p. 318). Direct interaction between officers and the community greatly influences residents' attitudes toward police.

Weisburd and Eck (2004) analyzed multiple studies of police organizations' efforts to reduce crime, disorder, and fear. While they found no consistent evidence that police–community partnerships had a significant effect on crime and disorder, it was apparent that community-police partnerships helped reduce citizens' fear of crime. Furthermore, they discovered that "when the police are able to gain wider legitimacy among citizens and offenders, the likelihood of offending will be reduced" (p. 59). More research is needed in this particular area, but the implications of this study show that police–community relations may indirectly have a positive effect on crime control in the community they serve.

As noted before, another key factor that determines resident involvement in policing efforts is neighborhood attachment. "The people likely to be involved in such 'anti-crime' groups are those that have a vested interest in the community—they tend to have children, own homes, and have lived in the neighborhood a long time" (Garcia et al., 2003, p. 4). The quality of life can be quantified as an indicator of neighborhood attachment. It is also significantly connected to the first factor, attitudes toward police. Higher levels of social disorder within the community equate to lower levels of satisfaction with the police. On the other side of the spectrum, residents who view their current neighborhood's quality of life as positive also express higher levels of satisfaction with the police (Reisig, 2002).

Disorder in the neighborhood impacts the quality of life. Public drinking, loitering youth, and street harassment are all forms of disorder that can affect the neighborhood. Skogan (1990) explained:

> Disorder not only sparks concern and fear of crime among neighborhood residents; it may actually increase the level of serious crime. Disorder erodes what control neighborhood residents can maintain over local events and conditions. It drives out those for whom stable community life is important, and discourages people with similar values from moving in. it threatens house prices and discourages investment. In short, disorder in an instrument of destabilization and neighborhood decline. (p. 3)

On the other hand, when there is less disorder, the quality of life is higher, and that can increase the probability of neighborhood attachment. Furthermore, a more organized neighborhood has greater motivation and a better ability to communicate concerns with the police (Greene, 2000). This makes neighborhood attachment, or quality of life, an important factor in determining the likelihood of participation in a variety of policing efforts.

To maintain the momentum of partnership initiatives between the police and the community, communication is vital. Continued partnerships throughout times of concern for crime and safety as well as during times of relative calm is important to maintain positive police–community relationships. The long-term goal of increasing neighborhood quality of life and ultimately reducing overall crime and disorder requires continuing collaborative efforts (Diamond and Weiss, 2009b). All these efforts to increase rapport between the police and the community, to increase citizen involvement in crime reduction initiatives, and to develop awareness and understanding between the police and the citizenry fall under the commonly touted community policing model. We now turn our attention, more specifically, to the adoption of community policing practices and their impact on citizen views of police.

Assessing Community Policing Efforts

The community policing approach has grown in popularity throughout the United States, and it has become a more widely used law enforcement strategy (Sadd and Grinc, 1996). Assessment plays an important role in developing or revising future plans and goals of the community policing initiative (Davis and Ford, 2002). "Ongoing input, evaluation, and feedback from both inside and outside the police organization are essential to making community policing work" (CPC, 1994, p. 28). Various types of assessments include crime reports data, officer self-evaluations, measures of the level of community health (such as home ownership, business startups, use of public places, etc.), and community perceptions of police and safety (Greene, 2000).

For the most part, crime report data are self-explanatory. It is easily assumed that when crime reports go down, then current practices are sufficient in controlling crime. However, it has been established that crime statistics are not infallible. A number of other factors, such as the amount of crime that goes unreported, may contribute to the crime rate at any given time. Therefore, the numbers' rise or fall may not directly reflect on the police department's current organizational structure, level of service, or citizen willingness to report. Maguire (2007) explains that crime statistical data should be considered evidence about, not proof of, the changes in crime or disorder that are taking place.

Officer evaluations can also contribute vital assessment information about community policing efforts. By evaluating an officer's understanding and perceptions of their community policing efforts, this assessment can identify any problems that may exist within the department. For example, in a study evaluating a small police department, Sumner (2008) found that while the community policing philosophy was defined, the implementation in practice did not reflect the identified goals and practices. Because of individual officer assessments, researchers were able to identify the problems that existed within the program.

Citizen opinions are a very important part of evaluating community policing efforts, and surveys are the most common form of collecting community feedback (Reisig, 2002). Partnerships can be utilized in the design and the distribution of neighborhood surveys. Officers and volunteers can help ensure that the survey reaches as many individuals as possible in the community. Local media can also be utilized to alert citizens of the survey and illustrate the importance of community input. The survey itself is another form of enhancing police–community relationships, as it gives residents an opportunity to express opinions. Finally, obtaining information on the citizens' level of fear, quality of life, and satisfaction with police will help shape the future of the local community policing effort.

It should be pointed out that, in many cases, the attempts to measure the effects of long-term goals, such as the result of a specific community problem-solving activity (for example, reduction of loitering and vandalism in a specified area), often cannot accurately depict the overall effectiveness of community policing within an agency (Diamond, 2006). As such, surveys designed to measure neighborhood quality of life and attitudes toward the police are considered more useful assessments of community policing practices as opposed to surveys designed to evaluate a single specific action. This is because community policing consists of a wide range of day-to-day behaviors and interactions that are ongoing and cannot all be specifically included or measured by a single survey and/or by most other data sources. Rather, it is the composite of the effective transfer from philosophy to practice that makes this approach ultimately transfer to visible outcomes in the community.

Assessments can give community policing partners a sense of direction. By evaluating what works and what needs work, the police and the community can focus their efforts on effective means of reaching their mutually decided goals. Finding whether changes are occurring as planned and what changes still need to be made are important to any community policing initiative. Furthermore, ongoing assessments help the process of the reevaluation of community needs and priorities. Encouraging community input from surveys, as well as other sources, can help to further strengthen community and police relationships as well (CPC, 1994; Greene, 2000).

The CPC (1994) gave three criteria for assessment—effectiveness, efficiency, and equity. Effectiveness is measured not in terms of arrests or crime-fighting data, but it should measure the crime-prevention methods. Some tools to measure the effectiveness of community policing efforts are surveys to determine fear of crime and quality of life in the neighborhood. Other measures include the number of partnerships created and maintained and the level of resident participation in the community efforts. In another vein, the measurement of equity should be considered. *Equity*, as a concept, is a process by which all citizens have equal access to voice their opinions about police. The community survey is one way to ensure that residents have an equal chance to evaluate any improvements or changes within their neighborhood.

A police agency's decision to conduct a community-wide survey is consistent with the steps to ensure that the efforts to improve community relations are successful and that community policing practices match the intended philosophy. Surveys allow citizens to express their opinions on their community and their attitudes about police. Evaluation is an important step in the community policing effort. This study examines citizen perceptions of their community and attitudes about the police who provide service to their area.

An assessment of community policing in Chicago by Skogan et al. (2000) found that a neighborhood's ability to solve community problems was directly correlated to that community's social and economic status. "Problem-solving capacity was strongly linked to affluence" (p. 10). Neighborhoods with higher social organization have a greater capacity to communicate with the police and participate in the community policing effort (Greene, 2000). As such, the higher organization of the community tends to result in higher quality of life, and, as a result, a higher opinion of the police (Reisig, 2002). Given this information, it is possible to assume that the income of the persons in a community not only may impact the problem-solving ability in that community, but would also be reflective of the citizen perceptions of police activity

A

in the community. A higher quality of life results in higher satisfaction with the police. Thus, our first hypothesis will test for respondent income as a determining factor for citizen satisfaction with police in this study. Victims of crime include those who reported and those who did not report the crime. For either, it is assumed that those who have been victims of crime are likely to have lower opinions of police than those who have not been a victim. Prior victimization consistently lowers citizens' approval of the police to a significant degree (Maxson, Hennigan, and Sloane, 2003). Therefore, hypothesis 2 will test for significant differences in responses between crime victims and noncrime victims. While it is expected that victims of crime will have significantly lower opinions of the police than those who have not been victims, for purposes of this study, our second hypothesis will only test for significantly different responses between both groups.

Hypotheses

After identifying the concerns of administrators regarding agency and citizen relations, it was determined that two areas of specific interest should be addressed: socioeconomic factors as well as prior experiences with victimization. Each of these respondent characteristics had an impact on the feedback that was provided during the administration of the survey. Therefore, our hypotheses were crafted along these two areas of interest:

H01: The income of survey respondents will be correlated with perceptions of police activity in the community.
H02: Perceptions of police activity will be less positive for crime victims.

Methodology

The community-wide evaluation of citizen attitudes and perceptions has been conducted in a manner that is consistent with the monograph entitled *A Police Guide to Surveying Citizens and Their Environment*, published by the Bureau of Justice Assistance (BJA) in 1993. In conducting this project, we believed that it was important to utilize some type of guidelines and/or precedent that had been established by an official body or agency involved with police–community-oriented surveys. We also referred to another BJA monograph entitled *Surveying Communities: A Resource for Community Justice Planners*. This document included specific examples of items used on other surveys that were similar to the one designed for this project. Although these BJA documents are a bit dated (it is 16 years old), the vast majority of guidelines and recommendations are still sound since they are steeped in a number of classic methodological approaches regarding survey research.

Furthermore, since this document was directly related to the type of project that our current citizen attitudes and perceptions survey has entailed, the document is a good fit as a point of reference regarding our approach to completing this project. This project was a joint effort between the faculty and the students of the University of Louisiana at Monroe and the officers and the volunteers of a local municipal police department. As such, this project also utilized the experiences and the input of numerous individuals who collectively helped to ensure the quality of the survey project and its ethical administration throughout the community. In the process, other official documents available from the Department of Justice were utilized, when appropriate.

All of this is mentioned only to demonstrate that the construction of the survey instrument used in this project as well as the methodology employed in administering the survey were grounded in past efforts that have been proven successful. While our own survey design and our own collection efforts were created to meet the unique needs of the local municipal police agency, we mirrored and replicated past survey designs and collection efforts to achieve consistency and congruence with prior research. Nevertheless, while we may have referred to other documents and examples freely offered by the federal government (being classified as public domain), our own project and survey design were constructed for our own particular evaluative purposes.

Survey Construction

The faculty of the Department of Criminal Justice at the University of Louisiana at Monroe constructed the survey instrument that was used to measure attitudes and opinions of citizens regarding local municipal police in an outlying jurisdiction. The survey instrument was designed to address several key points of inquiry, as promulgated by the CALEA requirements, included in Chapter 45, Section 2, Standard 4, as follows:

1. Overall agency performance
2. Overall competence of agency employees
3. Citizens' perception of officers' attitudes and behavior
4. Community concern over safety and security within the city limits
5. Citizens' recommendations and suggestions for improvements

The survey instrument included at least two or more items intended to generate data for each of the mentioned categories of interest. In addition, other items were included as requested by the police agency and/or as per the discretion of the researchers who were tasked with the design of the survey.

Prior to the finalization and the adoption of the instrument, various police agency administrators reviewed the instrument and ensured that all points of interest were included in the survey.

The instrument was designed to be simple and easy to administer. It was also intended that citizens would, in many cases, be in circumstances where they might fill out the survey on their own. Thus, simplicity and brevity were desired while, at the same time, addressing the need to capture as much relevant data as possible. In order to achieve this, the researchers referred to prior community surveys that had been implemented in the region, and they replicated the format and/or the content of various items included on the survey instruments available from the federal government. This was desirable because such information is public domain and free of copyright concerns and because federally published instruments are likely to at least possess face validity, at a minimum.

The Planning Stage

The planning stage consisted of a discussion as to how the survey would be administered. The coordination of volunteer activities, police personnel, researchers, and so forth was conducted during this time. It was also determined that multiple times of data collection should be conducted and that these efforts should be conducted through numerous types collection processes. Lastly, it was specifically noted that efforts would be made to garner data from all areas of the city, including those areas where more calls for police service are made and/or areas that include citizens of low income. This was important to ensure that the sample would be genuinely reflective of the overall city population. Such efforts likewise added to the integrity of the design and the results of the overall evaluation of citizen attitudes and opinions regarding police in their area.

Data Collection and Sampling

The police organization generated a media campaign, two weeks before data collection began, to inform citizens throughout the city of the possibility that they might be asked to provide their input on a survey of local police performance. This campaign informed citizens that their data would be anonymous, would not be collected or analyzed by police, and that both their negative and positive critiques were welcomed as feedback to improve police–community relations in the area. From this point, a variety of agency volunteers, faculty, and students from the University of Louisiana at Monroe began data collection efforts. Data were collected by four primary methods. These methods were the use of door-to-door interviews in neighborhoods of various citizens, the use of personal face-to-face interviews at participating business establishments, the use of the U.S. Postal System to deliver surveys to randomly selected residences.

The use of face-to-face interviews, using the survey instrument, was the primary means of collecting data for this study. According to the Bureau of Justice Assistance (BJA) (1993), face-to-face surveys are the most expensive means of administering a survey, but this type of data collection also tends to be the most accurate out of all the options available. Because this type of administration is thought to produce the most accurate data, we chose to use this approach as our primary means of data collection. A total of 466 surveys were collected from a variety of regions throughout the city using this technique. To ensure representativeness, data collection personnel were sent to all regions of the city.

In addition, mailed-out surveys were employed by selecting every 33rd person/residence listed in the local phone book. A cover letter, a copy of the survey, and a self-addressed stamped envelope was sent to residents within the city limits. This list of potential respondents totaled approximately 390 persons. The surveys were sent to those persons in the list. Upon completion of the data collection period, 67 surveys had been returned. This equates to a 17% response rate. As has been noted in other forms of survey-based research, the response rate for mail-based surveys tends to be low.

No telephone interviews were conducted. According to the BJA (1993, p. IX), "telephone surveys . . . automatically exclude citizens without telephones," and they also require questioners trained to administer them by telephone (BJA, 1993). Because a sample from the local phone book had already been obtained for the mail-out surveys, the use of phone interviews was eliminated. While this may have been a good opportunity for follow-up data collection, the researchers wished to avoid obtaining data from the same respondents who might respond to both techniques. In addition, the human resources utilized for the face-to-face interviews and the monetary resources used for the mail-out made additional data collection a challenge.

Results

The data in Table 9.1 show that slightly more than half of the respondents (55.5%) were female and 44% were male. Two respondents failed to indicate their gender on the survey and are recorded as missing data. This demographic information is not particularly noteworthy but does demonstrate that the sample was not skewed toward one gender or the other. The sample has enough of a composition so as to ensure that representativeness of both men and women exists.

The age range of the respondents was fairly evenly distributed. From the data in Table 9.2, it can be seen that respondent ages were fairly well dispersed

Table 9.1   Gender of Survey Respondents

	Frequency	Percentage	Cumulative Percentage
Male	235	44.1	44.1
Female	296	55.5	99.6
Missing	2	0.4	100.0
Total	533	100.0	100.0

Table 9.2   Age Categories of Survey Respondents

	Frequency	Percentage	Cumulative Percentage
18–25	67	12.6	12.6
26–40	132	24.8	37.4
41–60	168	31.5	68.9
61 or older	166	31.1	100.0
Total	533	100.0	100.0

among categories ranging from 18 years old to 61 years or older. Perhaps the first category (ages 18–25) was a bit low in relation to the other categories, but this would generally be expected among persons of this age; they are typically not a high-response group whether the data collection activity is based on mailservices or face-to-face administration. This tends to be also true since this group is less likely to be settled into their own domicile that are the other groups. Thus, the smaller number of respondents is somewhat as would be expected. Nevertheless, each age category includes more than 10% of the overall respondent sample, showing that all age categories in the population were reached through survey administration.

Table 9.3 shows that the overall racial composition of the sample was fairly representative of the population throughout the city. Indeed, the most recent published census data indicate that Caucasians account for 74.5% of the population and that African Americans account for 23.5% of the population. These two racial groups account for nearly 98% of the population for this municipality. Our survey sample consists of 74.3% Caucasians and 20.5% African American respondents. This is very close to the demographic composition of the city's population. Furthermore, the category of *Other*

Table 9.3   Racial Categories of Survey Respondents

	Frequency	Percentage	Cumulative Percentage
African American	109	20.5	20.5
Caucasian	396	74.3	94.8
Other	28	5.3	100.0
Total	533	100.0	100.0

includes persons from the Latino, Native, and Asian American racial groups. Collectively, these individuals only made up 5.5% of the sample. In many respects, it is good that this segment was oversampled to ensure that diversity exists within the sample. However, it is unfortunate that no group exceeded a count of 2% or more so as to warrant the possibility of distinguishing between these various combined groups. Lastly, it should be pointed out that this sample includes a percentage of the minority population that is consistent with the census data. This adds further strength to this particular survey since it is clear that all demographic groups, present within the city limits, were likely reached by these survey efforts.

When considering the marital status of the respondents (see Table 9.4), it is clear that the largest number are married (47%) with the next highest category consisting of single persons (28.3%). These two groups accounted for 75.3% of the entire sample, with other marital statuses accounting for the remaining 25%. Of some note is the fact that 9.3% were widowed; this reflects many of the residents who responded in areas of the city where elderly persons were predominant (remember that 31.1% of the sample consists of persons age 61 and older).

Next, the income of the survey respondents was examined. This information is obviously of importance from a demographic standpoint, but it is also important for later hypothesis testing with H01. Figure 9.1 provides an illustration of the general income levels among respondents of the West Monroe Police Department (WMPD) citizen attitudes and perceptions survey. It is fairly clear from the data in Figure 9.1 that the income levels of respondents are somewhat evenly spread out across categories ranging from $10,000 to $90,000 per year. Although there are, of course, fluctuations between categories, each is fairly well represented, and it would appear that approximately a third of the respondents made $40,000 or more per year. This is fairly well reflective of the region, including the jurisdiction under the city of West Monroe as well as the broader Ouachita Parish region that surrounds the city.

The next demographic variable to be examined was the status as a crime victim or a noncrime victim. A total of 66 respondents indicated that they

Table 9.4 Marital Status of Respondents

	Frequency	Percentage	Cumulative Percentage
Single	151	28.3	28.3
Married	251	47.0	75.3
Widowed	50	9.3	84.6
Divorced	49	9.3	93.9
Separated	13	2.4	96.3
Missing	19	3.6	100.0
Total	533	100.0	100.0

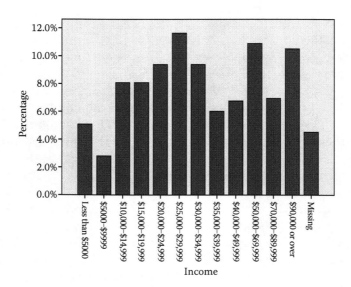

Figure 9.1 Income of survey respondents in municipality.

have been a crime victim during the past three years (see Table 9.5). This means that approximately 12.4% of the total sample of respondents were crime victims during the past 36 months (Table 9.5). The data from Table 9.5 show that among those who did report victimization, the majority reported some type of theft (approximately 41%) or a burglary (approximately 20%). Two other categories, vehicle theft and fraud, both similar in nature to theft and burglary (the intent to steal), accounted for another 15.2% of the crime victims who responded. Vandalism accounted for another 9.1% of the experiences of crime victims.

Among the personal and/or dangerous crimes, domestic violence accounted for 9.1% of the victimization that was reported among respondents. Robbery accounted for 4.5%, and serious assault accounted for 1.5%.

Table 9.5 Type of Crime Victim

	Frequency	Percentage	Cumulative Percentage
Theft	27	5.1	40.9
Vehicle theft	5	0.9	7.6
Vandalism	6	1.1	9.1
Burglary	13	2.4	19.7
Fraud	5	0.9	7.6
Serious assault	1	0.2	1.5
Domestic violence	6	1.1	9.1
Robbery	3	0.6	4.5
Total	66	12.4	100.0

Thus, when considering all 66 citizens who reported victimization, approximately 15% reported being a victim of a personal crime that had a potential to be physically injurious. The breakdown in the types of crime that are reported is actually a bit better than that found nationwide by the BJS in 2008. In the National Crime Victim's Survey, it was found that 23% of all crime victimizations were crimes of violence (BJS, 2008). In this city, it would appear that among those who are victimized, there are lower odds of that experience being violent.

Statistical Analyses Related to Hypothesis Testing

Data in Table 9.6 are produced from the use of linear regression analysis. In this case, linear regression was used to determine the predictive ability of citizen income on the perceptions of police activity. The specific dependent variables examined, as a measure of citizen perception of police activity in the community, were derived from items 8, 9, 10, 11, and 13 of the Citizen Attitudes and Opinions Survey (see Appendix). From Table 9.6, it can be seen that the level of income for citizens in this municipality was a significant predictor of perceptions related to police response, police competence, professional attitudes and behaviors on the job, and overall happiness with police presence in the community.

Oddly enough, the perceptions of overall agency competence were not predicted by the income level of the citizen and were therefore not significant. Regardless, it is clear that in four out of five dependent variables related to perceptions of police activity in the community, four of these were significant at the .05 level. Thus, citizen income serves as a significant predictor of perceptions related to police activity. This relationship is such that, as income level increases among citizens, the views of police activity tend to become increasingly positive. Thus, there is a positive relationship with citizen income that is statistically significant among four out of five dependent variables in Table 9.6.

Data in Table 9.7 are the result of a between-subject ANOVA comparing the means between noncrime victims and crime victims. Only two groups,

Table 9.6 Summary of Regression Analysis for Income as a Predictor Variable for Perceptions of Police Activity ($N = 533$)

Dependent Variables	B	SE B	β
Police response	0.125	0.022	0.240[a]
Police performance	−0.004	0.013	−0.012
Police competence	0.038	0.019	0.089[a]
Police attitudes	0.081	0.021	0.171[a]
Happy with police presence	0.042	0.013	0.138[a]

[a] $p < .05$.

Table 9.7   Analysis of Variance for Crime Victims (N = 533)

Source	df	F	SS	P
		Between Subjects		
Police response	2	9.690[a]	315869.230	0.001
Police performance	2	33.499[a]	324163.750	0.001
Police competence	2	15.055[a]	319076.814	0.001
Police attitudes	2	11.766[a]	316739.352	0.001
Happy with police presence	2	33.504[a]	324245.290	0.001

[a] $p < .01$.

crime victim and noncrime victim, were analyzed; both violent and non-violent crime victims were analyzed as one group due to the fact that only 10 respondents indicated being a victim of a violent crime. Furthermore, the total number of crime victims included only 66 respondents out of the 533 from whom information was collected. Nevertheless, ANOVA was used to analyze the mean differences between these two groups rather than a t-test for significance, simply because the two analyses are essentially the same when comparing two groups, and the researcher's own knowledge of the more recent 2010 Statistical Package for the Social Sciences (SPSS) application more readily lends itself to an automated ANOVA rather than the t-test. As can be seen, there are indeed significant differences in the overall group mean in the perceptions of police activity. From Table 9.7, it can be determined that this significance is at the .01 level of significance. The high level of significance makes this outcome very clear and distinct. In this case, crime victims report less favorable perceptions of police activity than do citizens who are not crime victims.

As with the linear regression analysis in Table 9.6, the dependent variables for this analysis were derived from items 8, 9, 10, 11, and 13 of the Citizen Attitudes and Opinions Survey (see Appendix). These variables include perceptions related to police response, agency performance, police competence, professional attitudes and behaviors on the job, and overall happiness with police presence in the community. These findings show that across all variables, significant differences in perceptions exist, and these differences are quite pronounced.

Discussion

It was found that support exists for H01 based on the regression output that examined the income as a predictor of perceptions related to police activity in the community. Four of the five variables tested showed significance in perceptions of police as divided by income. Perceptions of police response, attitudes and behavior of police, and being happy with police performance were very significantly related to income. Perceptions of police competence were also significant, but income was not significant in relation to citizen perceptions of agency performance. For the purpose of this study, we will accept H01 and reject the null hypothesis.

It was also found that support exists for H02 based on the use of ANOVA to test for different mean responses between crime victims and noncrime victims regarding their perceptions of police activity in the community. Not only was prior victimization found to be an important factor, it is very significant. The lower the number in the significance column, the more significance it contains, and the decimal level is literally off-the-charts low. Victims and nonvictims have very significant differences in their perceptions of police, including police response, performance, competence, attitudes, and happiness with police presence. Thus, we accept H02 as highly significant and again reject the null hypothesis.

Because income is a factor in satisfaction with police, it is recommended that police increase efforts to focus on less advantaged areas of the community. Reaching out with programs to help the less advantaged neighborhoods may increase citizen satisfaction with police. Skogan et al. (2000) explained that the challenge exists in implementing effective community policing programs in disadvantaged or low-capacity areas, although "doing so would help worse-off areas become better off" (p. 12). Therefore, giving more focus on community policing programs in disadvantaged neighborhoods can increase citizen satisfaction of police.

Classification as a crime victim is very significant in citizen satisfaction with police. Therefore, it is recommended that special attention be given to this group. In a study by Brandl and Horvath (1991), it was found that, for victims of property crime, the greater investigative effort on the part of police, the higher the victims' satisfaction with police. In the same study, it was found that gender, income, and education were not related variables in regard to victim satisfaction with police; however, younger victims were less likely to be satisfied with police than older victims. In evaluating a project "Bringing Victims into Community Policing," Herman et al. (2003) found that community policing is enhanced when collaborative problem-solving relationships with victims and victim service organizations are built. Given the information gathered from this study, in conjunction with the two mentioned earlier, it is recommended that police departments make a concerted effort to increase positive relationships with victims and victim service organizations.

Conclusion

In summary, it is recommended that this police agency continue to emphasize the importance of police–community relations in general and that they increase community policing programs in less advantaged areas, in particular, to help balance the socioeconomic divide in perceptions of the police. It is also recommended that this agency devote more attention to victims, including follow-up with victims and coordinating efforts with victim service organizations. An increased emphasis on community policing programs in less advantaged areas will likely improve relationships with lower income citizens through increased positive interactions. Likewise, increased interactions with victims of crime and victim service organizations will also likely improve the perceived gap in response, follow-up, and concern among these citizens. Lastly, we would like to note that overall and when taken in total, the results of this survey demonstrated that, overall, the relations between the police agency and the community were very good. Despite this, this agency's administration made it clear that they wished to identify areas of performance where they could improve; this is a testament to the ethical grounding of the organization. While these administrators could have simply hailed their positive findings without any further analysis, they chose to identify key areas that are commonly cited as problematic among other agencies, transparently present, and make public these data and to ensure that future work of the agency would work toward improving these areas of service delivery. Such efforts are laudable because they hold to the spirit of ethical policing, the true integration of the practitioner–researcher model, as well as many of the fundamental notions of policing by consent. In cases such as these, it is the citizenry of the region who are the final arbiters of police effectiveness in the community, and, in this case, this agency has utilized the input of their community to identify the means to provide a continuing and ever-improving model of policing for years to come.

Appendix

Citizen Attitudes and Opinions Survey

Section 1: Background Information

1. I am a resident of West Monroe: _____ Yes or _____ No
2. Please indicate the region that most closely describes the location of your residence in West Monroe:

Northside	Southside	Eastside	Westside	Outside city limits

3. How many people are there in your household? _____
4. Gender: _____ Male; _____ Female

5. Age: _____ 18–25; _____ 26–40; _____ 41–60; _____ 61 or over
6. Race/Ethnicity: _____ Black; _____ White; _____ Native American; _____ Asian; _____ Latino; _____ Other
7. Is English your first language? _____ Yes; _____ No
8. Marital status: _____ Single; _____ Married; _____ Widowed; _____ Divorced; _____ Separated
9. Education: _____ No school; _____ Elementary school; _____ Junior high; _____ High school; _____ Some college; _____ College graduate; _____ Graduate or professional degree
10. Total household income for the previous year

_____Less than $5,000	_____$30,000–$34,999
_____$5,000–$9,999	_____$35,000–$39,999
_____$10,000–$14,999	_____$40,000–$49,999
_____$15,000–$19,999	_____$50,000–$69,999
_____$20,000–$24,999	_____$70,000–$89,999
_____$25,000–$29,999	_____$90,000 or over

11. Current employment status
_____ Employed full-time
_____ Employed part-time (including students with assistantships)
_____ Self-employed
_____ Unemployed (Please specify: _____ Full time student; _____ Retired; _____ Homemaker; _____ Other)

Section 2: Perceptions of Neighborhood/Community
1. In general, how do you feel about the city of West Monroe as a place to live or work? (circle one):

Very unsatisfied   Unsatisfied   Undecided   Satisfied   Very satisfied

2. Over the past year, how would you rate the quality of life in the neighborhood? Is the quality of life (circle one):

Very bad   Bad   Undecided   Good   Very good

3. I am concerned about the safety and security of my community (circle one):

Strongly   Disagree   Undecided   Agree   Strongly agree
disagree

4. Knowing what I know about my neighborhood or community, the police services seem to be adequate for people in my own local area (circle one):

Strongly   Disagree   Undecided   Agree   Strongly agree
disagree

5. My community is a peaceful place to live (circle one):

Strongly   Disagree   Undecided   Agree   Strongly agree
disagree

Section 3: Contacts with Police

6. I would characterize the relationship between the police and the community as (circle one):

Very negative   Negative   Neutral   Positive   Very positive

7. If needed, services at the police station are easy to access and/or obtain (circle one):

Strongly   Disagree   Undecided   Agree   Strongly agree
disagree

8. In your experience, police response is (circle one):

Very bad   Unsatisfactory   Undecided   Satisfactory   Very good

9. The overall agency performance of the West Monroe Police Department is good (circle one):

Strongly   Disagree   Undecided   Agree   Strongly agree
disagree

10. The overall competence of agency employees of the West Monroe Police Department is good (circle one):

Strongly   Disagree   Undecided   Agree   Strongly agree
disagree

11. The police officers of West Monroe exhibit professional attitudes and behaviors (circle one):

Strongly   Disagree   Undecided   Agree   Strongly agree
disagree

12. It is important for police agencies to be sensitive and understanding of different cultural groups in my community (circle one):

Strongly   Disagree   Undecided   Agree   Strongly agree
disagree

13. I am happy with the overall police presence in the area that I live (circle one):

Strongly   Disagree   Undecided   Agree   Strongly agree
disagree

Section 4: Experiences with Crime

14. I have been crime victim in the past three years.
    _____ Yes   _____ No
    The crimes committed against me would be (select all that apply):

_____ Forcible rape   _____ Robbery   _____ Serious assault
_____ Burglary   _____ Theft   _____ Vehicle theft
_____ Arson   _____ Vandalism   _____ Sex offense
_____ Domestic violence   _____ Fraud

15. Consider the crime problems that may exist in your community. After each issue, state whether it is a
    1—Very big problem; 2—Big problem; 3—Minor problem; 4—Not a problem

1	2	3	4	Public drug sales
1	2	3	4	Fighting in public
1	2	3	4	Public drug use
1	2	3	4	Public drinking
1	2	3	4	Mugging
1	2	3	4	Littering
1	2	3	4	Prostitution

(Continued)

1	2	3	4	Begging and panhandling
1	2	3	4	Domestic violence
1	2	3	4	Child neglect or abuse
1	2	3	4	Residential burglary
1	2	3	4	Vandalism
1	2	3	4	Shoplifting
1	2	3	4	Garbage on the streets
1	2	3	4	Graffiti
1	2	3	4	Gang crimes
1	2	3	4	Poor street repair/poor street lighting
1	2	3	4	Abandoned property

Section 5: Recommendations

16. Please provide any recommendations or suggestions for improvement within the West Monroe Police Department.

_____

Thanks for your participation!

References

Brandl, S. G., and Horvath, F. 1991. Crime-victim evaluation of police investigative performance (Abstract). *Journal of Criminal Justice.* 19(3): 293–305.

Bureau of Justice Assistance. 1993. *A Police Guide to Surveying Citizens and Their Environment.* Washington, DC: Bureau of Justice Assistance.

Bureau of Justice Statistics. 2008. *Criminal Victimization in the United States, 2008 Statistical Tables*. Washington, DC: U.S. Department of Justice.

Community-Oriented Policing Services. 2009. *Community Policing Defined*. Washington, DC: U.S. Department of Justice.

Community Policing Consortium. 1994. *Understanding Community Policing: A Framework for Action*. Bureau of Justice Assistance Monograph No. NCJ 148457. Washington, DC: U.S. Department of Justice.

Davis, C. A., and Ford, J. K. 2002. Using assessment tools to jump-start the move to community policing. In *The Move to Community Policing: Making Change Happen*. Morash, M., and Ford, J. K. eds. Thousand Oaks, CA: Sage Publications: 15–42.

Diamond, D. 2006, July. Examining and assessing your community policing: A self-assessment tool. Presented at the 2006 COPS Conference: Community Policing: Leading the Way to a Safer Nation. Accessed August 12, 2010. Retrieved from http://www.cops.usdoj.gov/files/RIC/Publications/diamond-27.pdf.

Diamond, D., and Weiss, D. M. 2009a, May. *Advancing Community Policing Through Community Governance: A Framework Document*. Washington, DC: U.S. Department of Justice, Community Oriented Policing Services.

Diamond, D., and Weiss, D. M. 2009b, May. *Community Policing: Looking to Tomorrow*. Washington, DC: U.S. Department of Justice, Community Oriented Policing Services.

Garcia, L., Gu, J., Pattavina, A., and Pierce, G. 2003, April. Determinants of citizen and police involvement in community policing, final report. *National Criminal Justice Resource Service*. Accessed July 22, 2010. Retrieved from http://www.ncjrs.gov/pdffiles1/nij/grants/199367.pdf.

Greene, J. R. 2000. Community policing in America: Changing the nature, structure, and function of the police. In *Criminal Justice 2000*. Horney, J., ed. Washington, DC: National Institute of Justice: 299–370.

Hanser, R. D., Gallagher, C., Kuanliang, A., and Carlson, K. 2012. Community crime prevention initiatives and criminal investigations. *Journal of Sociology Studies*. 2(4): 278–91.

Herman, S., Anderson, D. R., Johnson, D., Dempsey, K., Weisburd, D., Greenspan, R. et al. 2003. *Bringing Victims into Community Policing*. Washington, DC: U.S. Department of Justice, Office of Community Oriented Policing Services.

Maguire, M. 2007. Crime data and statistics. In *The Oxford Handbook of Criminology*, fourth edition. Maguire, M., Reiner, R., and Morgan, R., eds. Oxford, UK: Oxford University Press: 241–300.

Maxson, C., Hennigan, K., and Sloane, D. C. 2003, June. *Factors That Influence Public Opinion of the Police*. National Institute of Justice Research for Practice No. NCJ 197925. Washington, DC: U.S. Department of Justice.

Reisig, M. D. 2002. Citizen input and police service: Moving beyond the "feel good" community survey. In *The Move to Community Policing: Making Change Happen*. Morash, M., and Ford, J. K. eds. Thousand Oaks, CA: Sage Publications: 43–60.

Reisig, M. D., and Parks, R. B. 2002, October. *Satisfaction with Police—What Matters?* Research for Practice No. NCJ 194077. Washington, DC: U.S. Department of Justice, National Institute of Justice.

Sadd, S., and Grinc, R. M. 1996, February. *Implementation Challenges in Community Policing: Innovative Neighborhood-Oriented Policing in Eight Cities*. National Institute of Justice Research in Brief No. NCJ 157932. Washington, DC: U.S. Department of Justice.

Schuck, A. M., Rosenbaum, D. P., and Hawkins, D. F. 2008, December. The influence of race/ethnicity, social class, and neighborhood context on residents' attitudes toward the police. *Police Quarterly*. 11(4): 496–519.

Skogan, W. G. 1990. *Disorder and Decline: Crime and the Spiral of Decay in American Neighborhoods*. New York: Free Press.

Skogan, W. G. 2005, September. Citizen satisfaction with police encounters. *Police Quarterly*. 8(3): 298–321.

Skogan, W. G., Hartnett, S. M., DuBois, J., Comey, J. T., Kaiser, M., and Lovig, J. H. 2000, April. *Problem Solving in Practice: Implementing Community Policing in Chicago*. National Institute of Justice Research Report No. NCJ 179556. Washington, DC: U.S. Department of Justice.

Sumner, G. E. 2008, February. Community policing: A critical analysis of a small police department. *Professional Issues in Criminal Justice*. 3(1): 19–37.

Vito, G. F., Walsh, W. F., and Kunselman, J. 2005, December. Community policing: The middle manager's perspective. *Police Quarterly*. 8(4): 490–511.

Weisburd, D., and Eck, J. E. 2004, May. What can police do to reduce crime, disorder, and fear? *The Annals of the American Academy of Political and Social Science*. 593: 42–65.

Transformations in Policing

10

Two Decades of Experience in Community Policing in Slovenia

BRANKO LOBNIKAR
GORAZD MEŠKO
MAJA MODIC

Contents

Abstract

In this chapter, the authors present the development of community policing in Slovenia over the last two decades. In the early 1990s, community policing was introduced as part of the democratization process and the process of transferring concepts of police work from the West, although some elements of community policing had existed in the Slovenian police since the end of World War II. After Slovenia gained its independence in 1991, the old practices of social/state control over the inhabitants were abandoned and, as described in the introduction, various reforms were implemented. In 1992, the police started to implement new foundations of police prevention and community policing as part of the Public Safety project, which in 1995 became the Police Project. One of the basic characteristics of preventive police work should be constant, active communication with the public with the goal of increasing public safety awareness and involving other public services and citizens in controlling disruptive and dangerous occurrences. In the process of reorganizing the police at the local level, in 1992, from 635 safety districts, there emerged 318 newly created police districts headed by community policing officers (CPOs). The appointed community-level police officers were expected to perform mainly preventive tasks. The new strategy on community policing was adopted in 2013, reinforcing the concept of community policing as an organizational strategy and a day-to-day operational tactic. Implementation has become the responsibility of all police officers including those responsible for criminal investigation tasks. CPOs perform not only preventive but also some repressive police tasks, using all police powers as part of problem solving in the local communities where they perform their work.

Introduction—About Slovenia and the Slovenian Police

Slovenia is a central European country covering 20,237 km^2 and bordering Italy to the west, Austria to the north, Hungary to the east, and Croatia to the south. As regards to natural landscape, Slovenia is alpine (the highest mountain is 2864 m high), Dinaric, Pannonian, and Mediterranean (with 46.6 km of coastline along the Adriatic Sea). The Republic of Slovenia is a parliamentary democratic republic. The National Assembly consists of 90 deputies—88 of them are elected representatives of the parliamentary parties and two representatives are elected from the Italian and Hungarian national communities. The National Council consists of 40 elected representatives of employers, employees, farmers, tradesmen, self-employed, noncommercial sector, and local interest groups.

Throughout history, Slovenians were governed within various multinational authorities: until 1918 within the Austro-Hungarian Empire, and between the years 1918 and 1941 within the *State of Slovenes, Croats, and Serbs*, followed by *The Kingdom of Yugoslavia*. During the Second World War (1941–1945), the territory of present-day Slovenia was occupied by Germany, Italy, and Hungary. After the Second World War, Slovenia joined the new Socialist Federal Republic of Yugoslavia, where it remained until June 25, 1991, when it gained its independence following the results of a plebiscite on sovereignty and independence, when Slovenes overwhelmingly voted for independence. The declaration of independence was followed by a 10-day armed conflict between the combined Slovenian military and police forces on the one hand and the Yugoslav armed forces on the other. This conflict led to the departure of the Yugoslav People's Army from Slovenia in October 1991. The Constitution of the Republic of Slovenia was adopted at the end of 1991, and in the following months, Slovenia gained wide international recognition. In the next two decades, Slovenia became a member of major global political, security, and economic organizations (United Nations, European Union [EU], North Atlantic Treaty Organization, Council of Europe, Organization for Security and Co-operation in Europe, Organisation for Economic Co-operation and Development [OECD], etc.) and also presided over some of them (Government Communication Office, 2012a; *Statistical Portrait of Slovenia in the EU 2011*, 2011).

Its gross domestic product (GDP) per capita increased from 8,150 Euro in 1995 to 18,437 Euro in 2008, when Slovenia was at the peak of its GDP growth—in 2011, it was 17,620 Euro (Statistical Office of the Republic of Slovenia, 2012a). In 2014, Slovenia joined the European Union and adopted the Euro as its currency in 2007. Despite the fact that in the period of global economic and financial crises, its GDP growth nearly stopped, the number of unemployed doubled (from 4.4% in 2008 to 8.2% in 2011), and many people are already below the at-risk-of-poverty threshold (13.6% in 2011), some statistical indicators still do not perceive this (Statistical Office of the Republic of Slovenia, 2012b). The human development index for 2011 puts Slovenia in 21st place in the world (United Nations Development Programme, 2011), and according to the Gini coefficient of inequality (0.24 in 2011*), Slovenia is supposed to have the lowest level of social disparities in the EU (OECD, 2012).

According to the population clock, Slovenia has 2,062,374 inhabitants (Statistical Office of the Republic of Slovenia, 2012c†), and the gender ratio is 1:1.02 in favor of women. According to the 2002 census, the ethnic composition of the population was as follows: Slovenians, 83.1%; Croats, 1.8%; Serbs, 2.0%; Bosnians, 1.6%; Hungarians, 0.3%; Italians, 0.1%; others, 2.2%; unknown, 8.9%. The official language is Slovenian, and in the areas where indigenous minorities live, the official languages are also Italian and Hungarian. The 2002 census revealed that 58% of inhabitants belong to the Roman Catholic religion. In Slovenia, there are 42 registered religious communities. The capital city is Ljubljana, with 280,080 inhabitants (Government of the Republic of Slovenia, 2012).

The average age of people living in Slovenia has grown from 32.0 in the 1960s to 36.4 in 1991, and today the average age in Slovenia is 41.8 years old. From 2004, the number of elderly people has been greater than the number of young people. In 2011, 17.5% of the population had tertiary education; one-third of the population, with finished technical or general upper secondary

---

* The Gini coefficient is based on the comparison of cumulative proportions of the population against cumulative proportions of income, and it ranges between 0 in the case of perfect equality and 1 in the case of perfect inequality. For comparison, in the OECD countries, the Gini coefficient is 0.31 (OECD, 2012).
† Data are as of September 24, 2014. Data are estimated on the basis of the certain assumptions for the third quarter of 2014. These are the following assumptions: a child is born every 22 minutes and 35 seconds; a person dies every 28 minutes and 48 seconds; and due to migration, the population decreases by one person in 43 hours and 4 minutes (Statistical Office of the Republic of Slovenia, 2012b).

education; 23.1%, with short-term vocational or vocational upper secondary; and 24.7 people, with primary education. Less than 5% of people in 2011 were without any education or with incomplete primary education. Slovenia is ranked fifth in the EU as regards to the share of people aged 25–64 speaking at least one foreign language. About two-thirds of the people in Slovenia are fairly satisfied with their lives and 20% are very satisfied, while about 13% of people are not satisfied.

There are 6031 settlements in Slovenia and more than a half of them (3801) are populated by 50–499 people. There are only two settlements populated with more than 50,000 people (the capital city Ljubljana and the second largest city Maribor). The population density in Slovenia (101.0 residents per km^2) is lower than the average for European countries (116.6 residents per km^2). Half of the people in Slovenia live in cities and suburban areas (Hren, 2011; Statistical Office of the Republic of Slovenia, 2012d).

The Local Self-Government Act (Zakon o lokalni samoupravi, 2007) provides that the basic self-governing local community is a municipality, with at least 5000 inhabitants. The authorities of a municipality comprise the mayor, the municipal council as the highest decision-making body, and the supervisory committee to oversee the disposal of municipal property and public expenditure. The mayor is a directly elected official who represents and acts on behalf of the municipality and presides over the municipal council (Government Communication Office, 2012b).

Slovenian municipalities (there are 211* municipalities in Slovenia) are very heterogeneous in terms of surface area—the smallest municipality is one-eightieth the size of the largest (the municipality of Odranci at 7 km^2 versus the municipality of Kočevje at 555 km^2), as well as in terms of population—312 people live in the smallest municipality (Hodoš), while 280,080 live in the largest (Ljubljana) (Statistical Office of the Republic of Slovenia, 2009).

Slovenian National Police

The beginnings of the Slovenian police go back to the period of the Austro-Hungarian Empire, when the Gendarmerie Corps was founded in 1849. After World War I and the disintegration of the Austro-Hungarian Empire, Slovenia along with its existing gendarmerie, became a part of the newly established Kingdom of Serbs, Croats, and Slovenes. Between the year 1945 and 1991, the Slovenian police was a part of the Yugoslav police force, called the *Milica* (militia). At that time, the Slovenian police force was subordinated directly to the Slovenian Secretariat of the Interior and was decentralized—police

---

* Data are as of July 1, 2014 (Statistical Office of the Republic of Slovenia, 2014).

station commanders were appointed by local authorities with the approval of the secretary of the interior. After 1991, when Slovenia gained its independence, the period of institutional changes began—in 1992, the militia was renamed the *police*, and in 1998, the Police Act (Zakon o policiji, 1998) came into force, representing the legal basis for current police work (Kolenc, 2003; Meško and Klemenčič, 2007; Meško and Maver, 2010).

The Slovenian police force employs 8300 personnel—5564 uniformed police officers, 1648 plain-clothed police officers, and 1088 other police personnel, or one police officer per 285.82 inhabitants (Police, 2014a).

Through the Police Act of 1998, the Slovenian police service became a body within the Ministry of the Interior and performs its tasks at three levels—national (General Police Directorate), regional (eight police directorates), and local (police stations), with its headquarters located in Ljubljana, the capital city of Slovenia. The Police Act introduced the office of the director general of the police, while formerly the minister of the interior had been the head of the police force. Since 1998, this position has been reserved for a professional and not a political appointee (Meško and Klemenčič, 2007). The director general of the police is a public servant and is appointed and dismissed by the government, upon the proposal of the minister of the interior. At the beginning of 2013, a new police legislation was adopted, namely the Police Tasks and Powers Act (Zakon o nalogah in pooblastilih policije, 2013) and the Organisation and Work of the Police Act (Zakon o organiziranosti in delu v policiji, 2013).

The bodies responsible for performing various tasks within the General Police Directorate are the service of the Director General of the Police, Uniformed Police Directorate, Criminal Police Directorate, National Forensic Laboratory, Police Specialties Directorate, Police Academy, and IT and Telecommunications Office. The Uniformed Police Directorate is responsible for coordinated, professional, efficient, and lawful work of the uniformed police (Police, 2014b). The Criminal Police Directorate is a specialized division for fighting crime, which coordinates, monitors, analyzes, and evaluates situations in the field of criminal offenses. It ensures the effective and lawful implementation of activities against various forms of crime and closely cooperates with uniformed police officers (Police, 2014c). Within the Criminal Police Directorate, a National Bureau of Investigation was established in 2010, as a specialized criminal investigation unit with the mission to detect and investigate economic crime, corruption, and other forms of serious crime. The bureau will gradually employ around 80 investigators from within and outside the police (Jevšek and Meško, 2011; Police, 2014d).

Police stations are headed by commanders and classified according to the tasks they perform: police stations, traffic police stations, border police stations, maritime police stations, airport police stations, mounted police stations, service dog handler stations, and police stations for compensatory measures (Police, 2014e). The area of each police station is divided into police districts, which comprise the jurisdiction of one or more municipalities, or only a part of the municipality. Police districts are headed by community policing officers (CPOs) who are responsible for preventive tasks within local communities and for the implementation of the social role of the police (Kolenc, 2003; Police, 2014e).

Community Policing in Slovenia

In Slovenia, community policing was introduced as part of the democratization process and the process of transferring concepts of police work from the West (Lobnikar and Meško, 2010; Meško, 2009). However, some elements of community policing existed in the Slovenian police from the end of World War II. According to the National Militia Act of 1946, the basic unit of the national police was a militia station, and the area of the station was divided into patrol districts. Despite the centralized management, one of the tasks of the militiapersons was to get to know people and the environment of their station. In 1950, combined patrolling was introduced, which enabled militiapersons to show more self-initiative. This form of work also influenced the establishment of information networks in patrol districts, which was important for obtaining information even when militiamen were not on the beat. In 1953, a new form of field service was introduced—the sector service. A sectoral militiaperson performed work in his/her sector according to his own discretion; in addition to the traditional repressive tasks, he/she performed preventive tasks and cooperated with residents. In the 1960s, the area of the militia station was divided into new patrol districts, which coincided with the areas of newly established local communities that were parts of the municipalities. The head of the patrol district was primarily responsible for public safety, with an emphasis on broader and more genuine partnership with the citizens in the local community. After 1976, the head of the security district (former patrol district) took over a set of new tasks mainly related to the development of social self-protection and provision of public safety within his district (Police, 2014f). The described factors of the social self-protection system in the 1970s represented the beginnings of the current role of the CPO and the partner cooperation in the field of providing security. Such preventive role of the police did not fully come to life at that time probably because it was institutionalized, ideologically oriented, and a regulatory imposition of self-protective behavior (Kolenc, 2003; Police, 2014f).

After Slovenia gained its independence in 1991, the old practices of social control were abandoned and the Slovenian police started to implement new foundations of police prevention and community policing. As in many other postcommunist countries, at the declarative level, the concept of community policing in Slovenia was followed along the lines of the United States and Great Britain. However, it seems that the implementation of community policing has not been satisfactory (Meško and Lobnikar, 2005; Meško and Klemenčič, 2007), and especially, its beginnings were accompanied by organizational, personnel and substantive issues (Pečar, 2002), as a consequence of the haste and the lack of understanding of the underlying philosophy and basic requirements, in particular legal regulations that do not give the police such wide discretion as in the countries where community policing originated (Meško, 2009; Meško and Klemenčič, 2007).

The police started to implement new foundations of police prevention and community policing in 1992 with the project of Public Safety, followed by the Police Project in 1995. The cornerstone of preventive police work should be constant active communication with the public that seeks to raise public safety awareness and involvement of other public services and citizens in controlling disruptive and dangerous occurrences (Žaberl, 2004). As a result of the reorganization, from 635 safety districts, 318 newly created police districts emerged in 1992 (Meško and Lobnikar, 2005; Žerak, 2004).

Laws and Bylaws on Community Policing in Slovenia

Before being defined in the legislation, community policing was defined in some strategic and operational documents of the Ministry of the Interior and the police. The document entitled *Basic Guidelines for the Preparation of a Medium-Term Plan for Police Development and Work for the Period from 2003 to 2007* (Ministry of the Interior, 2003a) explicitly states that the guiding principle of the Slovenian police is to perform community policing, while its mission is to help people, ensure their safety, and the safety of their property, and its vision is to provide a safe life for people through partnership with individuals and communities.

In the *Annual Work Plan of the Police in 2003* (Ministry of the Interior, 2003b), the strategic goal is to develop partnerships with individuals and communities, while the other goals include the establishment and the development of partnership between the police and the citizens in all local communities, constant consideration of the direction of policing in communities, and directions for implementing preventive work and development of prevention programs for community safety.

The current *Basic Guidelines for the Preparation of a Medium-Term Plan for Police Development and Work for the Period from 2003 to 2017* (Ministry of the Interior, 2012) comprise seven strategic goals that are considered to be of key importance for further development of the police. One of the goals—establishment of coresponsibility for security provision together with local communities—stresses preventive police work and development of partnerships with the community, along with increased police visibility. It is emphasized that without cooperation and help from citizens, the police are less successful, since problems cannot be solved solely by repressive work.

The annual *Guidelines and Mandatory Instructions for the Preparation of the Annual Plan of Police Work in 2012* (Ministry of the Interior, 2011) states that the annual plan of police work should reflect the strengthening of preventive activities and community policing as a priority, further emphasizing the need to increase police visibility and police–community partnership. The current *Guidelines and Mandatory Instructions for the Preparation of the Annual Plan of the Police Work in 2014* (Ministry of the Interior, 2013) dictates the establishment of the communities' coresponsibility for local safety provision, with the emphasis on strengthening police cooperation with the municipal warden service.

Along with the new police legislation, the new strategy of community policing was also adopted (Police, 2013a) at the beginning of 2013. The strategy follows the legislative provisions, especially by emphasizing the independence of police stations—they must adapt their activities to the needs and the interests of local communities concerning security. The new strategy declares that community policing is a comprehensive police approach, based on preventive work, but not excluding repressive work. Although CPOs are in charge of community policing, it should be performed by every member of the police force.

At criminal policy level, community policing in Slovenia has been mentioned in the *Resolution on the Prevention and Suppression of Crime* (2006). This document states that for crime at the local level, situational preventive tasks may be successfully accomplished by the police, who years ago began implementing a strategy of community policing. The emphasis is on the methods and the forms of work, such as consultancy, working in consultative bodies, working in police offices, education of children and adults, and informal ways of socializing and connecting with people. The role of the CPO is especially important. To achieve a greater sense of security among citizens and demotivation of potential offenders, police officers should be physically present at the local level, and they should be integrated into the local environment (awareness of problems; personal contact with problematic people, particularly young people; verbal counseling; and warning), as well as being a good example to others. The *Resolution on the National Program of Prevention and Suppression of Crime for the Period 2012–2016* (2012) states that community policing currently represents one of the central concepts in the (police) prevention of crime and reducing fear of crime.

As regards to the legislative level, at the beginning of 2013, a new police legislation was adopted: the Police Tasks and Powers Act (Zakon o nalogah in pooblastilih policije, 2013) and the Organisation and Work of the Police

Act (Zakon o organiziranosti in delu v policiji, 2013). Both acts entered into force on May 4, 2013, replacing the former Police Act (1998), ensuring the transparent and clear regulation in the area of policing. The new Police Tasks and Powers Act introduces some important new features, including new police powers to ensure safety and order at sporting events and modified conditions for the use of service dogs as well as firearms. With the Police Tasks and Powers Act, the use of firearms is further restricted and can be used only to prevent an unlawful assault directed concurrently against police officers or any other person that puts lives in jeopardy. The new legislation also introduces the distinction between the temporary restriction of movement and the deprivation of liberty. As regards to community policing, the Organisation and Work of the Police Act emphasizes the decentralization and the strengthening of the independence and the autonomy of police directorates (regional level) and defines the cooperation between the police and the local community with the emphasis on the role and the importance of community policing. Integrity is mentioned for the first time in the legislative context—the police should ensure the organizational and personal integrities of its employees. To do so, a new department responsible for the systematic examination of strategic proposals, innovations, questions, and issues in the field of ethics and integrity was established within the police academy.

Alongside police legislation, the Local Police Act (Zakon o občinskem redarstvu, 2006) and the Local Self-Government Act (Zakon o lokalni samoupravi, 2007) deal with some aspects of community policing and will therefore be presented. The Local Police Act provides that municipal councils should adopt a municipal security program that is based on assessed security conditions, and set out the types and the scope of tasks of the local police. Article 9 provides that municipal wardens, in accordance with their tasks and powers, cooperate with police officers. The Local Self-Government Act represents the enactment of the possibility to establish a formal police–local community partnership, since Article 29 enables the mayors to set up consultative bodies for dealing with problems in the local community (municipality). For this purpose, councils, advisory committees, commissions, and other forms of cooperation may be established.

Local Safety Councils

An important element of the local safety policy and community policing in Slovenia is local safety councils, situated within the local administration as a consultative body for crime and safety issues. The Organisation and Work of the Police Act (2013) and the Local Self-Government Act (2007) provide the legal basis for the establishment of such councils; however, these provisions are not binding, but merely recommendatory.

Within the municipalities in Slovenia, there are 182* local safety councils. The members of the local safety councils are representatives of both public and private agencies—police officers, municipal wardens, mayors, members of municipal councils, local government civil servants, representatives of social service organizations, schools, local business, media, political parties, and nongovernment organizations (Meško, 2004; Meško and Lobnikar, 2005). The local safety council should be a body that brings together the local community, the police, and other local interest groups in search of common solutions to improve safety at the local level. While the Slovenian police force has contributed much to the operation of local safety councils and community policing in general, the main challenge remains how to induce citizens to take part in addressing common security issues in their local communities (Meško, 2006a). Local safety councils deal with traffic safety, maintenance of public order and peace, and crime prevention. Their operation includes an analysis of the security situation in the local community, the development of safety strategies, the implementation of projects, the execution of a fund raising for their own operation (since the funding for their operation is not formally guaranteed, individual councils draw funds from the state budget, receive donations, accept contributions from businesses, organizations, and individuals [Kolenc, 2003]), the setting up of working groups at the neighborhood level (e.g., residential quarters), the issuance of preventive materials (leaflets, posters), the organization of round tables and public forums, and the raising of public awareness on their work (Kolenc, 2003; Police, 2013b).

Community Policing Officers

Those in charge of community policing are the CPOs, who are responsible for the cooperation with other police officers, residents, representatives of local communities, associations, organizations, businesses, institutions, bodies, and other interest groups (Meško and Lobnikar, 2005). In the scope of their own actions, which are mostly of a preventive nature, they also cooperate in preventing and detecting criminal offences and offenders, identifying and monitoring crime hot spots, raising awareness of crime and violations, reminding and advising citizens on crime prevention, lecturing in schools and kindergartens, visiting injured parties and victims, returning found or seized items, and obtaining information through interviews (Kolenc, 2003). CPOs' duties are defined in the police rules, the community policing strategy, guidelines for the implementation of preventive work, measures to improve community policing, and the basic guidelines for the preparation of

* Data are as of November 2013 (Police, 2013b).

a mid-term plan for police development and work for the period 2003 to 2007 (Meško and Lobnikar, 2005; Virtič and Lobnikar, 2004).

The CPO is considered a safety partner of citizens, to whom he is available for advice and help. The CPO post is usually reserved for police officers with years of experience and communication skills. The official website of the Slovenian police* includes the names of all 317 CPOs and their districts,† basic information on their duties, their contact information, and an appeal to citizens to help create favorable safety conditions in local communities (Kolenc, 2003; Lobnikar and Meško, 2010).

Studies on Community Policing in Slovenia

The findings presented in Table 10.1 illustrate the outline of Slovenian community policing development and indicate the problems emerging in the process of implementation. These findings are derived from studies on community policing in Slovenia, conducted on various samples of police officers, citizens, mayors, and municipal council members from 1998 onward.

In 1998, a survey was conducted among the residents of various locations in Slovenia (e.g., the town of Metlika, the Severna Primorska region, and the capital city Ljubljana). Respondents evaluated their attitudes toward the preventive work of the police. The findings indicate that people expect the police to cooperate with them and are willing to participate in police work—they expressed a willingness to help police officers and provide information, but they would not let police officers enter their home (Meško et al., 2000).

The finding from the study on the differences between police officers and citizens of Ljubljana regarding their attitudes toward community policing and citizens' willingness to cooperate with police indicated that police officers as well as citizens are more in favor of community policing than traditional police methods. It is noteworthy that citizens are much more willing to cooperate with the police than the latter perceive (Pagon and Lobnikar, 2001).

A study on police station commanders' perspectives on community policing was conducted in 2003 (Kosmač and Gorenak, 2004). It was found that commanders are relatively satisfied, with the CPOs' work motivation, community policing strategy content and crime prevention guidelines, but they are much less satisfied with the preventive work instructions. In their opinion, CPOs are well acquainted with community prevention documents and perform less repressive tasks. They take the view that the police have an

---

* http://www.policija.si/eng/index.php
† A police district is a basic geographic area where community policing officers perform their duties (Kolenc, 2003).

Table 10.1 Review of Studies on Community Policing in Slovenia

Title and Authors	Year	Sample	Subject of Research
Strah pred kriminaliteto, policijsko preventivno delo in javno mnenje o policiji (Fear of crime, police preventive work and public opinion on the police) (Meško et al., 2000)	1998	Residents of Metlika, Severna Primorska region, and Ljubljana (*n* = 343)	Fear of crime; threatening occurrences; attitudes toward police preventive work
V skupnost usmerjeno policijsko delo v mestu Ljubljana: Ugotavljanje potreb za ustanovitev mestne policije ali redefiniranje dela državne policije (Community-oriented policing in the city of Ljubljana: Assessment of needs to establish municipal police or to redefine state police work) (Pagon and Lobnikar, 2001)	2000	Police officers (*n* = 95) and residents of Ljubljana (*n* = 75)	Attitudes toward COP; citizens' willingness to cooperate and perception of willingness to cooperate with the police
Zagotavljanje varnosti v lokalni skupnosti (Security provision in the local community) (Meško, 2006a)	2003 2004	Members of local safety councils (*n* = 178)	Establishment, performance, and role of local safety councils; responsibility for solving local security issues; role of the police in crime prevention on the local level; partnership; feelings of insecurity and fear of crime
Stališča komandirjev policijskih postaj do policijskega dela v skupnosti (Police station commanders' attitudes towards community policing) (Kosmač and Gorenak, 2004)	2004	Police station commanders (*n* = 53)	Satisfaction with particular work segments; satisfaction with the content of basic community policing documents; assessment of CPOs' performance

(Continued)

Table 10.1 (Continued) Review of Studies on Community Policing in Slovenia

Title and Authors	Year	Sample	Subject of Research
Raziskava o ocenah in stališčih prebivalcev obmejnih območij do dela policistov na bodoči schengenski meji (Research on residents' attitudes towards the work of police officers on the future Schengen border) (Lobnikar et al., 2005)	2005	Residents of Slovenian–Croatian border region (*n* = 533)	Attitudes toward police work—trust and satisfaction with police work; feelings of security; willingness to cooperate with the police
Razhajanje med oceno stanja in med pričakovanji ljudi do policije z območja PU Maribor (Discrepancy between citizens' assessment of the current state and their expectations from the police of Maribor Police Directorate) (Virtič, 2006)	2005	Residents from the area of Maribor Police Directorate (*n* = 1006)	Assessment of police work; feelings of security; trust in police; assessment of police legitimacy; satisfaction with police work
Policing in a post-socialist country: Critical reflections (Meško, 2006a)	2006	Police officers (*n* = 847)	Police professionalism; police culture; management support; communication within the police organization; police perception of citizens' willingness to cooperate with the police; job satisfaction; attitudes toward community policing
Raziskava stanja na področju v skupnost usmerjenega policijskega dela—Stališča občinskih varnostnih sosvetov (Research on community policing—Attitudes of local safety council members) (Ministrstvo za notranje zadeve [Ministry of the Interior], 2010)	2010	Municipalities where local safety councils are established (*n* = 117)	Community policing; members' attitudes toward cooperation between local community, police, and municipal warden service

(Continued)

Table 10.1 (Continued)   Review of Studies on Community Policing in Slovenia

Title and Authors	Year	Sample	Subject of Research
Javnomnenjska raziskava o ocenah in stališčih prebivalcev Republike Slovenije o delu policije 2010 (Public opinion survey on police work) (Černič et al., 2009)	2010	Adult residents of Slovenia ($n = 2007$)	Trust in police; satisfaction with police work; opinion on police oversight; assessment of police performance; willingness to cooperate with the police; assessment of police cooperation with the local community; assessment of preventive actions
Zagotavljanje varnosti v lokalni skupnosti (Security provision in the local community) (Gorenak and Gorenak, 2011)	2010	Mayors and local safety council members ($n = 520$)	Assessment of police work; willingness to cooperate with the police
CRP—Občutki ogroženosti in zagotavljanje varnosti v lokalnih skupnostih (Feelings of safety and the role of police in local security provision) (Meško et al., 2012)	2012	Police officers (581), citizens (961), police chiefs (24), and mayors (24)	Extent of police engagement within local communities, police, and local community partnership in the process of identifying and solving security issues, existing forms of community policing, performance of local safety councils in police response to threats perceived by citizens

Source: Jere, M. et al., *Revija za kriminalistiko in kriminologijo.* 63(1): 3–13, 2012.

adequate legal grounding for work in safety councils; the commanders themselves are also involved in setting up the safety councils, but they feel that there is too little support from local communities for work in safety councils.

Meško and Lobnikar (2005), in their study on local safety councils, found that establishing local partnership through local safety councils is a great progress toward success, although it has not yet yielded the desired outcomes. The greatest burden of responsibility for problem solving still lies with the police. According to the respondents, the police are seen as having the greatest responsibility for local crime control and safety problems, followed by the local city administration, individuals, schools, social services, and family. Respondents are of the opinion that the impediments for the successful performance of local safety councils are related to the unclearly defined roles of the participants, the incomprehension of partnership, the lack of interest, and the centralization. The authors also found that preventive activities on a local level have more effect on the reduction of fear of crime than on the actual reduction of crime and disorder in local communities.

In 2005, a survey on attitudes toward police work was conducted among residents of the Slovenian–Croatian border region (before the implementation of the Schengen regime). The respondents expressed the need for better cooperation, communication, and help from the police. Findings show that respondents are generally quite willing to cooperate with the police, with the exception of activities that traditionally do not involve civic cooperation—joint patrols, assessment of effectiveness, and legitimacy of police work (Lobnikar et al., 2005).

The findings of a study on the discrepancy between the citizens' assessment of the current state and their expectations from the police conducted in 2005 among the residents from the area of Maribor Police Directorate show that people are satisfied with the work of the police, but police officers still do not entirely meet their expectations. However, more than half of the respondents are willing to cooperate with the police (Virtič, 2006).

The results of the study on the professionalism of the Slovenian police (Meško, 2006b) show that almost two-thirds of police officers in a sample of more than 900 police officers responded that community policing is not a waste of time and is useful for the police and the people in the communities. All CPOs answered this question positively. The problems they mentioned were that there are few people willing to cooperate with the police in solving problems in the neighborhoods where they live (28%) and even fewer people are willing to cooperate in providing information in the investigation of crimes (21%), but they are willing in somewhat greater numbers to call the police and inform them when they see something suspicious (35%). The problem reported by the CPOs is the lack of police officers at police stations, which means that the CPOs also perform other police functions and therefore have limited time for community policing.

At the beginning of 2010 the Ministry of the Interior sponsored a public opinion survey on the police (Černič, Makarovič, and Macur, 2009), which yielded results similar to those of previous public opinion surveys and shows that citizens are satisfied with the police–local community cooperation. Police officers' efforts in problem solving are rated very highly, while police visibility received the lowest rates. The cooperation between CPOs and residents is satisfying, and the level of public trust in the police is quite high (3.50 in a range of 1–5, with the higher value indicating a higher level).

Under the auspices of the Ministry of the Interior, an analysis of safety councils members' perspectives on various aspects of cooperation between the local community, the police, and the municipal warden service was conducted in 2010 (Ministry of the Interior, 2010). The members of the local safety councils reported that they usually meet from one to three times a week; in their opinion, the police force is the first in line to provide safety on the local level, followed by the municipal warden service and the private security companies.

In 2010, a study on local security provision was conducted among mayors and local safety council members from 42 Slovenian municipalities. Among various areas (satisfaction with police work, police effectiveness, feelings of safety, willingness to cooperate with the police, police–community cooperation, interpersonal competences of police officers), they rated willingness to cooperate with the police very high, while police–community cooperation and feelings of safety received lower ratings (Gorenak and Gorenak, 2011).

In 2011, a nationwide research among Slovenian citizens and police officers was conducted on the quality of life in local communities, the perception of threats, the community policing, and the various aspects of local safety provision. Both police officers and citizens perceive factors of uncertainty (unemployment, poverty), illegal drugs and alcohol, organized crime, and threats to traffic safety as the most threatening to local safety; however, citizens in general feel safe. Citizens exhibit the highest level of trust in their families and friends, fire fighters, and rescue services, while police officers trust the police the most. Based on interviews with police chiefs, CPOs, and mayors, it was found that the cooperation between the police and the municipal administrations mainly exists on an informal basis, depending on the willingness of the individual mayor, the police chief, the CPO, and others. Mayors rate community policing very highly, while police chiefs and CPOs stress that community policing should be the priority of all police officers, not only CPOs (Meško et al., 2012).

In the survey from 2011 (Meško et al., 2012), respondents were asked to express their attitudes toward community policing ("Community policing is a waste of time and is useless"). Results of a t-test, presented in Table 10.2 indicate that there are statistically significant differences between police officers' perceptions in 2006 (Nalla et al., 2007) and in 2012 (Meško et al., 2012)

Table 10.2   Police Officers' Attitudes toward Community Policing in 2006 and 2011

Variable on Community Policing	2006		2011		
	Strongly Agree/Agree (%)	Mean/SD	Strongly Agree/Agree (%)	Mean/SD	t-Value
"Community policing is a waste of time and is useless."	2.0/5.2	3.86/0.99	1.3/4.8	4.16/0.97	−5.85[a]

Note: 1 = strongly agree; 5 = strongly disagree.
[a] $p \leq .001$, two-tail probability.

regarding community policing ($t = -5.85$; $p = .000$). Police officers' attitudes have changed in the compared years, so from 2011 they hold more positive attitudes toward community policing.

Conclusions

At the very beginning, the community policing implementation process was marked by organizational, staffing, and content-related problems (Pečar, 2002) and later on impeded by the poor adaptation of the imported model to the Slovenian legal and social contexts as well as by conceptual problems in the philosophy of community policing (Meško and Klemenčič, 2007). The community policing activities that were in practice before 1991 were more ideologically oriented, in terms of the comprehensive social and political controls of citizens. During the political system of socialism, all former Yugoslavian states shared the so-called System of General People's Defence and Social Self-protection. This can be understood as a form of socialist community policing, with cooperation between the police and the local community as a crucial element of public security provision (Meško, Tominc, and Sotlar, 2013). The experiences and the memories of the communist regime can thus positively influence the public's willingness to participate (or as Seagrave [1996, p. 5] states the term *community policing* brings up "warm romantic images of policing from the past when police officers were viewed in a positive light"), but they can also dissuade people from participating. Particular practices are redolent of total state control, while others are commonly accepted as basic factors of community safety and maintenance of public order (Meško, 2009; Meško and Klemenčič, 2007).

From the users' point of view, there is still some room for improvement. The proposals of citizens for more effective community policing primarily refer to police patrols in the local environment, presence and accessibility of police officers in the streets, improvement of communication and cooperation between police officers and the local population, development of communication and interpersonal skills, and improvement of the skills of police officers in cultural diversity.

It is evident that policing in Slovenia has changed significantly over two decades of Slovenian independence; moreover, changes in the field of police work are still taking place. Meško et al. (2013) note that the Slovenian police are trying to balance two (often conflicting) concepts of policing—community policing and intelligence-led policing. Concepts such as intelligence-led policing and establishment of specialized investigative institutions (e.g., the National Bureau of Investigation) influence the politicians and the public to perceive the police as primarily repressive with the main purpose of providing excellent evidence for effective prosecution. This is particularly enhanced during the present economic crisis.

We can conclude that the main protagonists of community policing in Slovenia are police officers who are supported by local residents and, to some extent, and in principle also by the representatives of local self-government. Community policing is relatively well defined in the strategic and operational documents of the Ministry of the Interior and Police; however, mere definition is not sufficient for the implementation of the philosophy. Substantial changes at the organizational level are yet to be implemented, namely, changes in work organization and performance evaluation. Community policing is most clearly manifested in the work of CPOs and local safety councils. The main challenges for the future remain how to attract local residents to participate in the efforts to improve safety, how to consolidate the implementation and practice of the community policing philosophy, and how to ensure high levels of integrity on both sides of the partnership.

References

Černič, M., Makarovič, M., and Macur, M. 2009. *Javnomnenjska raziskava o ocenah in stališčih prebivalcev Republike Slovenije o delu policije—2009* [Opinion poll on assessments and attitudes of the residents of the Republic of Slovenia towards the work of the police—2009]. Nova Gorica, Slovenia: Fakulteta za uporabne družbene študije.

Gorenak, V., and Gorenak, I. 2011. Dejavniki pripravljenosti lokalnih skupnosti za sodelovanje s policijo v Sloveniji [Factors of the readiness of local communities to cooperate with the police in Slovenia]. *Revija za kriminalistiko in kriminologijo.* 62(3): 253–62.

Government Communication Office. 2012a. Official gateway to information on Slovenia. Retrieved from http://www.slovenia.si/en/.

Government Communication Office. 2012b. Local self-government. Retrieved from http://www.slovenia.si/en/slovenia/state/local-self-government/.

Government of the Republic of Slovenia. 2012. About Slovenia. Retrieved from http://www.vlada.si/en/about_slovenia/.

Hren, K. ed. 2011. To Slovenia for its 20th birthday—Slovenian statisticians. Ljubljana, Slovenia: Statistical Office of the Republic of Slovenia. Retrieved from http:// www.stat.si/eng/pub.asp.

Jere, M., Sotlar, A., and Meško, G. 2012. Praksa in raziskovanje policijskega dela v skupnosti v Sloveniji [Community policing practice and research in Slovenia]. *Revija za kriminalistiko in kriminologijo.* 63(1): 3–13.

Jevšek, A., and Meško, G. 2011. The Slovenian National Bureau of Investigation—An attempt to respond to contemporary unconventional forms of criminality. In *Policing in Central and Eastern Europe: Social Control of Unconventional Deviance: Conference Proceedings.* Meško, G., Sotlar, A., and Winterdyk, J., eds. Ljubljana, Slovenia: Faculty of Criminal Justice and Security: 243–58.

Kolenc, T. 2003. *The Slovene Police.* Ljubljana, Slovenia: Ministry of the Interior of the Republic Slovenia, Police, General Police Directorate.

Kosmač, F., and Gorenak, V. 2004. Stališča komandirjev policijskih postaj do policijskega dela v skupnosti [Police station commanders' attitudes towards community policing] 5. In *Slovenski dnevi varstvoslovja.* Lobnikar, B., ed. Ljubljana, Slovenia: Fakulteta za policijsko-varnostne vede: 714–26.

Lobnikar, B., and Meško, G. 2010. Responses of police and local authorities to security issues in Ljubljana, the capital of Slovenia. In *Police, Policing, Policy and the City in Europe.* Cools, M., De Kimpe, S., Dormaels, A., Easton, M., Enhus, E., Ponsaers, P. et al., eds. The Hague: Eleven International Publishing: 161–79.

Lobnikar, B., Pagon, M., Umek, P., Sotlar, A., Bučar-Ručman, A., Tominc, B. et al. 2005. *Raziskava o ocenah in stališčih prebivalcev obmejnih območij do dela policistov na bodoči schengenski meji* [Research on residents' attitudes towards the work of police officers on the future Schengen border]. Ljubljana, Slovenia: Fakulteta za policijsko-varnostne vede.

Meško, G. 2004. Local safety councils in Slovenia. In *Urban Safety: Problems, Governance and Strategies.* van der Vijver, K., and Terpstra, J., eds. Enschede, The Netherlands: IPIT, Institute for Social Safety Studies, University of Twente: 133–44.

Meško, G. 2006a. Perceptions of security: Local safety councils in Slovenia. In *Invisible Threats: Financial and Information Technology Crimes and National Security.* Gori, U., and Paparela, I., eds. Amsterdam: IOS Press: 69–89.

Meško, G. 2006b. Policing in a post-socialist country: Critical reflections. In *Understanding Crime: Structural and Developmental Dimensions, and Their Implications for Policy* (Plenary address at the annual conference of the ESC). Tübingen, Germany: Institut für Kriminologie der Universität Tübingen.

Meško, G. 2009. Transfer of crime control ideas: Introductory Reflections. In *Crime Policy, Crime Control and Crime Prevention—Slovenian Perspectives.* Meško, G., and Kury, H., eds. Ljubljana, Slovenia: Tipografija: 5–19.

Meško, G., and Klemenčič, G. 2007. Rebuilding legitimacy and police professionalism in an emerging democracy: The Slovenian experience. In *Legitimacy and Criminal Justice.* T. Tyler, R., ed. New York: Russell Sage Foundation: 84–115.

Meško, G., and Lobnikar, B. 2005. The contribution of local safety councils to local responsibility in crime prevention and provision of safety. *Policing: An International Journal of Police Strategies & Management.* 28(2): 353–73.

Meško, G., and Maver, D. 2010. On police and policing in Slovenia: Obstacles and challenges. In *Police without Borders: The Fading Distinction between Local and Global.* Roberson, C., Das, D. K., and Singer, J. K., eds. Boca Raton, FL: CRC Press: 87–109.

Meško, G., Lobnikar, B., Jere, M., and Sotlar, A. 2013. Recent developments of policing in Slovenia. In *Handbook on Policing in Central and Eastern Europe.* Meško, G., Fields, C. B., Lobnikar, B., and Sotlar, A., eds. New York: Springer: 263–86.

Meško, G., Sotlar, A., Lobnikar, B., Jere, M., and Tominc, B. 2012. *Občutek ogroženosti in vloga policije pri zagotavljanju varnosti na lokalni ravni* [Feelings of insecurity and the role of police in local safety provision]: *CRP(V5-1038 A: Poročilo ciljnega raziskovalnega projekta.* Ljubljana, Slovenia: Fakulteta za varnostne vede.

Meško, G., Tominc, B., and Sotlar, A. 2013. Urban security management in the capitals of the former Yugoslav republics. *European Journal of Criminology.* 10(3): 284–96.

Meško, G., Umek, P., Dobovšek, B., Gorenak, V., Mikulan, M., Žaberl, M. et al. 2000. *Strah pred kriminaliteto, policijsko preventivno delo in javno mnenje o policiji: Raziskovalno poročilo* [Fear of crime, police preventive work and public opinion on the police: Research report]. Ljubljana, Slovenia: Visoka policijsko-varnostna šola.

Ministry of the Interior. 2003a. *Temeljne usmeritve za pripravo srednjeročnega načrta razvoja in dela policije v obdobju 2003–2007* [Basic guidelines for the preparation of a medium-term plan for police development and work for the period from 2003 to 2007]. Ljubljana, Slovenia: Ministrstvo za notranje zadeve, Policija.

Ministry of the Interior. 2003b. *Letni načrt dela policije za leto 2003* [Annual work plan of the police in 2003]. Ljubljana, Slovenia: Ministrstvo za notranje zadeve, Policija.

Ministry of the Interior. 2010. *Poročilo o raziskavi stanja na področju v skupnost usmerjenega policijskega dela—Stališča občinskih varnostnih sosvetov* [Report on the current state of community policing survey—Local safety councils' perspectives]. Ljubljana, Slovenia: Ministrstvo za notranje zadeve, Policija.

Ministry of the Interior. 2011. *Usmeritve in obvezna navodila za pripravo letnega načrta dela policije v letu 2012* [Guidelines and obligatory instructions for the preparation of the annual work plan of the police]. Ljubljana, Slovenia: Ministrstvo za notranje zadeve, Policija.

Ministry of the Interior. 2012. *Temeljne usmeritve za pripravo srednjeročnega načrta razvoja in dela policije v obdobju 2013–2017* [Basic guidelines for the preparation of a medium-term plan for police development and work for the period from 2013 to 2017]. Ljubljana, Slovenia: Ministrstvo za notranje zadeve, Policija.

Ministry of the Interior. 2013. *Usmeritve in obvezna navodila za pripravo letnega načrta dela policije v letu 2014* [Guidelines and mandatory instructions for the preparation of the annual plan of police work in 2014]. Ljubljana, Slovenia: Ministrstvo za notranje zadeve, Policija.

Nalla, M. K., Meško, G., Lobnikar, B., Dobovšek, B., Pagon, M., Umek, P. et al. 2007. A comparison of officers' perceptions of the police organisational climate in large, midsize, and small cities in Slovenia. In *Policing in Emerging Democracies: Critical Reflections.* Meško, G., and Dobovšek, B., eds. Ljubljana, Slovenia: Faculty of Criminal Justice and Security: 101–26.

Organisation for Economic Co-operation and Development. 2012. *OECD Factbook 2011–2012: Economic, Environmental and Social Statistics.* Paris: OECD Publishing. Retrieved from http://www.oecd-ilibrary.org/content/book/factbook-2011-en ?contentType=&itemId=/content/chapter/factbook-2011-31-en&container ItemId=/content/serial/18147364&accessItemIds=&mimeType=text/h.

Pagon, M., and Lobnikar, B. 2001. *V skupnost usmerjeno policijsko delo v mestu Ljubljana: Ugotavljanje potreb za ustanovitev mestne policije ali redefiniranja dela državne policije: Končno poročilo s popravki* [Community-oriented policing in the city of Ljubljana: Assessment of needs for establishment of the city police or redefinition of the work of state police: Final report]. Ljubljana, Slovenia: Visoka policijsko-varnostna šola.

Pečar, J. 2002. Preprečevanje kriminalitete in policija [Crime prevention and the police]. *Varstvoslovje.* 4(2): 122–31.

Police. 2013a. Policijsko delo v skupnosti. [Community Policing] Doc. no. 2214-41/2012/4 (207–07). Ljubljana, Slovenia: MNZ, GPU.

Police. 2013b. Posvetovalna telesa [Safety councils]. Retrieved from http://www .policija.si/index.php/dravljani-in-policija/posvetovalna-telesa.

Police. 2014a. About the police. Retrieved from http://www.policija.si/eng/index .php/aboutthepolice.

Police. 2014b. Uniformed Police Directorate. Retrieved from http://www.policija.si /eng/index.php/generalpolicedirectorate/75-uniformedpolicedirectorate.

Police. 2014c. Criminal Police Directorate. Retrieved from http://www.policija.si/eng /index.php/generalpolicedirectorate/93-criminal-police-directorate.

Police. 2014d. National Bureau of Investigation. Retrieved from http://www.policija .si/eng/index.php/areasofwork/1073-national-bureau-of-investigation.

Police. 2014e. About police stations. Retrieved from http://www.policija.si/eng/index .php/aboutthepolice/organization/69.

Police. 2014f. Zgodovina in razvoj v skupnost usmerjenega policijskega dela [History and development]. Retrieved from http://www.policija.si/index .php/dravljani-in-policija/zgodovina-in-razvoj.

Resolution of the national plan on preventing and combating crime for the period 2012–2016. 2012. *Uradni list RS*, (83/12).

Resolution on the prevention and suppression of crime. 2006. *Uradni list RS*, (43/06).

Seagrave, J. 1996. Defining community policing. *American Journal of Police.* 15(2): 1–22.

Statistical Office of the Republic of Slovenia. 2009. Slovene municipalities in figures 2009. Retrieved from http://www.stat.si/doc/pub/Obcine2009/OBCINE%20 2009.pdf.

Statistical Office of the Republic of Slovenia. 2012a. Gross domestic product, quarterly data. Retrieved from http://www.stat.si/eng/indikatorji.asp?ID=12.

Statistical Office of the Republic of Slovenia. 2012b. Slovenia in figures 2012. Retrieved from http://www.stat.si/eng/pub.asp.

Statistical Office of the Republic of Slovenia. 2012c. Population clock. Retrieved from http://www.stat.si/eng/preb_ura.asp.

Statistical Office of the Republic of Slovenia. 2012d. Territorial units and house numbers, Slovenia, 1 July 2012—Final data. Retrieved from http://www.stat.si/eng /novica_prikazi.aspx?ID=4856.

Statistical Office of the Republic of Slovenia. 2014. Administrative territorial structure. Retrieved from http://www.stat.si/eng/novica_prikazi.aspx?id=6407.

220   Global Issues in Contemporary Policing

Statistical Portrait of Slovenia in the EU 2011. 2011. Ljubljana, Slovenia: Statistical Office of the Republic of Slovenia. Retrieved from http://www.stat.si/eng/pub.asp.
United Nations Development Programme. 2011. *Human Development Report 2011: Sustainability and Equity: A Better Future for All*. New York: Palgrave Macmillan. Retrieved from http://www.unodc.org/documents/justice-and-prison-reform /crimeprevention/10-52410_Guidelines_eBook.pdf.
Virtič, F. 2006. Razhajanje med oceno stanja in med pričakovanji ljudi do policije iz območja PU Maribor [Discrepancy between citizens' assessment of the current state and their expectations from the police of Maribor Police Directorate]. In *Raznolikost zagotavljanja varnosti, VII. dnevi varstvoslovja*. Lobnikar, B., ed. Ljubljana, Slovenia: Fakulteta za policijsko-varnostne vede: 646–56.
Virtič, F., and Lobnikar, B. 2004. Implementacija policijskega dela v skupnosti v slovenski policiji [Implementation of community policing in the Slovenian police] 5. In *Slovenski dnevi varstvoslovja*. Lobnikar, B., ed. Ljubljana, Slovenia: Visoka policijsko-varnostna šola: 745–50.
Žaberl, M. 2004. Vodja policijskega okoliša—Slovenski policist za preventivo [Community policing officer—Slovenian police officer for prevention]. In *Preprečevanje kriminalitete: Teorija, praksa in dileme*. Meško, G., ed. Ljubljana, Slovenia: Inštitut za kriminologijo pri Pravni fakulteti: 271–85.
Zakon o lokalni samoupravi [Local Self-Government Act]. 2007. *Uradni list Republike Slovenije*, (94/07).
Zakon o nalogah in pooblastilih policije [Police Tasks and Powers Act]. 2013. *Uradni list Republike Slovenije*, (15/13).
Zakon o občinskem redarstvu [Local Police Act]. 2006. *Uradni list Republike Slovenije*, (106/06).
Zakon o organiziranosti in delu v policiji [Police Organization Act]. 2013. *Uradni list Republike Slovenije*, (15/13).
Zakon o policiji [Police act]. 1998. *Uradni list Republike Slovenije*, (49/98).
Žerak, A. 2004. V skupnost usmerjeno policijsko delo v severno primorski regiji: Primerjava mnenja policistov in prebivalcev [Community policing in the northern Primorska region: A comparison of police officers' and citizens' opinions]. In *Slovenski dnevi varstvoslovja*. Lobnikar, B., ed. Ljubljana, Slovenia: Visoka policijsko-varnostna šola: 751–60.

Policing by Consent
Exploring the Possibilities of Functional Linkage between Local Police Station and Panchayat*

11

SONY KUNJAPPAN

Contents

Abstract

The Police Act of 1861, a colonial relic, still continues to govern the police in India. This legislative instrument is viewed with a degree of mistrust by the public, which has resulted in a mutual alienation of the police and the public. Analogous to the police station is another local institution that has created a drastic change in local governance. The Panchayats were a result of the 73rd Constitutional Amendment, whose objective was to deepen

* This chapter is an extract from the report submitted to Bureau of Police Research and Development (BPRD). The study was funded by BPRD, Ministry of Home Affairs, Government of India. Ideas expressed are of the author and not of the funding agency (BPRD).

221

the democracy through the decentralization of powers to the local bodies. While this act decentralized the power to the Panchayats, the local police stations, on the other hand, remained a closed archaic institution.

This creates a need to reexamine the mutual benefits of a law-implementing agency (the police stations) and the local self-government (Gram Panchayat). Unless these two are in a mutually beneficial relationship, an empowered and independently functional local government is not possible. Jayal and Prakash (2006) emphasizes the need for a relationship between locally elected institutions and administrative structures. This mutually beneficial relationship will ensure to a great extent the possibility of policing by consent. It will also be instrumental in preventing terrorism and other crimes at the local level. Furthermore, the fifth report of the Second Administrative Reforms Commission, titled *Public Order*, envisages an ultimate transfer of most of the police functions along with the personnel to the local self-governments over a period.

This chapter examines the possibility of a functional relationship between the police station and the local self-government (at the level of Gram Panchayat). The study is based on a case study conducted in Adat and Pananchery Gram Panchayat of the Thrissur district. The analysis was done on the basis of the study and various secondary data such as reports of police commissions and committees and the recommendations of the Second Administrative Commission Report on public order. This study proposes some well-researched suggestions for police reforms. It identifies the ways and the means through which the involvement of the local community can ensure the fulfillment of police roles, responsibilities, and accountability. This would not only bridge the gap between the police and the village citizens who are struggling to access justice, but also enhance the public delivery system in terms of criminal justice administration.

Community policing integrates image management as an essential ingredient of good policing. It encourages accountability and public scrutiny. Community policing is thus central to the prevention of repression of poor people in communities. This chapter highlights how a transfer of best practices in community policing can ensure better accountability and reduce mistrust. Thus, through an effective amendment of the Police Act, this chapter advocates the need to bring in a mandatory mutual beneficial linkage between the local self-government and the local police station.

Introduction

In India, the Panchayati raj and the police play a very important role in the lives of ordinary people. Several committees and commissions were appointed to look into their functioning to ensure greater participation of the people. However, there exists an asymmetry in that while the Panchayati raj as an institution has grown with powers devolved from the state, the police has remained a closed colonial institution. The Indian Police system has a colonial history and has evolved from pre-Mughal days. Its role was mostly to maintain oppressive power structures that were more intent on perpetuating its rule, rather than seeking the welfare of the masses. Due to this historical baggage, even today, the police is viewed with a degree of mistrust.

Village policing was essentially done by the village *Patel* (headman) assisted by the *chowkidar* (watchman). The spread of regular policing in rural areas was comparatively thin. The third report of the National Police Commission noticed defects in this system. The chowkidars had no minimum educational qualifications, no eligibility conditions with regard to age or physical condition, no perception of their duty in collecting and reporting information to police, no regular pay, and no specified chain of command, and in many places, they merely served the role of menial servants at the local police station. However, the chowkidar did serve the role of a useful point of information in a village. The Indian Police Commission Report in 1902 states the impossibility of policing using just the regular police force. It recommended the separation of the village police from the regular police and the relegation of the trial of petty offences to the village headmen and the Panchayat. The recommendations were either not followed or not implemented efficiently.

Effective police administration in this context must be based on the recognition and the enforcement of the responsibility of the village headman. This forms the basis of section 45 of the Criminal Procedure Code, which grants a greater devolution of powers to the village headman. The lack of financial devolution is an impediment in empowering the Panchayats, with only a few states having accepted the recommendations of the first State Finance Commissions, and with none of them having disbursed the funds. The Panchayat has grown in power with the 73rd Constitutional Amendment, but nothing had been done to improve the functioning of the police at the grassroots level, i.e., the local police station has failed to keep pace with the local Panchayat to ensure effective service delivery to the citizens.

After the declaration of independence of India, ideals such as democratic governance, accountability, transparency, and participation of the people were not being incorporated into the existing Police Act of 1865, which resulted in an alienation of the police and the public. Recommendations of the various committees and commissions (Shah Commission, National Police Commission, Rebeiro Committee) in this matter could not be implemented. Following the issuance of seven directives by the Supreme Court to the central and state governments requiring compliance, a Police Act Draft Committee (PADC) was set up by the Union Home Ministry, which submitted a draft outline for the enactment of a new Police Act on August 25, 2006.

It envisaged (1) professionalism in police; (2) public participation in policing; (3) insulation of the police from undue pressure/interference; (4) proactive policing, thereby enabling for police to face emerging challenges; and (5) empowerment of the lower functionaries. The state governments blindly followed only the seven directives of the Supreme Court and overlooked the essence of the draft outline brought out by the PADC, thus ignoring its fundamental aspect of reformation through inclusive governance.

Inclusive governance requires an approach, wherein the citizens (from all sections of society) also participate in the governance. In order for the police to cater to contemporary needs, its basic philosophy should be transformed into a different approach—*community- and problem-solving-oriented policing*. This approach emphasizes the need for building relationships between police and community/neighborhood residents in order to work together to prevent crime and solve problems. It also calls for new training practices that would augment the police–community linkages.

The fifth report of the Second Administrative Reforms Commission— Public Order—lays much emphasis on the local management of issues. It specifies the need for outsourcing many functions like service of summons, escort, and such general duties to appropriate agencies. The commission envisages the ultimate transfer of most of the police functions along with the personnel to the local self-governments over a period. The main issues pertaining to local governance and decentralization process are in regard to the need, the normative and material benefits, the nature of the exercise, and the experience of decentralization.

Community policing is one of the strategies used by the state to secure social order that matches or is shaped by the particular character of the political economy. It integrates image management as an essential ingredient of good policing. It encourages accountability and public scrutiny. It is gaining ground within the insipid police structure that is crumbling inside the failing state. Community policing is thus central to the prevention of repression of poor people in communities. Such communities are stronger agents of social control and information management from within the secretive armory of police steel frame.

Community policing arrived in India with the failure of the police to deal with crime. With decreasing transparency, increasing corruption, and nepotism, the space for honesty and commitment among police personnel has shrunk, hence the need for communities to enter the policing responsibilities. Central to this framework is the idea that image management is essential not only for the police but also for communities. If communities continue to think that they are in an irreparable state of disorder and indiscipline, then they would soon become one. Working together with the community much of this presumption about a state of disorder would get either absorbed in the collaborative efforts between the two or would be so marginalized that what would finally appear in rhetoric would be a friendly police and a supportive community.

This study looks into the Panchayat and the police. It is very much evident that there exists an asymmetry in the decentralization pattern or, in other words, the Panchayat in India are more decentralized compared to the police. Some degree of decentralization is required in order to function with local institutions such as the Panchayat. The basic elements of community policing are consultation with the community groups regarding their security needs, command devolution so that those closest to the community can determine how to best respond to their needs, mobilization of agencies (in the context of this study, the Panchayat) other than the police to assist in addressing those needs, and remedying the conditions that generates crime and insecurity through focused problem-solving. The central premise of community policing should be the public playing a more active part in enhancing public safety. This emphasizes the need for an effective network between the democratically elected local institution—the Panchayat—and the local police station.

Hence, this new approach of community-oriented problem-solving policing would involve *community involvement*, *problem solving*, and *organizational decentralization*. The participation from the local community is an essential component for effective policing, and for this to happen, we need to establish a working relationship between the local police station and the Panchayats.

This study highlights the need for creating a functional positive police–politician interface for public order maintenance. This can be achieved by reworking the police system and by taking all possible relationships with the Panchayati raj institutions into account. There are arguments in favor of the necessary relationship between locally elected institutions and administrative structures. This chapter explores the possibilities of relating policing with Panchayati raj institutions in India.

Rationale and Statement of the Problem

The police as an organized institution in this country came into existence with the Police Act of 1861. After the declaration of Independence of India, a few states have drafted new legislations. But still the ideals of democratic governance, accountability, transparency, and participation of people have not yet been incorporated. This has led to a severe alienation between the police and the public. The first national level commission came into existence (Government of India, 1977), to examine the excesses of power exercised during the emergency. The Shah Commission observed that the government must insulate police from the politics of the country. Therefore, the then Union Government set up the National Police Commission (NPC) in 1977 to examine the police with an in-depth analysis. The principal recommendations were basically focused on measures to free the police from a system of increasing political control. The most significant of these was the proposal to set up a statutory body in the states and at the center, to be called the State Security Commission. Later, the Reberio Committee was appointed in 1997 to examine NPC's recommendations to suggest further action regarding police reforms. The committee submitted its report in 1998–1999, but there was no action taken by the government. Later on, another committee was set up, under K. Padmanabhaiah, a former union home secretary. This committee also submitted the report in the year 2000. Now the present government has set up another committee to draft a new Police Act.

This study focuses on the reports of the NPC, the suggestions of related committees, the rural policing in India, and various researchers' works in the field, which have all unambiguously put forward suggestions regarding the structure of the system. In the research study conducted by Satya Narayan Pradhan, Indian Police Service (IPS) (director of the National Police Academy) on creating a functional positive police–politician interface for public order maintenance, he strongly placed the need of reworking the police system, by taking all possible relationship with the Panchayati raj institutions into account. There are arguments in favor of the necessary relationship between locally elected institutions and administrative structures (Jayal and Prakash, 2006). This study also explores the possibilities of relating policing with Panchayati raj institutions in India. The statements of problems are as follows:

- Alienation of socially and economically underprivileged people
- Respect for law and social ethics as suggested in the preamble of our Constitution
- Politicization of police that is preventing a meaningful reform initiative
- Police insulated from new developments in the market and technological spheres
- Ad hoc reform measures have failed to motivate the lower level officers such as constabulary toward modernizing Indian society
- Lack of political will in implementing the recommendations of National/State Police Commissions
- Lack of people's participation in policing in spite of the existence of a viable possibility with the help of the Panchayati raj institutions

Objectives of the Study

Although local self-government includes the Panchayat at three levels, viz., Gram Panchayat, block Panchayat, and district Panchayat, this study is trying to look only at the relationship between the Gram Panchayat and the police station. It has also looked at some of the initiatives of community policing at the urban level. Thus, this study focuses on the rural policing system and explores the possibility of a functional relationship of the local police station with the Panchayat at its jurisdiction. The specific objectives of this study are as follows:

- To analyze the recommendations and the suggestions of NPC and related commissions and committees on police reforms/public order in the light of suggested problems earlier
- To understand rural policing in India and redefine the roles, duties, power, and responsibilities of police and look at innovative strategies for individual and organizational development
- To explore a sustainable relationship between Panchayati raj institutions and local police station in villages
- To encourage the police toward the direction of legal reform, for greater access to justice

The Context

On April 23, 1994, and May 30, 1994, the Panchayati raj and the Municipality Act came into effect, respectively, on the basis of the 73rd and 74th Amendment Acts of the Indian Constitution. Local governments are dependent on the state governments and are "nothing more than their agencies" (Bandyopadhyay et al., 2003). Local self-government implies the decentralization of powers so that the elected bodies can function independently with authority and resources to bring about economic development and social justice.

In the aftermath of the amendments to the legal framework of the Panchayati raj system, the Kerala experience has been a unique one. The name Local Administration Department of Kerala was changed by the government to Department of Local Self-Government. In order to facilitate the administration, the rural development department was integrated to the local self-government department, and certain changes were incorporated in the secretariat pertaining to the administrative issues of urban areas. The Department of Urban Planning was changed to the Department of Town and Country Planning. Not able changes were made in the Urban Development Financial Corporation and the Rural Development Board. The local self-government plays a significant role in the formulation of policy and the implementation of developmental works at the grassroots level through the Gram Sabhas. The director of the Panchayat and the director of municipal administration constitute the two field departments of the Local

Administration, Department of the local self-government of Kerala. A secretary to government heads this department.

The local self-government of Kerala exercises great power and is effective in implementing developmental programs in the state. The decentralization through people's mobilization sought not only to devolve power from the state to the local level, but also to elicit people's participation in the process of development. The objective of the people's campaign for decentralized planning is not simply to draw up a plan from below. It was expected to bring about a transformation in the attitudes of the participants themselves (Thomas and Franke, 2001). The people's campaign has been described in detail. In its first phase, efforts were made to create basic awareness and preparation for attending Gram Sabha meetings. It estimated that more than two million persons participated in Gram Sabhas and ward committees. This generated public debate on development all over Kerala (Sharma, 2003). In the second phase of the campaign, development seminars were organized in every Gram Panchayat and efforts were made to draw up development plans. Emphasis was laid on data collection and resource mapping. The third phase was concerned with the projectization of the development plans.

Undoubtedly, the Kerala experience gave new meaning to the exercise of decentralization in the country. The Kerala experience also highlights the critical role of the state government in activating the Panchayats. It demonstrated that decentralization is more than rules and laws but a different culture of development that requires the intensive mobilization of the public. The Kerala experience signifies the diversity in implementing public policies toward decentralization in India. The concept of democratic decentralization requires a movement beyond representative democracy. There is a need to create not only appropriate institutions and opportunities, but also necessary capabilities at the lower levels in order for ordinary citizens to participate in the decision making, implementation, monitoring, and sharing of the benefits and the responsibilities of governmental activities. Such popular participation would make the elected representatives continuously accountable to the citizens and would facilitate a transparent administration.

The description just presented closely corresponds with the principles of decentralization enunciated by the Committee on Decentralization of Power (popularly known as Sen Committee, after its late chairperson, Dr. Satyabrata Sen) appointed by the government of Kerala. The key principles are autonomy, subsidiarity, role clarity, complementarity, uniformity, people's participation, accountability, and transparency. The legislation is being backed up by a powerful campaign to mobilize the people for democratic decentralization. Fundamental reforms cannot be merely legislated. Legislations remain mere empty phrases unless powerful movements oversee their implementation. Legislation is necessary but not sufficient for decentralization. Kerala's success in land reform reinforces the argument. The laws were successfully implemented because they were backed by a powerful farmers' movement. This political conviction has given rise to a fascinating and unique experiment in social mobilization for decentralization. So a study in the decentralization policies and the roles, duties, power, and responsibilities of the Panchayati raj institutions in Kerala has its own significance. In the light of a successful decentralized society in Kerala (compared with other states of India), the study also tries to redefine the roles, duties, power, and responsibilities of the police with a refreshing need and innovative strategies for individual and organizational development. Also, it tries to explore a sustainable relationship between Panchayati raj institutions and local police stations in villages. It also tries to see whether we need to have any constitutional amendments for a uniform policy across the country in ensuring a bond between these two institutions. Moreover, Kerala, being the highest literate state in the Indian Union and having a strong Panchayati raj system in its own, needs to make efforts to create a functional relationship between the local police and the local self-governments.

Methodology

This study proposes some well-researched suggestions for police reforms. It identifies the ways and the means through which the involvement of the local community can ensure the fulfillment of police roles, responsibilities, and accountability. This would not only bridge the gap between the police and the village citizens who are struggling to access justice, but also enhance the public delivery system in terms of criminal justice administration. This study would also look into the possibilities of having a functional relationship between the local police and the Panchayat. The selection of the method of the study was based on the commitment to the theoretical considerations presented earlier.

A case study of two Panchayats are conducted to understand the relationship between Panchayat and police station. They are as follows:

- Adat Gram Panchayat the Thrissur district in Kerala
- Pananchery Gram Panchayat at the Thrissur district in Kerala

For the case study of the two Panchayats (Adat and Pananchery), random sampling was done from a selection of the various respondents such as (1) 40 police officers at the local police station and (2) 40 Panchayat officials/elected representatives from the two Panchayats. The data for this study were collected through primary and secondary sources. For the first two case studies, the data are collected using secondary sources. Questionnaires, semistructured interviews, and focus group discussions were used for collecting primary data for the case study (Adat and Pananchery Panchayats). Thematic content analysis technique was used for the analysis of data.

Case Study: Two Gram Panchayats

The Adat Gram Panchayat of the Thrissur district was selected as the best Panchayat of the State in 2006 (Swaraj Trophy). At the national level, Adat Panchayat had received Nirmal Gram Puraskar award in 2008. This Panchayat has also pioneered various schemes and projects that have been taken as the model for the Kerala state, viz., (1) waste disposal scheme (2) Elamkulam Manakkal Sankaran (E. M. S.) Bhavana Nirman Padhathi, and (3) medical insurance for all below-poverty-line families. The governance of this Panchayat is by a political party, which is at present in opposition to the ruling party in the state.

The second Panchayat, Pananchery Panchayat has been selected because it is the only Panchayat in Kerala where the Jagratha Samithi (vigilance committee) of Gram Panchayat is being run smoothly for the past two years. Pananchery is also one of the largest Panchayats in Kerala. It is governed by the present ruling party of the state. This study explores the possibilities of relating policing to the Panchayati raj institutions. This study is primarily an overview of the concurrent interrelationship between Panchayati raj institutions and policing. It highlights the practical and functional correlations between the local Panchayat institutions and the police stations.

Observations

From the study so far, we have seen that it is required to have new ways of looking at the old problem of policing civil society. We have seen that innovative strategies of action are often required to tackle problems that could not be dealt with in existing procedures. Some of these include setting apart some of the police modernization funds for awareness programs especially in terms of the projects/welfare schemes of the Panchayat, for which a committee at the local level with adequate representation of Panchayat members and local police officers is required to be formed.

There is already a shortage of police personnel at the local police station, and then considering the jurisdiction of the police station and the new additional role of functional association with the Panchayat, there needs to be an increase in the number of police personnel in the local police station. The strength of local police station to give service to the people could be increased in Kerala, if the armed reserve and local police are merged and integrated. This brings about an increase of 20% more police at the cutting edge, dealing with people.* This increase in police personnel at the local police station

* Proposal for integration of local police and armed reserve police into civil police in Kerala, submitted by Dr. Alexander Jacob, Indian Police Service (IPS) dated October 22, 2009 to the Direct General of Police (DGP) of Kerala.

could be utilized to effectively divide the workload. Once the shortage of personnel at the local police station is addressed, then the local police station as well as the police officers will be in a position to deal with the responsibilities in relation to Kerala Panchayat Raj Act and to have a better working relationship between these two institutions at the local level. The strongest recommendation is that there should be one police station per Panchayat in order to have better working relationship and sharing of budget and other schemes between these two institutions at the local level. Other strategies that should be considered essential include conducting classes related to traffic, law and order, and other legal issues, with participation from both the Panchayat and the police station.

This study clearly points out the requirement for an effective functional relationship between the local police and the Panchayat. It also points out that the roles, duties, powers, and responsibility of the police need to be redefined with refreshingly new and innovative strategies both at the individual and at the organizational level. Section 52 of the Kerala Panchayat Raj Act (1994) defines the responsibilities of the local police officers. It held that the police should convey the complaints of violation of any of the sections of the Act to the president and the secretary of the Panchayat without any delay. The police officer is also responsible for giving proper legal aid, if the Panchayat president or secretary or any Panchayat officials/members requests for the same. If the police officer does not provide it, then he or she will be considered in violation of the law according to Section 41 of the existing Kerala Police Act 1960.

Chapter 23, Section 362 of the Draft Model Panchayat and Gram Swaraj Act defines the powers and the responsibilities of the police in respect of offenses and assistance to the Panchayats. Every police officer shall give immediate information to the Panchayat of an offense coming to his knowledge, which has been committed against this act or any rule or bylaw made thereunder and shall assist all members, officers, and servants of the Panchayat in the exercise of their lawful authority (Government of India, 2009).

The major observations of the study are as follows:

- One police station per Panchayat needs to be implemented through constitutional amendment.
- The accountability of the local police station and the Panchayats needs to be redefined by having an effective mechanism between the two for proper check and balance.
- There is a need for a functional harmony between the different stakeholders such as the legal framework, the civil administration, the police system, the criminal justice system, the civil society, the nongovernment organizations, and the media for effective delivery of service.

- Policing is required to be oriented in terms of the demand from its citizens.
- Police is arguably dysfunctional because of overcentralization. So there is a need for decentralization, and it should be through the effective participation of civil society.
- There is a need for outsourcing the functions of service of summons, escort, and such general duties to appropriate agencies. There is also an urgent need for increased involvement of the local government in the functioning of the police.
- The police functions such as traffic control and solving minor law and order problems should come under local self-governments. In order to achieve this, an ultimate transfer of most of the police functions along with the personnel to the local self-governments over a period is required.
- Enough steps should be taken to try and ensure that the local population is adequately represented in the police.
- The possibility of having an amendment to the Constitution for a mandatory relationship between the local police station and the local Panchayat, for effective delivery of public service to its citizens, should be further looked at.

Conclusion

This chapter entailed a qualitative research strategy considering the objectives it proposed. As the study attempts to examine the functional relationship between the Panchayati raj institution and the local police station, it also needs to deal with the real-life experience of the public with these two institutions, and their impacts for effective service delivery to citizens.

This chapter looks into the asymmetry between the two institutions (Panchayat and police) and calls for a similar degree of decentralization between the two, for effective networking, thereby better governance. It also looks into the aspects of community policing and points toward the idea of how it should be implemented. This study explores the possibility of having a sustainable relationship between the Panchayat and the police. This could bridge the gap between the police and citizens, whereby including the organizations the Panchayati raj institutions in village where the majority of poor are looking for access to justice.

It highlights how lack of financial devolution is an impediment in furthering the intentions of the amendments. Panchayats are to a great extent dependent on the states for grants. Even though the first state finance commissions were constituted by all the states, the acceptance of their recommendations has been uneven. Kerala, Madhya Pradesh, Punjab, Rajasthan, Tamil Nadu, Uttar

Pradesh, and West Bengal are among the states that have accepted the report in full. However, none of the states have disbursed funds according to the recommendations (*Panchayati Raj Update*, 2000, pp. 6–7). The 11th Finance Commission sanctioned Rs 1600 crores annually for Panchayats and Rs 400 crores for municipalities to be distributed among the states. It is clear that the states are reluctant to share their powers and resources with the Panchayats.

Local government institutions must share the responsibility for finding workable solutions to problems that detract from the safety and the security of the community. Effective policing depends on optimizing positive contact between the police organization and the community members. Law enforcement agencies alone will not have the resources to address all contemporary problems. But a police–local government partnership can work as a catalyst for mobilizing resources at the national, state, and local levels to impact the problems more effectively.

The six themes that have been identified have been drawn from the theoretical framework and the objectives of this study. Thus, it would be appropriate to conclude by looking at the objectives of this study and the areas that it had tried to address. The first objective of analyzing the recommendations of the NPC, the related committees on police reform, and the report on public order is being dealt with in the literature review. The second objective on understanding the rural policing in India is explored in the analysis of the third case study of the Panchayats, where the redefined roles, duties, power, and responsibilities of police with innovative strategies for individual and organizational development is detailed upon in the analysis of the first two case studies. The third objective of exploring a sustainable relationship between the Panchayati raj institutions and the local police stations in villages has been covered in the analysis of all the three case studies through the six themes. Finally, the last objective toward a legal reform, for greater access to justice, is attained through the analysis of data of the three objectives. The necessity of a constitutional amendment for a mandatory functional relationship between these two institutions (police and Panchayat) cannot be ruled out. Moreover, considering the strength of the police and its jurisdiction over a wider area covering many Panchayats, and for better delivery of public service, it is necessary for there to be one police station per Panchayat.

This study evaluates the need for a sustainable functional relationship between the Panchayati raj institutions and the local police stations. For the same, there should be a constitutional amendment that assures a healthy sharing of responsibilities between the Panchayat and the police station. Also, there is a need for proper decentralization of power from the state level administration to the local government institutions. The police administration will need to undergo modernization from the lowest level and also change from its traditional policing methods to a new and efficient citizen-centric service-oriented organization.

Many commissions and committees have been constituted for framing an effective way to apply decentralization and to study the various aspects of the participation of the police and the local governing bodies in policing. But most of the recommendations have failed to make a strong impact, and they remain mute spectators. This chapter is therefore trying to analyze the various possible aspects to have a strong police–Panchayat participation in effective policing. Hence, the importance of a constitutional amendment of ensuring the concept of *one police station per Panchayat* is most essential. Along with this concept, a mandatory functional relationship is required between the local police station and the Panchayat for effective delivery of service to the citizens.

Article 243G of the Constitution of India mandated that the legislatures of a state may, by law, endow the Panchayats with such powers and authority as may be necessary to enable them to function as institutions of self-governance. It further listed 29 subjects in the 11th schedule with reference to which powers and functions could be devolved to the Panchayats. The intention of the amendment was that these institutions would be able to act autonomously within the domain delegated to them by the state laws. The emphasis of the planning commission in improving governance in the country is on building state capacities, strengthening public service delivery mechanism, and creating effective institutions for decentralization. Governance is concerned with a network of relationship between the state and the civil society. In this context, it is the network or the relationship between two institutions (Panchayat and police station) and thereby a network of relationship between the state and its citizen is being established.

This study clearly points out that an effective functional relationship is required between the local police and the Panchayat. It also points out that the roles, duties, powers, and responsibility of the police need to be redefined with refreshingly new and innovative strategies both at the individual and at the organizational level. Community policing encourages accountability and public scrutiny and is thus central to the prevention of repression of poor people in communities. Thus, through an effective amendment of the Police Act, this chapter advocates the need to bring in a mandatory mutual beneficial linkage between the local self-government and the local police station; therefore, we could transfer some best practices in community policing, which remains only in some parts of our country, for better policing by consent. In this chapter, we have seen the limitations in the present scenario of governance and policing. Research has been done in overcoming these; however, even more ground has to be covered in reviewing the existing literature and in further research endeavors. The need of the hour is for the government to ensure an effective implementation of the recommendations of the various committees and commissions, taking into consideration the views of all the stakeholders, to ensure a truly democratic functioning of our civic institutions.

Bibliography

Reports and Commissions

Government of India. 1975. *Report of the Shah Commission*. New Delhi: Ministry of Home Affairs.

Government of India. 1977. *Report of the Shah Commission*. New Delhi: Ministry of Home Affairs.

Government of India. 2009. *Draft Model Panchayat and Gram Swaraj Act*. New Delhi: Ministry of Panchayati Raj.

Gore, M. S. et al. 1971. *The Gore Committee report on Police Training*. New Delhi: Ministry of Home Affairs.

Books

Ahern, J. 1972. *Police in Trouble*. New York: Hawthorn.

Ali, A. 1994. The role and range of police training. In *Police Training: Problems and Perspectives*, Sankar, S., and Saxena, A. K., eds. New Delhi: Rawat Publications.

Ayres, L. 2008. Semi-structured interview. In *The Sage Encyclopedia of Qualitative Research Methods*. Given, L. M., ed. Thousand Oaks, CA: Sage Publications, Inc.

Bandyopadhyay, D., Amitave, M., and Mitali, G. S. 2003. *Empowering Panchayats Handbook for Master Trainers: Using Participatory Approach*. New Delhi, India: Concept Publications.

Barlow, H. 1996. *Introduction to Criminology*. New York: HarperCollins.

Baxi, U. 1994. A human rights curriculum design for police academies. In *Police Training: Problems and Perspectives*, Sankar, S., and Saxena, A. K., eds. New Delhi: Rawat Publications.

Bayley, D. H. 1969. *The Police and Political Development in India*. Princeton, NJ: Princeton University Press.

Bayley, D. H. 1994. *Police for the Future*. New York: Oxford University Press.

Bhargava, K. N. 1982. Issues in inservice training. In *Issues in Inservice Training*. Mathur, H. M., ed. New Delhi: IIPA.

Blatter, J. K. 2008. Case study. In *The Sage Encyclopedia of Qualitative Research Methods*. Given, L. M., ed. Thousand Oaks, CA: Sage Publications, Inc.

Bloor, M., and Wood, F. 2006. *Key Words in Qualitative Methods: A Vocabulary of Research Concepts*, London: Sage Publications Ltd.

Buerger, M. E. 1994. The limits of community. In *The Challenge of Community Policing*. Rosenbaum, D. P., ed. Thousand Oaks, CA: Sage Publications, Inc.

Clarke, C. 2008. Democratic policing: The Canadian experience. In *Comparative Policing: The Struggle for Democratisation*. Haberfeld, M. R., and Cerrah, I., eds. Thousand Oaks, CA: Sage Publications, Inc.

Fuller, J. 1998. *Criminal Justice: A Peacemaking Perspective*. Boston: Allyn and Bacon.

Gupta, A. 1979. *The Police in British India: 1861–1947*. New Delhi: Concept Publishing Company.

Hadenius, A. 2001. *Institutions and Democratic Citizenship*. Oxford, UK: Oxford University Press.

Haralambos, M., and Heald, R. 1980. *Sociology Themes and Perspectives*. New Delhi: OUP.

Jayal, N. G., Prakash, A., and Sharma, P. (eds.) 2006. *Local Governance in India Decentralization and Beyond*. New Delhi, India: Oxford University Press, p. 8.

Jha, S. K. 1995. *Raj to Swaraj: Changing Contours of Police*. New Delhi: Lancer Publication.

Kelling, G., and Moore, M. 1988. From political to reform to community: The evolving strategy of police. In *Community Policing: Rhetoric or Reality*. Greene, J., and Mastrofski, S., eds. New York: Cambridge.

Kholi, A. 2004. *State-Directed Development: Political Power and Industrialization in the Global Periphery*. New York: Cambridge University Press.

Long, M., and Cullen, S. 2008. United Kingdom: Democratic policing—Global change from a comparative perspective. In *Comparative Policing: The Struggle for Democratisation*. Haberfeld, M. R., and Cerrah, I., eds. Thousand Oaks, CA: Sage Publications, Inc.

Manning, P. 1991. Community policing as a drama of control. In *Community Policing: Rhetoric or Reality*. Greene, J., and Mastrofski, S., eds. New York: Praeger.

McNabb, D. E. 2004. *Research Methods for Political Science: Quantitative and Qualitiative Methods*. New York: M. E. Sharpe.

Oliver, W. M. 1998. *Community-Oriented Policing: A Systemic Approach to Policing*. Upper Saddle River, NJ: Prentice Hall.

Osborne, D., and Gaebler, T. 1993. *Reinventing Government, How the Enterpreneurial Spirit Is Transforming the Public Sector*. New York: Ringwood.

Pepper, D. A. 1984. *Managing the Training and Development Function*. Aldershot, UK: Gower.

Platt, T., Frappier, J., Cooper, L., Currie, E., Ryan, B., Schauffler, R., Scruggs, J., and Trujillo, L. 1982. *The Iron Fist and the Velvet Glove: An Analysis of the US Police*, third edition. San Francisco: Synthesis Publications.

Raghavan, R. K. 1999. The Indian Police: Expectations of a democratic polity. In *Transforming India: Social and Political Dynamics of Democracy*. Frankel, F. R., Hasan, Z., Bhargava, R., and Arora, B., eds. Oxford, UK: Oxford University Press.

Rao, A. V. 1994. Managing a training institute: Essential requirements. In *Police Training: Problems and Perspectives*, Sankar, S., and Saxena, A. K., eds. New Delhi: Rawat Publications.

Rondinelli, A. D., and Shabbir, C. 2003. *Reinventing Government for the Twenty First Century*. Bloomfield, CT: Kumarian Press.

Sankhdher, M. M. 1975. *The Concept of Welfare State*. New Delhi: University of Delhi.

Skolnick, J., and Fyfe, J. 1993. *Above the Law: Police and the Excessive Use of Force*. New York: Free Press.

Skolnick, J., and Fyfe, J. 1995. Community policing would prevent police brutality. In *Policing the Police*. Winters, P. A., ed. New York: Greenhaven Press.

Thomas, I., and Franke, R. 2001. *Local Democracy and Development: People's Plan Campaign for Decentralised Planning for Kerala*, New Delhi, India.

Trojanowicz, R., and Bucqueroux, B. 1990. *Community Policing: A Contemporary Perspective*. Cincinnati, OH: Anderson Publishing.

United Nations. 1966. *Handbook of Training in the Public Service*. New York: United Nations.

Verma, A. 2005a. The police in India: Design, performance and adaptability. In *Public Institutions in India Performance and Design*. Kapur, D., and Mehta, P. B., eds. New Delhi: OUP.

Verma, A. 2005b. *The Indian Police: A Critical Evaluation*. New Delhi: Regency Publication: 223.

Willig, C. 2008. *Introducing Qualitative Research in Psychology: Adventures in Theory and Method*. Buckingham, UK: Open University Press.

Wilson, J. 1968. *Varieties of Police Behavior: The Management of Law and Order in Eight Communities*. Cambridge, MA: Harvard University.

Yin, R. K. 2003. *Case Study Research: Design and Method*. Thousand Oaks, CA: Sage Publications, Inc.

Articles

Bandhyyopadhyay, J., and Shiva, S. 1988. Political economy of ecological movements. *Economic and Political Weekly*, June 11. pp. 1223–31.

Barlow, D. E., and Barlow, M. H. 1999. A political economy of community policing. *Policing: An International Journal of Police Strategies and Management*. 22/4: 646–74.

Birokracij, L. M. 2005. Bureaucracy. *Financial Theory and Practice*. 29(3): 267–72.

Braun, V., and Clarke, V. 2006. Using thematic analysis in psychology. *Qualitative Research in Psychology*. 3: 77–101.

Garland, D. 1997. Governmentality and the Problem of Crime: Foucault, Criminology, Sociology, Theoretical Criminology. 1(2)s: 173–214.

Joseph, J. 2000. *Review on Fabrication of Social Order: A Critical Theory of Police Power*, by Mark Neocleous. Archway Road, London: Pluto Press.

King, W. R., and Lab, S. P. 2000. Crime prevention, community policing and training: Old wine in new bottles. *Police Practice and Research*. 1(2): 241–52.

Samuel, P. 1983. Training for public administration and management in dfeveloping countries. World Bank Staff Working Papers Number 584: 41.

Schwartz, M. D., and Friedrichs, D. O. 1994. Postmodern thought and criminological discontent: New metaphors for understanding violence. *Criminology*. 32(2): 221–46.

Sharma, R. 2003. Kerala's Decentralization: Idea in Practice. *Economic and Political Weekly*. 38(36): 3832–5.

Wilson, J. Q., and Kelling, G. L. 1982. Broken Windows: Police and neighborhood safety. *The Atlantic Monthly*, March. 249: 29–38.

Newspapers

Deccan Chronicle. 2005, September 1. Reforming the police. Hyderabad.

Panchayati Raj Update. 2000, July. pp. 6–7.

Telegraph. 2006, February 14. Organizational independency for professional policing. Calcutta.

The Hindustan Times. 2006, October 6. Edgy J&K Policemen beat up NDMC official. New Delhi.

The Hindustan Times. 2006, October 11. Teach policemen trick of the trade. New Delhi.
The Statesman. 2007, October 24. Deviant police: Problem is with the system not the "rotten apple." New Delhi.
The Statesman. 2006, November 17. Reform or Deform-I: Renewed debate on the PC report. New Delhi.

Websites

Bureau of Police Research and Development. http://bprd.nic.in/.
Institute of Social Sciences. http://www.issin.org/.
Ministry of Home Affairs. http://www.mha.nic.in/.

The International Police Executive Symposium (IPES) was founded in 1994. The aims and objectives of the IPES are to provide a forum to foster closer relationships among police researchers and practitioners globally, to facilitate cross-cultural, international, and interdisciplinary exchanges for the enrichment of the law enforcement profession, and to encourage discussion and published research on challenging and contemporary topics related to the profession.

One of the most important activities of the IPES is the organization of an annual meeting under the auspices of a police agency or an educational institution. Every year since 1994, annual meetings have been hosted by such agencies and institutions all over the world. Past hosts include the Canton Police of Geneva, Switzerland; the International Institute of the Sociology of Law, Onati, Spain; Kanagawa University, Yokohama, Japan; the Federal Police, Vienna, Austria; the Dutch Police and Europol, The Hague, The Netherlands; the Andhra Pradesh Police, India; the Center for Public Safety, Northwestern University, United States; the Polish Police Academy, Szczytno, Poland; the Police of Turkey (twice); the Kingdom of Bahrain Police; a group of institutions in Canada (consisting of the University of the Fraser Valley, the Abbotsford Police Department, the Royal Canadian Mounted Police, the Vancouver Police Department, the Justice Institute of British Columbia, the Canadian Police College and the International Centre for Criminal Law Reform and Criminal Justice Policy); the Czech Police Academy, Prague; the Dubai Police; the Ohio Association of Chiefs of Police and the Cincinnati Police Department, Ohio, United States; and the Republic of Macedonia and the Police of Malta. The 2011 annual meeting with the theme of "Policing Violence, Crime, Disorder and Discontent: International Perspectives" was hosted in Buenos Aires, Argentina, on June 26–30, 2011. The 2012 annual meeting was hosted at the United Nations in New York with the theme of "Economic Development, Armed Violence and Public Safety" on August 5–10. The 2013 annual meeting with the theme of "Global Issues in Contemporary Policing" was hosted by the Ministry of Interior of Hungary and the Hungarian National Police on August 4–9, 2013. In 2014, there were two meetings: the annual meeting with the theme of "Policing by Consent" was hosted in Trivandrum (Kerala), India, on March 16–21, and the other with the theme of "Crime Prevention and Community Resilience" was hosted in Bulgaria's capital city Sofia (July 27–31).

There have also been occasional Special Meetings of IPES. A special meeting was cohosted by the Bavarian Police Academy of Continuing Education in Ainring, Germany, University of Passau, Germany, and the State University of New York, Plattsburgh, United States, in 2000. The second special meeting was hosted by the police in the Indian state of Kerala. The third special meeting with the theme of "Contemporary Issues in Public Safety and Security" was hosted by the Commissioner of Police of the Blekinge Region of Sweden and the President of the University of Technology on August 10–14, 2011.

The majority of the participants of the annual meetings are usually directly involved in the police profession. In addition, scholars and researchers in the field also participate. The meetings comprise both structured and informal sessions to maximize dialogue and the exchange of views and information. The executive summary of each meeting is distributed to participants as well as to a wide range of other interested police professionals and scholars. In addition, a book of selected papers from each annual meeting is published through CRC Press–Taylor & Francis Group, Prentice Hall, Lexington Books, and other reputed publishers. A special issue of *Police Practice and Research: An International Journal* is also published with the most thematically relevant papers after the usual blind review process.

IPES Institutional Supporters

APCOF, The African Policing Civilian Oversight Forum (Contact: Sean Tait), 2nd floor, The Armoury, Buchanan Square, 160 Sir Lowry Road, Woodstock Cape Town, 8000 South Africa. Tel: 27–21–461–7211; Fax: 27–21–461–7213. E-mail: sean@apcof.org.za.

Australian Institute of Police Management, Library, 1 Collins Beach Road, Manly, New South Wales 2095, Australia. Tel: +61–2–9934–4800; Fax: +61–2–9934–4780. E-mail: library@aipm.gov.au.

Baker College of Jackson (Contact: Blaine Goodrich), 2800 Springport Road, Jackson, MI 49202, U.S. Phone: (517) 841–4522. E-mail: blaine.goodrich@baker.edu.

Cliff Roberson, Professor Emeritus, Washburn University, 16307 Sedona Woods, Houston, TX 77082-1665, U.S. Tel: +1–713–703–6639; Fax: +1–281–596–8483. E-mail: roberson37@msn.com.

College of Health and Human Services (Contact: Mark E. Correia, PhD, dean), Indiana University of Pennsylvania, 216 Zink Hall, Room 105, 1190 Maple Street Indiana, PA 15705–1059 E-mail: mcorreia@iup.edu. Tel: 724-357-2555.

Cyber Defense & Research Initiatives (Contact: James Lewis), Limited Liability Corporation (LLC), PO Box 86, Leslie, MI 49251, U.S. Tel: 517–242–6730. E-mail: lewisja@cyberdefenseresearch.com.

De Montfort University, Health and Life Sciences, School of Applied Social Sciences (Contact: Dr. Perry Stanislas, Hirsh Sethi), Hawthorn Building, The Gateway, Leicester, LE1 9BH, U.K. Tel: +44 (0) 116-257-7146. E-mail: pstanislas@dmu.ac.uk, hsethi@dmu.ac.uk.

Defendology Center for Security, Sociology and Criminology Research (Valibor Lalic), Srpska Street 63,78000 Banja Luka, Bosnia and Herzegovina. Tel. and Fax: 387-51-308-914. E-mail: lalicv@teol.net.

Department of Criminal Justice (Contact: Dr. Harvey L. McMurray, chair), North Carolina Central University, 301 Whiting Criminal Justice Bldg., Durham, NC 27707, U.S. Tel: 919-530-5204, 919-530-7909; Fax: 919-530-5195. E-mail: hmcmurray@nccu.edu.

Department of Psychology (Contact: Stephen Perrott), Mount Saint Vincent University, 166 Bedford Highway, Halifax, Nova Scotia, Canada. E-mail: Stephen.perrott@mvsu.ca.

Edmundo Oliveira, Prof. PhD. 1 Irving Place, University Tower Apt. U 7 A, 10003.9723 Manhattan, New York, New York. Tel. 407-342-24-73. E-mail: edmundooliveira@cfl.rr.com.

Fayetteville State University (Contact: Dr. David E. Barlow, professor and dean), College of Basic and Applied Sciences, 130 Chick Building, 1200 Murchison Road, Fayetteville, North Carolina, 28301, U.S. Tel: 910-672-1659; Fax: 910-672-1083. E-mail: dbarlow@uncfsu.edu.

International Council on Security and Development (ICOS) (Contact: Andre Souza, senior researcher), Visconde de Piraja 577/605, Ipanema, Rio de Janeiro 22410-003, Brazil. Tel: (+55) 21-3186-5444. E-mail: asouza@icosgroup.net.

Kerala Police (Contact: Shri Balasubramaniyum, director general of police), Police Headquarters, Trivandrum, Kerala, India. E-mail: manojabraham05@gmail.com.

Law School, John Moores University (Contact: David Lowe, LLB programme leader), Law School, Redmonds Building, Brownlow Hill, Liverpool, L3 5UG, U.K. Tel: +44 (0) 151-231-3918. E-mail: D.Lowe@ljmu.ac.uk.

Molloy College, The Department of Criminal Justice (Contact: Dr. John A. Eterno, NYPD captain-retired), 1000 Hempstead Avenue, PO Box 5002, Rockville Center, NY 11571-5002, U.S. Tel: 516-678-5000, Ext. 6135; Fax: 516-256-2289. E-mail: mailto:jeterno@molloy.edu.

National Institute of Criminology and Forensic Science (Contact: Mr. Kamalendra Prasad, inspector general of police), MHA, Outer Ring Road, Sector 3, Rohini, Delhi 110085, India. Tel: 91-11-275-2-5095; Fax: 91-11-275-1-0586. E-mail: director.nicfs@nic.in.

National Police Academy, Japan (Contact: Naoya Oyaizu, deputy director), Police Policy Research Center, Zip 183-8558: 3-12-1 Asahi-cho

Fuchu-city, Tokyo, Japan. Tel: 81–42–354–3550; Fax: 81–42–330–3550. E-mail: PPRC@npa.go.jp.

Royal Canadian Mounted Police (Contact: Craig J. Callens), 657 West 37th Avenue, Vancouver, BC V5Z 1K6, Canada. Tel: 604–264–2003; Fax: 604–264–3547. E-mail: bcrcmp@rcmp-grc.gc.ca.

School of Psychology and Social Science, Head, Social Justice Research Centre (Contact: S. Caroline Taylor, professor and foundation chair in social justice), Edith Cowan University, 270 Joondalup Drive, Joondalup, WA 6027, Australia. E-mail: c.taylor@ecu.edu.au.

South Australia Police (Contact: Mal Hyde, commissioner), Office of the Commissioner, South Australia Police, 30 Flinders Street, Adelaide, SA 5000, Australia. E-mail: mal.hyde@police.sa.gov.au.

Southeast Missouri State University (Contact: Dr. Diana Bruns, dean), Criminal Justice & Sociology, One University Plaza, Cape Girardeau, MO 63701, U.S. Tel: (573) 651–2178. E-mail: dbruns@semo.edu.

The Faculty of Criminal Justice and Security (Contact: Dr. Gorazd Mesko), University of Maribor, Kotnikova 8, 1000 Ljubljana, Slovenia. Tel: 386–1–300–83–39; Fax: 386–1–2302–687. E-mail: gorazd.mesko @fvv.uni-mb.si.

UNISA, Department of Police Practice (Contact: Setlhomamaru Dintwe), Florida Campus, Cnr Christiaan De Wet and Pioneer Avenues, Private Bag X6, Florida, 1710 South Africa. Tel: 011–471–2116; Cell: 083–581–6102; Fax: 011–471–2255. E-mail: Dintwsi@unisa.ac.za.

University of Maine at Augusta, College of Natural and Social Sciences (Contact: Richard Myers, professor), 46 University Drive, Augusta, ME 04330-9410, U.S. E-mail: rmyers@maine.edu.

University of New Haven (Contact: Dr. Mario Gaboury, School of Criminal Justice and Forensic Science), 300 Boston Post Road, West Haven, CT 06516, U.S. Tel: 203–932–7260. E-mail: rward@newhaven .edu.

University of South Africa, College of Law (Contact: Kris Pillay, School of Criminal Justice, director and professor), Preller Street, Muckleneuk, Pretoria. E-mail: cpillay@unisa.ac.za.

University of the Fraser Valley (Contact: Dr. Darryl Plecas), Department of Criminology & Criminal Justice, 33844 King Road, Abbotsford, British Columbia V2 S7 M9, Canada. Tel: 604–853–7441; Fax: 604–853–9990. E-mail: Darryl.plecas@ufv.ca.

University of West Georgia (Contact: David A. Jenks, PhD), 1601 Maple Street, Pafford Building 2309, Carrollton, GA 30118, U.S. Tel: 678–839–6327. E-mail: djenks@westga.edu.

Index

A

Active listening, training on, 111–112
Agitator view, 165
Amazon AWS, 136
Analysis of variance (ANOVA), 55
Anonymous, 125
Application whitelisting, 134

B

Basic Law on Disaster Countermeasures
    (Japan), 18
Bifurcated mass murder, 15
Big data, 136
Border gateway protocol (BGP), 137
Bots, 128
Bring your own device (BYOD) to work,
    122
Bureau of Justice Assistance (BJA), 182,
    185
Bureau of Police Research and Development
    (BPRD), 221, *see also* Policing
    by consent (functional linkage
    between local police station and
    Panchayat)

C

CALEA, *see* Commission on Accreditation
    for Law Enforcement Agencies
Catastrophes, police response to, 18
Citizen satisfaction with police, 175–198
    citizen attitudes and opinions survey,
        192–196
    discussion, 190–191
    literature review, 176–182
        assessing community policing
            efforts, 179–181
        encounters with police, 177
        hypotheses, 182
        neighborhood quality of life, 177

methodology, 182–185
    data collection and sampling, 184–185
    planning stage, 184
    survey construction, 183–184
results, 185–190
    crime victim, types of, 188
    income, 187
    marital status, 187
    racial composition of sample, 186
    statistical analyses related to
        hypothesis testing, 189–190
    survey respondents, 186–187
    WMPD citizen attitudes and
        perceptions survey, 187
Cloud
    mitigation service providers, 137
    security providers, security provision by,
        136–137
    storage, 123
Collaboration
    importance of, 21
    with other justice agencies, 26–27
    research, 5
Command and control model, 163, 165–166
Commission on Accreditation for Law
    Enforcement Agencies (CALEA),
    149
Community-oriented policing (COP), 37
Community–police relations, using
    complaints against police to
    improve, 97–119
    comprehensive source for data-driven
        training, 116–117
        record what customers want when
            they lodge a complaint, 117
        train staff to ensure complaint
            information is recorded neutrally,
            116
    customer service, police focus on,
        99–100
        factors influencing customer service,
        99